BODIES

IAN WINWOOD

BODIES

Life and Death
in Music

faber

First published in the UK in 2022
by Faber & Faber Ltd
Bloomsbury House,
74–77 Great Russell Street
London WC1B 3DA

Typeset by Faber & Faber Ltd
Printed and bound by CPI Group (UK) Ltd, Croydon, CR0 4YY

The right of Ian Winwood to be identified as author of this work
has been asserted in accordance with Section 77 of the Copyright,
Designs and Patents Act 1988

Quotation on p. vii from 'The Fisher King Blues' (2013) by
Frank Turner, courtesy of Frank Turner; on p. 10, from 'All My Friends' (2020)
by Creeper, courtesy of the band

A CIP record for this book
is available from the British Library

ISBN 978–0–571–36418–3

2 4 6 8 10 9 7 5 3

For Eric

We're all broken boys and girls at heart;
Come together fall apart

Frank Turner, 'The Fisher King Blues'

CONTENTS

SLEEVE NOTES

In the course of writing this book I have spoken with numerous musicians, music industry experts, psychotherapists, academics, journalists, charities and more. Each of my interviewees gave generously of their time, and did so free of charge. For this, I am of course grateful. Over many hours of conversation their insights and wisdom have imbued the text with nuance and perspective that would otherwise be lacking.

When quoted, people with whom I have spoken specifically for the purposes of this book are referred to in the present tense – 'she tells me', 'he says', and so on. Quotes relevant to my story that I have taken from my files as a working journalist are presented in the past tense – 'so and so claimed', 'such and such revealed', and so forth. Bespoke interviewees are also referred to by their first names. On the rare occasions that I have been forced to mention it, Covid-19 is referred to as 'The Disease'.

Broadly speaking, the book can be divided into two sections. 'Side One' deals with excessive and disturbing behaviour from musicians I have interviewed in the field. 'Side Two' seeks to explain the high degree of addiction and mental turmoil in the music industry at large. In the opening half, I've tried to retain at least a sense of the naïvety of my younger years. After that, I'm wise to the game.

Everything you are about to read is true. Recounted in what I hope is sparkling dialogue, certain conversations are recalled from memory in good faith. In some cases I've changed the names of the guilty.

Ian Winwood, Camden Town, London

SIDE ONE

INTRODUCTION

I used to speak to my dad whenever I was at an airport. Standing on the pavement outside Heathrow or Gatwick, Stansted or City, I'd place a call to his small office just outside our hometown of Barnsley, in South Yorkshire.

'Hello, Triple Engineering,' he'd say.

To which I'd always reply, 'Hello, Triple Engineering.'

'*Eyup*, pal.'

'How we doing?'

'Fine. Fine.'

'Another customary call from the airport, Dad.'

That's what we called these brief exchanges of ours – *a customary call from the airport*. While Eric Winwood sat at his desk (in his slippers) estimating the cost of steelwork on construction projects tall and wide, down in the beautiful south his son was off to interview musicians on behalf of a national publication that *paid him to do so*. My father wasn't much interested in the bands and artists to whom I spoke, or, as far as I could tell, in the stories I wrote about them. But he did get a kick out of me visiting cities that had been revealed to him in the pages of a book.

'Where to this time?' he'd ask.

'New York, Dad.'

'Oh, right – the City That Never Sleeps.'

This 'oh' would last for two or three beats. The 'right' would rhyme with 'eight'.

'Chicago today, pal.'

'Oh, the Windy City. Good stuff.'

From my father, 'good stuff' was the highest praise.

'Pacific Northwest, Dad. All the way to Seattle.'

'Get in. Jet City.'

Eric knew the nickname of every place I went. San Francisco was the City by the Bay. New Orleans was the Big Easy. Milwaukee was Brew City. I sometimes wondered just how deep this seam of knowledge ran. If I'd have phoned him from Gatwick with the news that I was headed to Pilot Butte, Saskatchewan, would he have said, 'Now then,' – *nar then* – 'the Sand Capital of Canada'?

One Friday in summer I was bound for California with a record company press officer and an insufferable photographer. Like me, the pair were well used to spending vast swathes of the early twenty-first century in mid-air; unlike me, they seemed to regard this bounty of complimentary trans-global travel as a matter of cheerless mundanity. It gets worse. At Heathrow I learned that my companions had been gifted an upgrade to business class, while I – Muggins here, Mr Chopped Liver – remained at the rear of the plane. Estimating the scale of this injustice, with typical equanimity I judged it to be the worst thing that had ever happened.

'Hello, Triple Engineering.'

'Hello, Triple Engineering.'

'Eyup, pal.'

'A customary call from the airport.'

'Ooh . . .'

'Los Angeles.'

'City of Angels.' A pause. 'I must say, you don't sound particularly happy about it . . .'

He didn't miss much, my dad. A man of economical horizons, after leaving secondary modern at fifteen he inevitably followed his own father down the pit. Man and boy, a dawn chorus at Houghton Main. I remember him telling me that he hated every minute of his time underground. At a loss for a response, I asked for how long he'd stuck it out. Seven years, he said. *Seven years?* I don't think I'd have made it to elevenses. To be honest with you, I'm not sure miners take elevenses.

In the hope of learning something new, each day after work he took a paperback to a quiet corner of a traditional pub on the outskirts of Barnsley. Widely respected as an erudite arbiter of ale-house disputes – a shout across the bar: 'Eric! Who was it that wrote *The Gang That Couldn't Shoot Straight?*' – he carried himself with an authoritative intelligence that was rarely impatient and never unkind. When he and my mother divorced he would send letters to my new home in the south of England. Deprived of the conventional bulwarks of physical comedy – gesture, intonation, facial expression – I used to marvel at his ability to bring forth laughter using only the words on the page.

Beneath a headstone that reads 'Eric Ian Winwood: Son, Father, Brother, Friend – Mined from the Good Stuff', these days my dad is buried in a plot at Ardsley Cemetery. As well as giving me the gift of reading for pleasure, he bequeathed me a talent for placing words in an order that earns me my living.

Sometimes this living takes me to Los Angeles.

'Well, I'm *not* very happy about it, Dad, to be honest with you.'

'Oh. Right. Why on earth not?'

So I told Eric of the egregious assault on my human rights. Eleven hours cocooned with hundreds of other common-or-garden arse-scratchers in the cheap seats of an airborne dildo. 'I'm right at the back,' I told him. 'Right next to the toilets. There'll be coming and going and faffing about and bad smells and bad food and ... *all of that*. And I wouldn't mind, Dad, I really wouldn't, but the people I'm travelling with have been upgraded, and, I mean, I'm not being funny or nothing but, well ... well ... *they don't even deserve it.*'

A moment's silence. A question dangling on a hook. 'Do you know what *I'm* doing tonight, pal?'

I had no idea. The last film Eric saw at the pictures was *Indiana Jones and the Temple of Doom* (1984). A visit to a restaurant in town was by now an annual event.

Okay, I'll play. 'Dad, what are you doing tonight?'

'Funny you should ask, son,' he says. *Oh, God, he's starting his engines.* 'I'm heading into Barnsley for a couple of pints. And when I'm there, Ian, you'll be in Los Angeles.'

'Right.'

'*Right.* So shut the fuck up.'

There were a number of things I didn't share with my dad. I didn't tell him that the music business tolerates – *celebrates* – terrifying behaviour. I didn't divulge that after three days at the Reading Festival, his own stepson had remarked that the open-all-hours tomfoolery of me and my friends would have us sacked from any other line of work. When he asked me how things were going, I failed to mention that *things* were swerving out of control. A world of trouble was coming down the pipes. We didn't yet know it, my dad and I, but a terrible storm was headed our way.

In time, medically qualified women and men will tell me that I have Rapid Cycling Bipolar Affective Disorder, Impulse Control Disorder, Borderline Personality Disorder and Emotional Dysregulation Disorder. I also have Post Traumatic Stress Disorder. From a stylistic point of view, that's a lot 'disorder' for one paragraph. In starkly lit offices in Islington and Camden, I've explained my situation to at least two dozen therapists. I've taken so much medication that it's likely I'll be buried in a coffin with a childproof lid.

Divided in their diagnoses, the professionals agreed that I was gravely unwell. I've broken my bones and torn my flesh. Fearing me dead, the police have visited my home in the thick of the night. I've had the Old Bill in my back garden in the middle of the day. The purity of purpose with which I drove my needles into the red was a thing to behold; in a certain light, it looked like rage. Drugs, always drugs. Ablaze with paranoia, there were times when I was certain that an armed response unit sat waiting in the bushes in the back garden. I once moved so far from reality that I believed I was sharing my living room with a pair of kindly Nigerian strangers. Perched on the settee, I couldn't believe how *placid* they were. Turns out they were my cats.

Today I'm relieved to report that I've been well for almost three years. But for the longest time, my behaviour was given perfect cover by the industry in which I work. Out here, there's always plenty of company. Over the course of my career I've spoken with many scores of musicians whose behaviour might reasonably be described as deranged. Some are my acquaintances, and a number are my friends. I've written about people who, like me, have seen the insides of psychiatric care facilities. I've transcribed the words of performers who have since taken their own lives. Drink and drugs are everywhere. Like a magnet, the music business attracts people hardwired for self-destruction; as well as this, it provides an unsafe environment for those who might not otherwise give it a go. A perfect monster, it is both the chicken *and* the egg.

'There's a culture where music is linked to partying or having a good time,' Dr Charlie Howard tells me. Dr Howard is a consultant clinical psychologist who works in the music industry. 'So there are environments where the artists finds themselves [in places] where drinking or drug-taking happens,' she says. 'They get pulled into that and it becomes normal. So people will often say to me, "Oh, this is normal." And I'll say, "Well, hold on. Let's just question that for a moment. Because it might be normal in *your* world, but it's not *normal*."'

Scenting blood, I have written reams of articles that examine in precise detail the degradation of a hundred lives. I thrive on ruination. I will defend the tone of these pieces but I can hardly deny their existence; stacked up, they reach the height of a drum stool. In a luxurious apartment near Park Lane, Trent Reznor, of Nine Inch Nails, once told me of the time he was sectioned to a psychiatric institution after ingesting quantities of heroin and cocaine. Even as he spoke, I could hear trumpets in my ears. 'That's it, right there,' I thought. 'That's my intro. The rest will write itself.' And it was, and it did. Two days later the features editor at the *New Musical Express* told me it was my best piece yet.

I knew I was being played. I knew that Reznor *wanted* this story to appear in print. Selling the sizzle with screaming headlines and tales of horror, my trade offers a ringside seat for a circus at which the unlucky drop dead. People damaged beyond repair are eulogised as fallen heroes whose messy fates are largely unconnected to the dangerous terrain on which they practice their trade. Those who survive, or who seem to, will be written up as victors in a war whose rules of engagement are dangerously abstract. We never join the dots; working on a case-by-case basis, the full story is never told. So here goes. *There is something systemically broken in the world of music.* It's making people ill.

This book is my attempt to join the dots. In writing this story I don't wish to imply that people who work in other fields are unencumbered by mental illness or that their lives are spared the burden of addiction. As the twenty-first century approaches its first chorus, matters of the mind have become part of a mainstream conversation. Good. But there is, I think, something exceptional about our habit of romanticising the ghastly stories of my wing of the creative industries. Some of us are wedded to the idea that capable art should be underwritten by human suffering. Others bow to the image of the musician as an outlaw with license to do *anything*. When it comes to music played loud, this last one is particularly tenacious. How else to explain the ever increasing popularity of Mötley Crüe?

It's certainly no place for the faint of heart. Financially squeezed by a business model that has rendered recorded music all but worthless, for all but the most popular bands the road is the only place from which an income is guaranteed. Out on tour you'll find a dozen or more people living on a bus; its overworked residents run the risk of becoming co-dependent and infantilised. Brothers and sisters in arms, come the end of a tour they can barely stand the sight of one another. Believe me, I've seen 'em come and I've seen 'em go. If it is found at all, success can disappear in the space of a single album cycle. Bereft, artists are left to wonder what on earth just happened, or what they did wrong. (They did nothing wrong, or else everything.) Among them are people for whom a life in music is the only thing they've ever wanted. Going out of business in this way is a shock from which some will never quite recover.

Starved of time for conventional relationships, out in the field musicians form bonds that are tenacious and unwise. Lars Ulrich, from Metallica, once noted that he could tell that his group were going places when, in favour of cheaper alternatives, concert promoters began stocking their dressing rooms with bottles of Absolut vodka. There can't be many jobs that come with a free supply of hooch. Headline acts and support bands alike can be assured, upon request, of a backstage area stocked with crates of beer and bottles of wine and spirits. For those hoping to go off-piste, a discreet word in the right ear will secure refreshment in the form of pills and powders. In the music business, people who don't take drugs are tolerant of those who do. Nobody's against it. At its furthest remove, everybody knows somebody who knows *somebody* who can help.

So this is a book about all of that: about music, musicians, the industry, mental health, addiction, derangement, corrosive masculinity, monomania, overdoses, suicide and a hectare of early graves. Were he a bloodthirsty editor at a national publication, Eric Winwood would doubtless describe this as 'the good stuff'. As a journalist, I do too. But in writing this story, I've come to regard artists as victims and survivors of circumstance. In pursuit of a living wage, musicians are required to work themselves into the ground.

In the foothills of autumn in 2020 my fiancée and I travelled to the West Country for a short holiday. Dividing our labour, she undertook the task of keeping us alive – like many music writers, I've never driven a car – while I was anointed DJ. Cueing up the latest album by the emerging South Coast rock group Creeper, I allowed my mind to drift gently in the direction of the book, *this book*, that I was due to begin writing in just seven days' time. As the accents outside our little red car began to change, the CD in the stereo ended with a sad and fragile song of which I'm now reminded:

Getting high has got us so low.
All my friends.
All my friends.
All my friends hurt.

1: HAPPINESS IS EASY

I'm on my way to meet a band who have gone mad. In the spring of 2003 it's been twelve years since Metallica's eponymous fifth LP – known to all as '*The Black Album*' – found its way into the homes of thirty-one million listeners. Even by the blockbusting standards of the time, their assault on the mainstream was resonant and profound; the purest of breeds, the group's mass appeal was measurable by metrics of both size and weight. In a cover-story interview with frontman James Hetfield, *Rolling Stone* announced, with self-appointed legitimacy, 'The Leader of the Free World Speaks.' *The leader of the free world.* On the final leg of a two-year world tour, at stadiums across Europe supporters were offered the chance to purchase a t-shirt bearing the words 'Birth School Metallica Death'. Try as I might, I can think of very few bands that could justifiably make such a claim.

But now Metallica are in trouble. Six years since they last issued an album of new material, the group have been off the road since the turn of the century. With the position of bassist sitting vacant since 2001, it's been an age since they last spoke to the press. Profiling them in *Playboy* more than two years earlier, writer Rob Tannenbaum described how he'd 'spent a day with each of the four [performers] and I'd never seen a band so quarrelsome and fractious'. In the hope of addressing his enduringly dysfunctional relationship with alcohol, James Hetfield entered a rehabilitation clinic shortly afterwards. His absence from the ranks delayed the completion of Metallica's eighth album, *St Anger*, by more than a year. 'I haven't been really good at long-term goals,' the singer would later say. 'And long-term happiness was always pretty foreign to me. I'm going to be happy right now, because I want it now, because I feel like shit. And so the drink, the chick, whatever, was always the quick fix.'

On the long flight from London to San Francisco, I consider the prize that sits in my lap. *The World Exclusive*. After uncharted wanderings along lonely roads, Metallica have agreed to speak to one member of the European press. Writing for *Kerrang!*, that person is me. Heading west at no personal cost, over the course of an afternoon it is my job to discover exactly what has been furring the arteries of one of the most popular bands on the planet. It's been seven years since I first waved a tape recorder in Metallica's general direction. Aged twenty-five, aboard a private jet kitted out like a presidential suite, I accompanied them from their base in Paris to a concert at the Flanders Expo in Ghent. As the engines began to roar, James Hetfield invited me to stand up for takeoff. Hoping to establish my credibility, instead, like Wile E. Coyote before me, I learned an important lesson about the laws of physics. Cartwheeling backwards, the band's laughter accompanied me on my short but speedy journey to the rear of the plane.

In Northern California, Metallica run their operations from a labyrinthine complex in the North Bay commuter town of San Rafael. The size of a mid-scale production plant, the anonymous looking 'HQ' houses a recording studio, a production office, a fan club and well-stocked living quarters in which one might see out a routine Armageddon. At a counter in the kitchen area, guests sit on stools adorned with the words 'Metallica – San Francisco'. Two capacious rehearsal rooms creak under the weight of a battalion of amplifiers, many scores of guitars, a grand piano and numerous drum kits. Flags and banners from Metallica's vast army of world-wide constituents adorn the walls. *Don't tread on me.*

It's difficult not to be overwhelmed. Pacing the corridors, I review the questions written only in my head. Where has the time gone? Where did the band go? How is James Hetfield? *Who* is James Hetfield? Where is this new album? When will you tour? What went wrong? *What went wrong?* **What. Went. Wrong?**

'I've been in Metallica since I was nineteen years old, which is a very unusual environment for someone with my personality to be in,' Hetfield tells me in San Rafael. 'It's a very intense environment, and it's easy to find yourself not knowing how to live your life outside of that environment. Which is what happened to me. I didn't know *anything* about life. I didn't know that I could live my life in a different way to how it was in the band since I was nineteen, which was very excessive and very intense. And if you have addictive behaviour then you don't always make the best choices for yourself. And I definitely didn't make the best choices for myself.'

James Hetfield had tried to give up drinking once before. Believing himself cured of his need for excess, he began taking 'the occasional glass of wine' with dinner. From there it was but a short hop to prioritising a hunting trip to Siberia over his son's first birthday. In Russia, entire days were spent drinking vodka. Apart from shooting bears, there was 'nothing else to do'. Pitched out of the family home by his wife, Francesca, the singer checked himself into a rehabilitation clinic. Embarking on a process he would later describe to me as being like 'college for the soul', at last Hetfield's commitment was total. Anyone associated with Metallica was kept at bay for months on end.

The contrast with what had come before was jarring. This was the man who had mugged for the camera astride an inflatable bottle of vodka. He played in a band nicknamed 'Alcoholica'. He had a guitar on which were written the words 'more beer'. Intense and indomitable, the public face of James Hetfield would look in place on Mount Rushmore. That it had come to this was like overhearing

God on the line to the Samaritans. For the many millions drawn to his gunmetal persona, the inference was stark: if this can happen to him, what hope is there for the rest of us?

In the group's earliest days, Hetfield projected a public image of perfect invulnerability. 'That's what I wanted to be, that's what I needed in my life,' he tells me in San Rafael. 'That's what I wanted to see. That's what I wanted to portray. Through all the instability of childhood [following the death of his mother, the guitarist was raised by his father under the doctrine of a cultish church] I wanted something that was a rock, something stable. But at the end of the day we're all human and things change for a reason.' A number of the band's supporters were disappointed that he was no longer the person he used to be. 'How much that hurts me is so amazing,' he says.

In a room adorned with cartoon images of cars and racing drivers, James Hetfield speaks in the calm and measured tones of an apparently sensible man. It's me who's spooked.

Prior to my interview, I had been approached by a man who introduced himself as Joe Berlinger. Almost whispering, he told me that he and his colleague Bruce Sinofsky had been filming Metallica for the past two years. It's all there, he said, many hundreds of hours of footage of a group in various states of disrepair. The sudden departure and gradual re-emergence of James Hetfield; the musicians' bruised relationships; their stalled momentum; the pervading sense of creative insecurity; and the painfully hesitant, fractious and complicated recording of an album that was by now comically and expensively delayed – *it's all there*. In vainglorious Technicolor, at twenty-four frames per second, the footage unfolds like a train wreck. 'We'd like to film your interviews,' he told me.

'Right. What?'

'We'd like to film you talking to the band.'

To this end, my encounters with the members of Metallica are conducted in the presence of Joe Berlinger, a cameraperson and boom mic operator. As yet, no one can say what the footage is for. Certainly, they won't tell me. Most likely it'll be a six-part television series in the style of the (then) popular periodical *The Osbournes*. But, who knows, it might even be made into a film. *A film, eh?* Yeah, could be. Anyway, would I mind signing this release form? And posing for a Polaroid picture? 'It's nothing complicated,' Berlinger explains. 'It's just so we can use the footage in which you appear. You know, if it's suitable.' *Yeah, yeah, sure. No problem at all.* My eyebrows were rising. *And, um, might it be suitable?*

'Oh, yeah, I'd say so,' the director tells me. 'I mean, you're the first journalist the band has spoken to in years. This is the first time they've discussed any of this stuff to anyone outside of the camp.'

The feature film *Metallica: Some Kind of Monster* premièred at the Sundance Film Festival on 25 January 2004. With a running time of more than two hours, not one frame of Berlinger and Sinofsky's picture is graced with my presence. Upon reflection, probably it was unwise of me to spend every second of every day telling every person I knew, and a far from discountable number that I didn't, that I would be playing a pivotal role in a forthcoming production about Metallica's tortured revivification. *At the pictures and everything.* Sitting bemused in a screening room in Soho, I could only marvel at the filmmakers' ability to tell their story without me.

During my time as a journalist, two events have powerfully recalibrated public perceptions of what it means to be a member of a wildly successful rock group. Prior to the suicide of Kurt Cobain, from Nirvana, it had been widely assumed that happiness was index-linked to commercial success. The novel notion that the opposite could ever be true ignited frenzy among the ladies and gentlemen of the music press. I can still recall Cobain's already iconic image appearing on the front of a magazine beneath the strapline, 'I'm not gonna crack.' Right until the end, the stories were written as if this were somehow a game. *Why do you hate us?*

Why aren't you grateful? The bloodstained throne that Cobain left behind following his death on 5 April 1994 served as an enduring epitaph to the corrosive and distorting metric of public popularity.

I told you so.

Ten years later, the release of *Metallica: Some Kind of Monster* again served to disrupt conventional narratives about boys' clubs that play music. Without recourse to hindsight, the globally acclaimed feature portrays a group that fears for its life. James Hetfield is clearly terrified of losing both his sobriety and his family. Drummer Lars Ulrich is frightened for the future of a band that improved the quality of heavy music more than any other. Goosed by the notion that younger acts have stolen their crown, the musicians are stricken by a deeply pitiful sense of creative insecurity.

'Artists, musicians, band members, often they're looking over their backs thinking, "Who's the next band who's coming to take our place?",' the consultant clinical psychologist Dr Charlie Howard tells me. '"Who's coming to take our place in the charts?" Or whatever it might be. The relationships between band members can often be very fragile. People can be thick as thieves, but then something can be happening, or something can be bubbling or festering, and those relationships get damaged.'

Today, *Metallica: Some Kind of Monster* should be viewed as the first real-time document of a group in the throes of collective and individual mental illness. Beaten and ravaged by the weight of their creation, Metallica are broken from without and within. That the musicians would choose to cast light into such dark crevices strikes me as a remarkable and deeply honourable act.

'I don't understand who you are,' says Lars Ulrich to James Hetfield. Men who once shared hotel rooms, a house and, for more than twenty years, a band, theirs is a relationship at the end of its wits. 'I don't understand the [recovery] programme,' he says. 'I don't understand all this stuff.'

Ulrich then utters a sentence of such quiet devastation that it hardly ripples the water. 'I realise now that I barely knew you before.'

Aged fifteen, I'm on my way to see Metallica. The date is 21 September 1986, and my mother and stepfather are taking me from our home in Buckingham to the doors of the Hammersmith Odeon. When it comes to parenting, only one of these people is in charge; fortunately for me, she is instinctively inclined to indulge her only child's latest obsession. This is my first full year of live music. For now, and for decades afterwards, it is *on*.

These were the days when I would go and see *anything*. On the night before my English 'O' level, I travelled alone to the Electric Ballroom in Camden Town to see the then incomparable Bad Brains. Liking only one of their songs, I boarded a bus to watch Simple Minds at the Milton Keynes Bowl. Getting my bragging rights in early, I caught Queen at Wembley Stadium. My mum and I saw Dire Straits – it was me who was the fan – at the NEC in Birmingham. Missing the last train home after watching the English punk band The Stupids at a pub in the same city, I slept in the cold on a platform at New Street Station. In Nottingham and London, I caught up with Slayer on consecutive school nights. On dozens of occasions, my mum picked me up at Bletchley train station at one in the morning. Again, school the next day. Thinking back, I have no idea why social services weren't getting involved.

Like a blood red dawn, violent music was breaking over the wet concrete of my teenage imagination. *Speed* metal, reckless and loud. From there I made my way to the graffiti-strewn streets of hardcore and popular punk. Day trips to London, Milton Keynes, Aylesbury and Oxford harvested a record collection featuring Suicidal Tendencies, Dirty Rotten Imbeciles, Voivod, SNFU, Murphy's Law, the Misfits, Megadeth, Circle Jerks and dozens more. Breaking records for the amount of agro packed onto a single LP, an import copy of Slayer's swivel-eyed masterpiece *Reign in Blood* came to be mine before the end of autumn.

But tonight is something special. *Metallica in London*. Conquering the terrain at which punkish energy collides with virtuosic chops, it is they who are the masters. Authoritative and – what's the word? – *insouciant*, the San Franciscans are immune from the conventions to which others are required to adhere. Remarkably, thrillingly, the group's hostility to established norms is gaining traction. En route to west London I already know that, without any help from radio or MTV, their latest album, *Master of Puppets*, has sold more than a million copies in the United States alone. The true sound of liberty, everything about them is oppositional. Feral and troubling, the photograph adorning the record's inner sleeve is of a group that appears to have emerged from a plane crash: seated at a coffee table strewn with empty bottles, cigarette butts and the detritus of last night's takeaway, the musicians snarl at the camera in ripped clothing. The scene is chaotic, unwelcoming. A strewn copy of the *San Francisco Chronicle* announces that '[Rock] Hudson Has AIDS'.

Waiting for the band to strike up their set, at Hammersmith I read the tour programme. A double-page spread reveals the four members of Metallica bearing impish grins; a pull-quote from a grandly irritated American journalist is printed above them: 'They're dirty, noisy, obnoxious, ugly, and I hate them . . . but you can't deny their success.' Bet your boots, you can't. In the back rows of the balcony, on some level I understand that I am learning an important lesson about personal identity, about self-worth. Squinting at the page, this deliberate conjoining of image and words is just about the greatest thing I've ever seen. Thirty-five years later, I can still remember it. Emboldened, I am part of a rebellion.

To pay for all this music, I work two jobs. As the only child of a kind mother I am also the recipient of a good deal of maternal generosity. Each evening after school, I clean the branch of WH Smith in the centre of town. Six mornings a week I start work at the same shop at 5.30 a.m., sorting the day's papers and periodicals into fourteen delivery rounds. In the colder months, my day begins before dawn; plunged into a sink full of cold water, by the time I arrive at work my business-up-top-party-out-back mullet is an explosion of frozen shards. At the end of each shift I lend a hand in racking the papers and magazines, a service for which the shop's manager dispenses a torrent of unsolicited advice. 'Listen to what I'm saying to you, Ian, you'll thank me later,' he says. *I mean, I doubt it.* Mr Jones has a tendency to refer to parts of his life in the past tense. He used to like this band, and that band; he used to go to gigs here, and festivals there. But not any more.

Each morning I read the papers. A year earlier the Conservative government's decision to close (among others) Cortonwood Colliery in Barnsley had fired the starting pistol on the year-long Miners' Strike. By 1985 the struggle had become the bitterest industrial dispute of the past fifty years. (In my hometown, the event is known only as 'The Strike'.)

Heading home after my morning shift every other Saturday, my mum and I would drive north to see my dad. In the George & Dragon pub, on Summer Lane, I listened to the first-hand accounts of men who had spent months on the picket lines. Back in the south of England, on Monday mornings some of the papers described these people – one of whom had bought me a packet of crisps – as being a threat to the nation. It was a priceless education.

But even this formative gift was as nothing when compared to my discovery of *Kerrang!*. Lurking in a bundle of lesser publications – *Times Literary Supplement*, the *Economist*, *New Scientist* – then, as now, the weekly magazine featured only loud music: metal, punk, rock, alternative rock and even (occasionally) rap. It didn't matter that in 1985 I didn't yet care for many of the bands it covered; the reactionary old guard would soon be replaced by a tranche of livelier acts, anyway. I didn't mind back then that the magazine contained some of the most haphazard music journalism I'd ever read. All that mattered was that I'd found a title to which I was ideologically aligned. With its reckless energy, *Kerrang!* was the voice of the underdog. In other sections of the press, groups that give it some welly dined below the salt. Everywhere but here, ostentatious male writers told me that the Jesus and Mary Chain were more legitimate than Motörhead. Well, not any more. *Kerrang!* is never embarrassed by its beat. Even when it should be, it isn't. Denoting the sound of a guitar struck with force, its name comes with a free exclamation mark. Beat that for certainty.

'Can I buy this?' I ask Mr Jones.

'Course you can,' he says. 'You know, I used to enjoy this kind of music. Ever heard anything by Deep Purple? Never mind. I'll take it out of your wages.'

Around this time my mum asked me if I'd had any thoughts about what I might like to do with the next fifty years of my life. Despite a talent that might generously be described as ordinary, as a young child I thought I wanted to be an artist. What I actually meant was, I wanted to be my dad. Eric used to sit at the glass-top table at the rear of our family home at the foot of Prince Arthur Street, in Barnsley, patiently sketching superior images of film stars and landmarks. Marking his pad with heavy-leaded pencils – 'never anything less than 2B, Ian; 4B for dark' – sometimes he drew from memory. The work was its own reward; for him, praise held no currency.

'That's amazing!' my mother would say.

A shrug. 'Ah, not really. Look, here, the light's not quite right.'

'Love, it's *fantastic*.'

A tilt of the head. 'It's all right, I suppose.'

So anyway, one day my mum asked me if I'd had any thoughts about working a job. 'You know, when you leave school.'

Actually, I have. 'I want to write for *Kerrang!*'

To which she replied, 'Well, someone does those jobs. I don't see any reason why it shouldn't be you.'

And there they were, the most important words of my young life. If my mum thought it could be done, then it *could* be done. This was all it took to set me on my way. While the other lads at our secondary modern headed off to metal and woodwork shops, I joined the girls in typing class. On a typewriter the size of a church organ, over the course of two years I learned to touch type at a speed of sixty words per minute. I'm even faster now. In my earlier years as a music journalist, the first thing I would say to any student seeking my advice was, 'Teach yourself to type.' In the days before the QWERTY keyboard became familiar to all, the faster your speed the better your hourly rate. Even now, I can still tap-dance a sentence without once looking down. Back at school, hammering away at the reliably combative Underwood Touchmaster Five was like running a marathon in clogs.

Aged eighteen, somehow I talked my way onto the National Council for the Training of Journalists' (NCTJ) postgraduate course. Looking back, even at gunpoint I'd struggle to explain quite how I managed this. Oversubscribed by a ratio of six to one, the course was, and perhaps still is, widely recognised as being the most legitimate route into the world of print media. At the end of an entrance exam and, later, an interview with three stern interlocutors, on both occasions I sensed that I'd fared poorly. But apparently not. With the nights drawing in, by first class post I received an invitation to enrol at Sheffield University for a twelve-month calendar-year course in newspaper journalism. For the first time in almost a decade, I was to make my home in the People's Republic of South Yorkshire.

Living on the outskirts of Barnsley with my dad, his wife and a nine-year-old stepbrother, each morning I'm up with the milkman for a long commute to a cheerless college in Sheffield. In the black of

January 1991, the weather is persistently harsh. Spinning my wheels in the slush of February, one evening I say to my dad, 'Spring's on its way, Dad, isn't it? It'll be here soon, won't it?' What I need from him is just a few drops of paternal reassurance. Instead, Eric looks at me and says, 'Oh, Ian, I've known *many* a bitter March.' Great. Thanks, fella. A gift for life, as the coldest season prepares to clock off, each winter I'm reminded of these words.

With spring at last in the post, one evening at the family home on – yes, really – Coronation Street, my father answers a call from a pair of American evangelists punting bibles and invitations to a prayer meeting somewhere in town. Hanging on the frame of the front door with patient good grace, Eric bats away their genial enquiries as to the spiritual wellbeing of everyone who lives on the street. 'If they're at all religious, they keep it to themselves,' he says.

Recognising barren earth when he sees it, the younger of the two visitors begs one more question.

The quietest of sighs. 'All right. But just one.'

'Great, thanks.' *What is that accent? Texas? Tennessee?* 'Um, do you know anywhere I can get a Fat Willy's t-shirt?'

Defiant and robust, Barnsley is no place for the faint of heart. On its own the sight of two travelling evangelists from the red states of America is unlikely enough. That one of them has just asked if a man in the foothills of middle age knows of a source for a line of deeply garish beachwear advertising the non-existent 'Fat Willy's Surf Shack' shovels the exchange into the realms of the surreal.

'I've no idea,' says my dad. 'I don't even know where I can get a fat willy from.'

From the living room to his left, uproar. As our comic patriarch retakes his seat, I see in his face a quiet delight that I recognise today as my birthright. A weakness for the sound of other people's laughter.

Weekends and holidays are spent with friends in Buckingham. Following a surprisingly slow start, by now we're getting high. Loitering in Milton Keynes' pleasant shopping centre, we make the acquaintance of our first drug seller. A shoelace-thin swag bag of elbows and ribs, 'Bony Tony' dispenses casual conversation and a reliable supply of LSD and amphetamine sulphate. Dressed in Dr Martens boots, spacious jeans and an XL t-shirt that flies like a windsock, his look conforms to the 'postmodern grebo' style of the early nineties. His drugs, though cheap, are dependably potent.

We enjoy taking acid. Retiring to a pub back in Buckingham our little gang has been known to neck as many as six stamps of blotted paper in a single gulp. 'Are you feeling anything?' 'Not yet.' 'Are you feeling anything?' 'Dunno. Maybe a little bit.' 'Are you feeling anything?' 'I . . . think . . . I . . . am.' Like an orgasmic yawn, suddenly the evening is upon us. So long as we stay away from the bottomless void that is the mirror in the gents we're home and hosed. In the middle of the night the sound of music on MTV separates itself into a hundred layers; instrumental sections occupying four or eight bars somehow last for minutes. Broadcast at 4 a.m., movies that might otherwise be served as the focal point of a Christmas dinner are at once transformed into classics of the comic form.

But nothing compares to the surging electricity of amphetamine sulphate. *Speed*. Nasty and synthetic, the accelerating force is like being affixed to the wings of a space shuttle. *Whoosh*. Rapacious and wild, its initial rush can be felt in the hairs on my arms; I can feel it, even, in the breath held deep in my lungs. *Can't get enough.* Who knew that a chemical substance manufactured in a bucket from household cleaning products would be a source of such complicated wonder? Staying awake by re-upping my dose at regular intervals until the need for sleep overpowers me, in time I will learn to outrun the drug's steep hangover. With an ounce in my system, I once stayed awake for five days. In Buckinghamshire, already there are signs that I'm falling for this life harder than my friends. Failure to score fills me with something more than disappointment. To my nineteen-year-old mind, it feels like grief. *I was so wasted.* Cultivating a habit of refusing to acknowledge what awaits me on the other side of a high, I have no interest in saving myself from problems of my own making.

Heading north, Monday mornings were rarely pretty. Arriving in Milton Keynes with nothing more than coins in my pockets, on many occasions I was required to hoist my thumb in the air. As an alumnus of the final generation of hitchhikers, I hold fond and vivid memories of this once common and surprisingly dependable form of travel. But with an anxious new century heading our way, my time on the hard shoulder was almost up. At service stations and slip roads, already I was hearing stories from fellow travellers of uninvited sexual advances and physical danger from men (always men) behind the wheel. It was time to stop.

My final pickup was from a lorry driver named Sid. Peering out at the road from behind pop-bottle glasses, after an hour's chatter my friendly ride pulled his vehicle into Leicester Forest East for a spot of dinner, by which I mean lunch. Coloured by embarrassment, something inside me fell over. Was I not having anything? 'Ah, it's okay, I'm not very hungry.' 'You don't have any money, do you?' 'I don't, but it's all right.' In an act of kindness I will recall in detail until the day I die, my new Geordie friend filled a second tray with exactly the same items that graced his own. 'Don't worry,' he said. 'I can claim it back from the company. I just give them the receipt.'

'Um, Sid, it'll say you've eaten the exact same meal twice. Do you not think that they might see through this?'

The notion was extinguished with a wave of the hand. 'No they won't,' he said. 'If they ask, I'll just tell them I had two of everything.'

In a reference sent by post, the good burghers of the National Council for the Training of Journalists warn prospective employers that I have been a terrible student. About this, I can hardly complain. What began as an uneasy alliance between pupil and staff has in time metastasised into a silent but seething animus. A week before the end of my third and final term, word reaches the student body of a smattering of trainee places on the *Sun*. During my time in the Steel City, Sheffield's town hall has been the site of the ongoing Taylor Inquiry into the deaths of (at that time) ninety-five Liverpool supporters at Hillsborough in 1989. In a lesson far more valuable than anything the NCTJ has to offer, I well recall the paper's coverage of The Strike from six years earlier. *I don't want to write for the* Sun. Instead, what I want is what I now have: the confidence to come to London and chance my arm in the magazine game.

From a bedroom in Southgate, I launch what I imagine to be my assault on the capital. Lacking a plan worthy of the name, I know not a single person who writes for or edits any of the numerous music magazines published in the city. I've never met a full-time musician. Save for an unpaid article in a photocopied fanzine, I am entirely bereft of evidence to substantiate my claim that I can 'write a bit'. Really, it's difficult to imagine anyone within the borders of the M25 who is further from a piece of the Big City Action than I am.

I catch a wave. Reading *Kerrang!* at Paddington station in the cold January air I learn that the San Franciscan band Exodus are in town to record an album for Capitol Records. In like Flynn. The following morning at Battery Studios guitarists Gary Holt and Rick Hunolt grant me an hour of their time. Barely five years away from a dalliance with crystal methamphetamine that will rob him of everything but his life, Hunolt already looks like a skeleton. A voluble double act, the pair don't seem to mind, or even to notice, that their visitor is incapable of advancing their cause by even a single unit of sales. Having explained the nature of my business, they actually seem to want to help me become a music journalist. To this day I regard their generosity as being something close to altruism. Re-emerging into the dim light of an English winter, I have what I need to get me into the game.

Tongue protruding only slightly, like a novice skater clinging to the sides, I write my first ever feature. With stultifying simplicity, sometimes my own observations serve only to prepare the ground on which the musicians will say exactly the same thing. ('It's been a tough year for Bay Area heroes Exodus . . .' I write, to which Holt or Hunolt will duly reply, 'It's been a tough year for us . . .') Dividing the space equally between paragraphs of prose and quotes, this fiercely non-creative routine of call and response persists for more than two and a half thousand words. 'Tell you what,' I think. 'I haven't half got the hang of this.'

In a spasm of proactivity that still astonishes me, I head out onto the streets of London in search of work. First stop, *Kerrang!* Handing my photocopied article to a combative receptionist, without thinking I say, 'You will let me know if you decide to print this, won't you?'

'Is this the kind of thing you think that we do here?' she asks.

'I'm sorry, what?'

'Do you honestly think we'd take your story and just print it without telling you?'

'Um. No. I don't think that. I was just, um . . .'

'You were just what?'

'Um . . .'

As if in slow motion, the magazine's editor appears at her side. On sight, I know who he is. I could pick him out of a line-up of people who possess the authority to damage a career in music journalism that hasn't yet begun. There is a chance I'm going to burst into flames.

'Is there a problem here?'

Please, God, make it stop.

Four sheets of paper are jabbed in my direction. '*He* thinks we'll print this story he's written without even asking.'

Short of a criminal offence, it's difficult to imagine a means by which I might have made a lousier impression. I'm not imagining it, either; I'm not overplaying things in my mind. From a distance of yards, I can see the distaste on the editor's face. *Who the fuck is this kid?*

With a forlorn trudge I deliver my little story to the other publications on my list. Even now I can still recall my futile attempts to swat aside the overpowering sense of profound humiliation. The feeling of hopelessness is still within reach. *What am I doing here?* The world of music journalism is a citadel of cruelty to which I will not be permitted entry. And what business do I have here, anyway, if this is what the people within its walls are really like?

Why am I doing this?

By the end of the week I'm offered paid work by two national magazines.

2: WE ARE LONDON

Pearl Jam have given me tickets to the baseball. As the Seattle Mariners do battle with the visiting Los Angeles Angels of Anaheim, the bruised clouds blanketing the Jet City swell with the promise of rain. Not to worry. As the game unfolds, from high above a retractable awning slowly covers the field of play. I think of my dad, snoring up a storm in South Yorkshire. From an industrial estate on the fringes of Barnsley, twelve years earlier he had successfully estimated the cost of the steelwork on the renovated No.1 Court at Wimbledon. From a window seat in a plane descending over southwest London, in a little over twenty-four hours I will once again take the opportunity to look down at his work. *My dad helped make that.* Casting my eyes up to the blanket of metal now protecting thirty thousand people from the weather in Seattle, I briefly wonder if Eric has the chops to undertake a job of *this* size.

More than a month from the playoffs of 2009, the game takes place in what its participants call the 'dog days' of the season. As a writer for *Kerrang!* for the past nine years, I think I can sympathise with their disorientating schedule. Bouncing across the Atlantic, I was in Nashville earlier this week. Days before that, I landed in Toronto. In town to interview the disarming Canadian band Alexisonfire, that evening I joined three of the group's members at Rogers Centre for a tilt between the Toronto Blue Jays and – yes, indeed – the Los Angeles Angels of Anaheim. With fans funnelling into the stadium, our party was escorted to a suite of armchairs next to the visiting team's dugout. A front office representative in a shirt and a tie told me that this time yesterday Avril Lavigne had watched the same teams from the same spot. As with Ms Lavigne, in Canada the status of my hosts stands within touching distance of superstardom. To a chorus of applause, in the sixth innings their faces appeared on a giant scoreboard above the outfield. Seated between them, I was up there too. *Why am I on the Jumbotron?* Well, if the announcement over the public address system was to be believed, it was because I'd been mistakenly identified as a member of the group. Raising my arms in delight, it dawned on me that I had no idea what was going on. *Top of the world, Ma.* On the field of play, the Angels' first-base coach turned his head and, for a second, caught my eye.

In Seattle, I watch the game from an equivalent position. Three time zones west, the first-base coach is once again yards from my seat. From a few rows behind me a determined supporter attempts to win his attention. 'Hey, coach!' he shouts. 'Can I have a ball? Hey! *Fella!* Can I have a ball? It's for my kid. Yeah, it's for my kid . . . he's, um . . . he's got cancer.' This goes on for half an innings. The son has had an operation. No, two operations. Scratch that, *six* operations! Throwing out an indulgent smile, at last the uniformed coach turns round. As his eyes graze mine for the second time in ten days, I calculate the vanishingly thin odds of him thinking, 'Wait now, isn't that the fella from the game in Toronto? What the hell is he doing here?'

Back in the fervid year of 1991, Pearl Jam broke at the first time of asking. As their debut album *Ten* sold many millions of copies across the world, the group joined Nirvana, Soundgarden and Alice in Chains as leading members of a local scene attracting attention on a vast and terrifying scale. That this community of artists seemed wary of, and in some cases entirely unsuited to, the kind of fame that changes lives for ever did nothing to temper the rock world's sudden obsession with what until then had been a rainy second-tier city. (With appropriate elan, the author

Mark Yarm even titled his definitive book about the Seattle scene *Everybody Loves Our Town*.) Amid a feeding frenzy of berserk proportions, major label record companies rushed to open offices in the Pacific Northwest. Bands who would have struggled to get further than the reception desk a year earlier were suddenly garlanded with seven-figure recording contracts. Nihilism ran amok. A city awash with heroin, Seattle made drug addicts of many of its talented musicians. Several years earlier, a junkie cohort had told Duff McKagan to leave town or else risk becoming a victim of its intravenous plague. Moving to Los Angeles, he joined Guns N' Roses and became an addict all the same.

At Pearl Jam's compound near the centre of Seattle I'm granted a thirty-minute audience with Eddie Vedder. Chain-smoking American Spirit cigarettes, the singer is by now the team captain of a group that has somehow successfully managed to transform the gilded cage of fame into a force for liberation. Save for a smattering of early-day jukebox favourites, the music of this stadium-filling band rarely tugs at the sleeve of the casual listener. In eschewing fame in favour of something more substantial, Pearl Jam's five members have worked hard to sculpt a reality to which each is suited. I can see why they did it, too. In Seattle, the phrase 'adapt or die' resonates with literal force. Of the platinum-rated frontmen of the early nineties, Eddie Vedder is the only one who is still alive.

Determined to wreck the planet single-handedly, two weeks earlier I'd been in this very city listening to a singer tell me that he'd once seriously considered committing mass murder at Pike Place Market. 'I had a gun in my backpack,' he'd said. Just stood there stock still, apparently, ideating the carnage. *Right. Pretty quick to tell me all about it though, weren't you? I didn't even have to ask.* A likeable young man, he spoke of the years he'd spent addicted to heroin. Taking the air in the busy University District, I asked him how much time he would need to secure hard drugs, right now, from a standing start. Squinting in the sunshine, the look on his face changed. 'Fifteen minutes,' he reckoned. 'Tops.'

'Wow.'

Listening to Seattle's concrete surf, I shooed away a sudden urge to ask the young man to make a telephone call.

'Hey, do you know who Layne Staley is? he asked.

'Of course,' I said.

'Right. Okay. So do you see that block of apartments over there?' I followed his finger. 'Yep.'

'Well, that's where he used to live,' he said. 'And it's where he died.'

The frontman with Alice in Chains, Layne Thomas Staley, concluded his wretched march to the grave on 5 April 2002. Following two decades of heavy addiction to hard drugs, the singer spent his final years in a state of sordid isolation. Unable to wrest himself free of habits that first ruined his career, then his life, fears that had permeated the Seattle scene for years were heightened when his former manager received a call saying that Staley's bank account had been inactive for two weeks. Entering his apartment, the police discovered an eighty-six pound body in a state of advanced decomposition. An autopsy and toxicology report revealed that Layne Staley had died from a mixture of cocaine and heroin.

'I know I'm dying,' the singer told the Argentinian journalist Adriana Rubio months before his passing. 'I'm not doing well. Don't try to talk to my sister Liz, she will know it sooner or later . . . I know I'm near death. I did crack and heroin for years. I never wanted to end my life this way. I know I have no chance. It's too late.'

In an obituary published in the US music magazine *Spin*, Jason Cohen wrote, 'Heroin was Staley's demon and his muse, but what once fuelled his art also kept him from making any more. His death from an overdose . . . at the age of thirty-four was as inevitable as it was tragic . . . Staley had been through rehab several times and lost a former fiancée, Demri Parrott, to an overdose in 1996. In a 1993 *Spin* cover story, he discussed the many drug references in such [Alice in Chains] songs as "Junkhead" and "God Smack": "Maybe something this blatant and heavy . . . might steer people away from being excited about the idea of trying heroin." He made that point one last time.'

In the autumn of 1993 I was granted an interview with Layne Staley at the Royal Garden Hotel in Kensington. Unbeknownst to me, even then the singer was battling the practical difficulties of being a drug addict in an international touring band. Dressed in dirty blue jeans, a peach-coloured sweater and expansive black sunglasses, he silently accepted a copy of the magazine for which I wrote. As I watched him flick through its pages, his eye was led to a photograph of himself onstage in North America wearing clothes that suggested he got dressed in the dark. At the bottom of the picture was a captioned joke about the detrimental effects of hard drugs on one's sense of style. *Oh Christ, I'd forgotten about that.* In a voice that could barely be heard, he whispered the word 'asshole'. With a resonant sense of helplessness, my stomach sprinted to the window and threw itself to the pavement below.

The interview was for my second ever cover feature. Reviewing the story today, to my surprise I can see that I've already discovered ways of making music journalism work for me. I'm comfortable asking awkward questions; if required I will do so repeatedly. My employee is the reader, to whom I owe only good faith. Because I've never met him, or her, or them, *I* am that reader. Licensed to be many things – a booster, a storyteller, an assassin – it is unthinkable that I should allow myself to become an unpaid member of the group's public relations department. Mindful only of the story at hand, it is not my place to worry about preferred status or future access. More than anything, I appear to understand that, really, the job is no more complicated than making the distance between what I know and what I write to be as slim as possible. If nothing else, it's reassuring to know that I was as insufferable at twenty-two as I am now.

Seeking to outfox an editor who loathed copy bearing first-person pronouns, in the subsequent article I wrote how the woman handling press duties for Alice in Chains 'starts to tell you – and she hopes this doesn't impinge on your integrity – how the band doesn't really like doing interviews, how they're being persecuted at the moment, and how they keep being asked the same questions about . . . "About . . . Drugs?" you ask. Well . . . yeah. You know how these journalists can be. As proof of how these journalists can be, you're handed a verbal list of strong hints as to what it is and what it isn't okay to ask Alice in Chains.'

I told Layne Staley that I'd been warned not to ask him about drugs. As well as asking questions about drugs, I asked question after question about whether or not he was sick of being *asked* about drugs. I figured that ought to be enough to cover all eventualities. My apparent insubordination earned me a lifetime ban from interviewing any bands represented by the press officer's PR firm.

'Would you get sick of it?' he asked.

'Yeah,' I said. 'But no one's asking me.'

Layne Staley was the first obviously damaged person I'd ever met. Gravely unwell even then, the singer's questionable health – his *safety*, actually – was no match for the forward momentum of a breaking rock band. Whatever reservations he may have had about the wild adventure on which he was now embarked were as nothing compared to the shared promise of limitless possibilities. Seizing a moment, that's the key. Without the blessing of timing and opportunity a clutch of songs as good as those on the multi-platinum *Dirt*, the album Alice in Chains were promoting at the time, may as well be worthless. Unjust and perplexing, the history of rock 'n' roll is sinuous with music that didn't get its due. As likely as not, in the big leagues artists get one shot. Two at most. The diseased and vulnerable *will* be put to work.

It is, I suppose, worth saying that not everyone in music is determined to paint the town with their own blood. But if you *do* fancy giving it a go, I can think of no other industry that will make it quite so easy. Certainly I'll want to write about it. When a musician begins talking about difficult times, I hope for the worst. The death of a grandparent is no use to me at all – *oh, come on, that happens to everyone* – whereas an addict interviewee reduced to sleeping beneath a tarpaulin next to an overpass in a major metropolitan city (that's a real example, by the way) is a jewel. I'll make sure *that* gets polished up on the page, don't you worry. In print, it's me who has final cut; I'm the one who knows how to transform tragedy into a tastefully judged hyper-realistic vignette. If I can, I'll even bring it all together in a happy ending. I'm not like those cats on the internet. Out there in the new Wild West citizen journalists are able to explode carefully curated myths of rock 'n' roll inviolability in an instant. After briefly *dying* from an overdose of heroin, in 1989 Nikki Sixx, of Mötley Crüe, was able to write a career-defining hit ('Kickstart My Heart') that made the whole thing sound like enormous fun. *I'm just looking for another good time.* One wonders how the song might have been received had its source material been filmed by perfect strangers and broadcast on Twitter.

With forensic (non-visual) detail, no band has been quite as adept as Mötley Crüe at monetising their own dysfunction. Long after their star had fallen, the reanimating properties of the group's bestselling tell-all memoir *The Dirt: Confessions of the World's Most Notorious Rock Band* easily eclipsed their achievements on record. In collaboration with the writer Ian Gittins, Sixx issued his own memoir, *The Heroin Diaries: A Year in the Life of a Shattered Rock Star*, in which the degradations of untrammelled addiction are chronicled even more starkly. In a far from untypical extract, on 23 April 1987 the bassist writes, 'This is how low it gets . . . at three this morning I was crouched naked in my closet thinking the world was about to burst through my door. I peered out the closet and saw myself in the mirror. I looked like an Auschwitz victim . . . a wild animal. I was hunched trying to find a vein so I could inject my dick. Then the dope [heroin] went in my dick and I thought I looked fucking fantastic. I can't keep doing this, but I can't stop.' Well, that doesn't sound like much fun, does it? I don't think Sixx can be accused of trying to glamorise his own circumstances here. Dramatise, sure, but not glamorise. Instead, the work is being done by the gravitational pull of the dark side; in conjunction with the voyeuristic appetites of the reader, it adds up to a remarkably successful sales policy. Decades after their creative peak, the commercialisation of Mötley Crüe's antics has at last made them a stadium band.

'One thing we all agreed on very early was that we would be very honest about our lives,' Sixx once told me. 'So we'd do an interview and be asked what we did last night, and we'd answer, "Oh we did some cocaine, got into a fight and fucked a prostitute." And [the journalist] would look at us and say, "Who the fuck are these people?" But there were other people who were doing that who didn't want to talk about that stuff. I won't mention any names but there were quite a few bands who I talked to when I was doing *The Heroin Diaries* who I told were in my story and they said, "God, please don't let people know that we did that too." And that was just never Mötley's way. With us we were very open lyrically and in interviews, and it kind of took off from there.'

In what is by now a don't-bore-us-get-to-the-chorus cliché, books written (or ghostwritten) by troubled musicians invariably begin with scenes of squalid ruination. *The Dirt* opens with a description of Mötley Crüe's communal living quarters in West Hollywood in 1981. 'The place was crawling with vermin,' it reads. 'If we ever wanted to use the oven, we had to leave it on high for a good ten minutes to kill the regiments of roaches crawling around inside.' In the bathroom 'there would be tampons in the shower from girls the night before, and the sink and the mirror were black with Nikki's hair dye.' Never mind making a good first impression, Mötley Crüe are desperate that we understand that they were once the most repellent band in the world.

'A lot of interesting people do have the kind of stories that we do,' drummer Tommy Lee said to me in 2021. 'The ones that are fearless, and who do go to those levels to experience those things, have those stories, and I want to know what theirs are. They're fun to talk about and hear about. It's like when people go to the races to see a car crash. A lot of them aren't really there for the actual race. People are there to see an explosion . . . we all want that rush of wild stuff.'

The question of what best to do with struggling musicians is one that haunts the music industry. It's not always drugs that are the problem, either. When the Manic Street Preachers emerged at the turn of the nineties with music equipped with shock and awe, the band splattered bold colours onto an otherwise pallid domestic rock scene. For an audience of expressive outsiders too young to remember the reduce-to-rubble fury of the Sex Pistols, 'the Manics' were a tonic. But even at the start there were signs that one of their members was becoming unwell. Keen to defend his group's honour against the charge of inauthenticity, in an interview in 1991 with Steve Lamacq from the *New Musical Express* Richey Edwards carved the phrase '4REAL' into his arm with a razor blade.

'It wasn't as if I said, "You're crap. Now defend yourselves" or anything,' Lamacq later recalled in a piece for the *Guardian*. 'There was also no forewarning of what would happen next. Believe me, backstage, as Richey began to carve his arm open, I was as shocked as anybody was. But people always ask me: "Why didn't you stop him?" And there are two reasons, I think. One is that it happened so quickly. The cuts were deliberate but fast (and got faster and lighter as he neared the end). The second is: do you think he wanted me to stop him?'

In a characterful greasy spoon in Ladbroke Grove in the spring of 1993 Richey Edwards was my first British interviewee. It was a very British day, too; outside, the rain sounded like a drum solo. Amid a fug of smoke at a Formica table, I did my best to quickly reconcile the image of a firebrand rock star with the gentle twenty-five-year-old sitting opposite me. The kind of autodidactic intellectual to whom I remain drawn, at this point the Welshman was the most fascinating individual I'd ever met. He told me that he was 'not that precious about life: people are always up in arms about how precious life is – big deal. Stop smoking that cigarette, stop drinking that pint of beer. You're quite happy now but it means that you're going to die at sixty rather than eighty . . . I don't know one person who's genuinely concerned about their health.' Nodding my head in time to this nihilistic boilerplate, I thought I was listening to Joan Didion.

In a decision that makes me feel grubby to this day, a week later I agreed to sell the recording of our conversation to an acquaintance that wished to release it on CD. (To my relief, he never did.) Emerging from the World's End pub in Camden Town with sixty quid in my pocket, I used the money to buy six grams of speed. The following month, I said hello to Richey Edwards at a concert by the hardcore punk band Poison Idea at the new Marquee Club. Seeing as it was me who recommended that he watch the band, I sometimes wonder what he made of it all. But I never got the chance to ask.

At the nadir of an alarming decline, twenty-two months later the guitarist disappeared for ever. In 2008 his official status was changed from 'missing person' to 'presumed dead'.

It's difficult to overstate just how startling this new life was to me. Only months earlier, the people I was now interviewing were faces on music videos played late at night on MTV. At the start of the nineties, decisions about what someone like me could see or hear, or read about, were decided by radio programmers and DJs, television executives and magazine editors and journalists. The distance between artist and audience was codified and austere. Then, just like that, without having to pass any kind of entrance exam, I was one of their number. As insignificant as my standing may have been, my opinions were now deemed worthy of a place on the page.

To give it its due, the music industry welcomed me with a good show. As well as granting top-tier access to artists whose music I loved – not to mention a high number of those whose stuff I didn't care for at all – record companies threw parties all over London. Laminate stickers granting access to 'after show' happenings were dispensed to journalists queuing for complimentary concert tickets at the guest-list window. With drinks at the bar plentiful and free, alcohol was both currency and fuel. Forget about normal, being plastered at 1 a.m. on a Tuesday night was seen as a commendable achievement. If this all sounds uncommonly exotic, please understand that in many ways the music business is much like hundreds of other professions. As with insurance brokers and heating engineers, its workers gather off the clock to swap tedious stories and talk trade. It's the settings that are different, not to mention the severity of our behaviour. A friend of mine who today edits a popular magazine was once so wasted at a Metallica after show that he ended up asleep on platters of expensive food on the buffet table. What a guy. Once again, his efforts were widely and wildly applauded. I doubt you see *that* kind of thing at an orthodontists' convention.

This adolescent hoopla conferred a sense of counterfeit exclusivity. Whether at work or out on the lash, we were all *in*. I was twenty-two when I made the acquaintance of Layne Staley, by then a man whose artistry and dysfunction had made him a millionaire. Maybe it was confusing for both of us. *What was I doing talking to someone who was rich? Sensitive and unwell, what was* *he doing **being** rich?* This proximity to success and glamour could sometimes scramble the mind. Warped by the vicarious glow of the group's success, in 1993 Pearl Jam's press officer would answer the phone at his desk with the words, 'Pearl Jam do not want to speak to you.' For a good two years he seemed to believe that he was in fact a member of the band. In backstage corridors and after-show parties, journalists and public relations people brandished laminates and passes as if they were Olympic gold medals. You did hear me, right? We were the jet set. We were *in*. There we were at 2 a.m. on a January night waiting for the night bus to take us back to our distant bedsits and our box rooms in terrace houses rented with perfect strangers in Zone 4.

At an Offspring concert in the summer of 1993, I met a man named Chris Watts. It would perhaps be easier if I introduced him to you as my hero. Reading *Kerrang!* it was *his* spiky and expressive work that I revered the most. At that point I'd yet to meet a single person who wrote for the only music magazine that mattered to me. All I knew was that I'd spent eight years studying each writer's copy with an attention to detail that bordered on the obsessive. To me, *they* were the *real* rock stars. *They* were the chosen ones. In delivering my little photocopied article to its doors seventeen months earlier, I'd rather hoped that *Kerrang!* might give me a home. Instead, it had gifted me a sense of envy so profound that it often kept me awake at night. I'd managed to make the scene, sure, but not *their* scene. I wasn't one of *them*. I didn't imagine I ever would be.

'Chris?'

'Yes, mate.'

'Um, I love your work.'

'Right. Thanks.'

'Like, I really like it.'

'*O-K.*'

'May I buy you a drink?'

On account of him having no money, in point of fact Chris Watts allowed me to buy him seven or eight drinks. Probably I'd still be buying them now had the venue not called time at midnight. But try as I might, I could not convince him that I was right to hold his work in such high regard that the only thing I really wanted was to one day be considered his equal. Unwilling to come out and say that his sentences didn't merit the encomiums I was so breathlessly lavishing upon them, instead Watts let it be known that the world to which he had dedicated his talents was a place of stuff and non-sense. The whole thing was a waste of time. Really, I ought to have slapped him. I ought at least to have found a way to explain that my attraction had nothing to do with music – which I'm not sure he liked all that much, anyway – or his crippled sense of self-worth. It was about *prose*. It was about placing words in an order that set the page on fire.

He is rusting before my eyes.

'If you want my advice,' he told me. 'Don't be taken in by all this' – he waved an arm at the bar and the stage – 'stuff.'

'Okay.'

This is a warning sign.

'Listen to this. Do you want to know what I do, you know, to make ends meet?'

Make ends meet? 'What?'

'I drive a minicab.'

'Okay.'

'Here's another piece of advice for you. If you ever need to get out of a taxi without paying, do it before the driver has put the hand-brake on. The time it takes him to sort himself out will give you the time you need to make a clean getaway.'

Why would I need to that? 'It was nice meeting you, Chris.'

Today, the only thing I can really remember about Chris Watts's journalism is that he seemed willing to ask his interviewees *anything*.

If there were rumours that a musician took heroin, he'd ask if it was true. He didn't want to be their friend. Consciously inspired, in my first full year as a music writer for a minor-league magazine I learned that people would answer whatever question I asked. After almost thirty years of pronounced change, it pleases me greatly that today this part of the process remains more or less the same. Speaking to musicians, even very successful musicians, I'm afforded the latitude to ask whatever I please. As often as not, I'm given an hour in which to do so. Unlike film journalists, I'm not hustled in and out in seven minutes. I don't have a public relations person at my shoulder. With space in which to stretch my legs, like every other member of my profession I am at liberty to find a story.

Growing up, I always liked this one. In 1982 Ozzy Osbourne was arrested for urinating on the Alamo while visibly drunk and dressed in a colourful selection of his wife's clothes. He might have got away with it were it not for the screams of nearby tourists attracting the attention of local law enforcement. Recounted in his book *Can't Stand Up for Falling Down*, the British journalist Allan Jones recalls looking 'around to see a man and a woman, the latter with her hands to her mouth [while] her husband, or whatever he is, looks like he's well on his way to having a seizure of some kind'. Ozzy Osbourne couldn't understand what all the fuss was about. Placed under arrest by a Texas Ranger, he was told, 'Mister, when you piss on the Alamo you piss on the state of Texas. *That*'s what all the fuss is about.'

Writing this book, I've come to regard this misadventure as a bellwether for any aspiring rock 'n' roll delinquent. Ozzy was arrested for urinating on the Alamo. Wearing women's clothes. In the middle of the afternoon. *What have you got?*

In the spring of 2011 Ozzy Osbourne becomes my first interview since the death of my father. It's been exactly a week since the sun-soaked funeral at which Eric was lowered into the ground. At the graveside a large and loving gathering of mourners was each invited to toss a handful of dirt onto the coffin below. Much to my surprise, I found myself gripped by the sudden and certain belief that it was necessary for us all to partake in this strange ritual. Patrolling the crowd, I reminded friends and family members that had known me for as long as I had been alive that this was their last chance to say goodbye to a man no one could believe was dead. To the sad sound of dry earth hitting a wooden box, the last thing I did for my father was encourage people to bid him farewell.

'Bye, Eric.'

'Sithee, lad.'

'So long, Dad.'

'Take care, son.'

Now, waiting at a rural train station for a ride to the Osbourne home in rural Buckinghamshire, it occurs to me that I should give him a ring. My father doesn't have a mobile phone – of course he doesn't – but it's only just past lunchtime on a Friday afternoon so he'll still be at work. I can tell him that I'm on my way to interview Ozzy, a man so famous that even Eric will recognise the mononym. He'd like that, I think. A year or two earlier he'd seen one of the lads in the workshop at Triple Engineering reading an article about Muse that I'd written for *Kerrang!* By the sound of it, he couldn't get the words 'that's my son' out of his mouth quick enough. 'So, yeah,' I think, 'I'll ring him and tell him what my afternoon has in store.' *Oh. Yeah. Right.* Within a beat of my heart I remember that I won't be making the call because my dad is dead. Like the first plunge over the brow of a towering rollercoaster, the realisation turns me upside down.

Seated at an outside table, Ozzy Osbourne tells me about the time he woke up in the cells at nearby Amersham police station after attempting to murder his wife. He had no memory of how he got there, and neither do the writers who today conveniently air-brush the incident from their innumerable profiles portraying him as a National Treasure. He then tells me that he retains the ability to source drugs anywhere in the world inside of fifteen minutes. Fixing my gaze on the flock of sheep grazing in the undulating fields stretched out before us, I say, 'I bet you can't round here.'

At times during our interview, Ozzy Osbourne looks to be in a shocking state. Trails of dribble hang from his mouth; sputniks of spittle are sent flying through the air. Hearing my words, though, the singer looks me hard in the eye. With a clarity of purpose that I'll remember for the rest of my life, he asks, 'How much do you want to bet?'

As ever, I'm getting ahead of myself. Back in the twentieth century, I begin to flounder. Having failed to land a position on *Kerrang!*, I regard the publications who *are* willing to pay for my words with something approaching contempt. Talk about taking the piss. There is nothing standing in my way of requesting work from other magazines. In the hope of changing my circumstances, there is nothing stopping me exercising the kind of proactivity that landed me a seat at the table in the first place. But it doesn't occur to me to do this. It doesn't even cross my mind that I ought to approach *Kerrang!* for a second time. Instead, my days are filled with drift and mischief.

By now I'm shovelling down enormous quantities of drugs. Every Friday afternoon I catch a bus from an increasingly dishevelled two-room bedsit in Palmers Green to a pub near the top of Green Lanes in Turnpike Lane. The kind of establishment that looks to have been imported wholesale from a Cheech & Chong movie, in the saloon bar of the Queen's Head a former miner sells me an ounce of speed for a hundred quid. For ease of access, my purchase is packed to bursting inside a small zip-lock bag. Necking four or five grams of acrid powder in a cubicle in the gents, my entire body is consumed by an involuntary spasm. But it's okay. The promise is now in the post. *Four-day, five-day marathon.* To this day, the twenty-minute wait for the astonishing elevation of amphetamine sulphate is the most sublime pleasure I have ever known.

By now I'm signing on the dole. With housing benefit covering my rent, I am writing – illegally – less and less. In the eyes of my editors, my reputation for unreliability is growing. Walking away from the Queen's Head on a winter's evening, I remember thinking, 'This is the very last thing you need to be doing.' I also remember my sense of elation that such tedious concerns were mere minutes away from total obliteration. *It's okay – speed is about to run its sprints through my system.* For the next few days, nothing – and I *do* mean *nothing* – can touch me. Created by my own hand, I know that my problems are growing stronger. With great patience, they will be waiting for me on the other side of the hill.

Needing to raise funds, I've started selling CDs at the second-hand record shops of Soho and Islington. Decoupling from the intermittent responsibilities of the lazy music journalist, in 1998 I begin taking my stereo down to the nearest branch of Cash Converters. Transported in a shopping trolley, each visit pays fifty quid. A lovely system, the hi-fi was a gift from my mum; putting it in and pulling it out of hock is hardly an edifying look. Had I worked as hard at writing as I do raising a kitty for my seller at the Queen's Head, it's just possible that I might have prospered. With deadlines whistling by, instead I allow whatever talent I have to decay. One Thursday afternoon in spring, my exhausted sleep is pricked by the incessant trill of the telephone. On the far end of the line an exasperated section editor waits to tell me that my line of credit in the Last Chance Saloon is at an end. He's sorry, he really is, but I'm fired.

Hoping to wrestle my life into a semblance of order, I take a job at a bookshop. 'That'll be easy,' I think. 'I like books. I get along with people.' Evicted from my hovel in Palmers Green, each morning I walk from my new home in Islington to a branch of Books etc. in the square mile. No longer a jobbing music journalist, these days work begins as early as eight o' clock. Them's the breaks. I was only ever a minor league writer anyway, I tell myself; so long as I don't look backwards it (sometimes) doesn't feel as if I've lost all that much. Out on the shop floor, my new workmates are nice people who love books. They read the music press and sometimes go to concerts. A few of us have been known to head east to watch the London Knights play ice hockey at the London Arena. With the shop closed at weekends, whenever the team are in town I take one of the deputy managers to see Barnsley play. I don't dislike my new circumstances. For the first time in my life I feel like a respectable citizen.

The way I see it, the only real problem is that I'm a hopeless bookseller. Reliably bamboozled by all aspects of my new position, my determination to pose a clear and present danger to anyone hoping to purchase a paperback is total. It's not as if I'm not trying, either; people who diffuse bombs for a living don't concentrate as hard as this. Touch typing on a Jurassic computer system, my mind is like a firework display. But it's no good. Routine enquiries send me into paroxysms of panic. Books on order disappear into black holes of my own making. On the first of our many 'little chats' in a windowless office my stern but likeable manager tells me, 'In a bookshop – in *this* bookshop – there's nowhere to hide.' Sometimes I wonder if this is actually true. I haven't tried hiding in the space above the ceiling tiles, or beneath the floorboards. Now that I think about it, there's a giant skip out the back. I reckon I could hunker down in that easily enough. 'Come on, Ian,' I'm told, again and again. 'You should know this stuff by now.'

It's tempting to say that the only person from my life as a writer I remained in contact with was my friend Dan Silver. But in his refusal to be torched to a crisp in my scorched-earth policy towards the world of music journalism, it might be him who holds onto me. Three years earlier the two of us had been united – for life, I would say – on a work trip to the Pinkpop Festival in Landgraaf, on the Dutch border with Belgium. With the rain bouncing like tennis balls on a concrete court, between us we took the executive decision that the most likely salvation for our dismal Friday evening lay in engaging the services of the man patrolling the fringes of the main arena carrying a placard featuring a cartoon image of smiling fungi. *What's the worst that can happen?* The fact that neither of us had ever tried magic mushrooms did not detain us. It's difficult to pinpoint the exact moment that I realised that the drugs were *really* taking hold, but it might have been when a group of third-division American rap metal dullards suddenly began sounding like The Beatles. An hour later, as I stood whispering sweet nothings to a tumble-dryer sky, Dan came barking out of the festival's production office brandishing a pair of Access All Areas laminate passes – 'Triple A's', the gold standard – valid for the entire weekend.

'How the hell did you get these?'

'I don't believe I know. Something about us being English journalists. I might have been speaking fluent Dutch.'

(To this day, Dan still thinks he might have been speaking fluent Dutch.)

'These mushrooms are a revelation, aren't they?'

'I think we should see if we can get some more.'

This was the two of us doing our jobs. Back at the hotel bar we charged two hours' worth of whiskies to the room of an MTV presenter sitting at the next table along. This was the two of us at work. And now? Well, now I have a position in which my name gets written in a ledger of wrongdoing should I arrive a minute late on the tills. At the end of each day, colleagues rummage in each other's bags to make sure that nothing is being nicked.

Like the ghost of Christmas past, Dan comes to meet me at close of business on a Friday night so that the two of us can repair for a few pints down near Aldgate, or head off for a curry on Brick Lane. In a just and fair world, his flat on the nearby Whitechapel Road would be universally recognised as the site of the best all-night parties the world has ever known. On one particularly notable morning a music journalist friend was roused from a fully clothed coma on the living-room floor with the words, 'Shouldn't you be on your way to Paris?' '*What?* Oh *fuck!*' Grabbing his bag, off he went, a cloud of dust en route to Waterloo for a job of work in a different country. Oh, how we applauded. Now, when my best friend asks me what I've been up to I tell him I've been selling books.

I tell myself that I'm taking my medicine.

One Friday Dan informs me that he's landed the job of website editor at *Kerrang!*. I am of course (essentially – more or less – give or take) pleased that my closest comrade has bagged the kind of gig that his talents clearly deserve, even if it is at a publication for which I've yearned to write for half my life. With my own reputation residing in the clearance bins, I don't think to ask if he'll have a word with the commissioning editors on my behalf. I don't wish to embarrass him in that way, just as I don't want *them* to embarrass me. But having watched my incremental transformation into a vague approximation of a functioning adult human, under cover of silence Dan has already spent the summer months of 2000 on manoeuvres. Unbeknownst to me, he's been dropping my name into the ears of *Kerrang!*'s loveably psychotic features editor. There can be no question that the timing is perfect for everyone. Following the departure of its best and most prolific writer, bylines on Planet *K!* are suddenly going for a song. On a Friday night in September 2000, the three of us meet up for drinks in a pub on the Tottenham Court Road. For the first time I sense that I'm being watched. 'Just wait and see,' says Dan.

One week later, on my last day of work before a fortnight's holiday, the features editor calls.

'Look,' he says, 'we're going to give you a try out.'

Kapow! 'Wow. Thanks. Right. Cool.'

'So what sort of bands do you like?'

The screen goes blank. Faced with a question capable of changing the course of my entire life, I am unable to recall a single group whose music I enjoy. Truth is, during my fifteen months at the bookshop I haven't been paying attention to the sounds of what is by now a brand new scene. To do otherwise is just too painful. Realising that a poorly judged answer will blow apart the shaky façade of the person I'm now pretending to be, I urge myself to think. 'Um, well, I like the newer stuff, you know,' is my answer. 'I'm not really a big fan of, um, Iron Maiden, say.' 'That's good,' I think. 'That *is* good. I told the truth. I didn't lie.'

'Well, that's a shame,' he says. 'There's actually a trip to do Maiden in Seattle. You've shot yourself in the foot there.'

Because I don't yet know what life on *Kerrang!* is like, I assume he's joking. But he isn't. Dispatching young reporters across the world, the person to whom I am speaking is both a full-time commissioning editor *and* a part-time air traffic controller. As a music journalist for most of the nineties, I'd been sent to the United States on two occasions. Come the end of 2000, in the space of barely three months on Planet *K!*, I will have walked the streets of Los Angeles, Chicago, Pensacola, Louisville, New Orleans, Baltimore and Munich. The magazine is well on its way to overtaking the *NME* as the highest-selling music weekly in the world. Comrades, this is the Big Leagues. Friends, this is *The Show*.

'All right,' he says, 'let's see what else I've got.' I can hear the sound of papers being shuffled. 'Okay, how about this. There's a trip to LA, this time next week, to interview Downset. Do you like them?'

I have never heard of this band.

'Yeah, they're pretty good,' I say. 'If I'm being honest' – *honest!* –
'I don't think they're great, but they're all right.'

'Ace. I'll get their PR to give you a ring with all the details. What's your home number?'

To the sound of skyscrapers collapsing around me, I remember a piece of crucial information.

Tell him.

'I look forward to reading your piece, Ian.'

Tell him.

'Um, yeah. There is just one other thing.'

A sigh. 'Go on.'

'I haven't got a current passport.'

Another sigh. 'Well get yourself down to Petty France and fucking get one, then. Now fuck off.'

Seven days later, aboard an all but deserted plane, I flew to Los Angeles for four nights. Interviewed at the studio in Van Nuys at which Nirvana made *Nevermind*, Downset's singer told me we were in a sketchy neighbourhood. *Really?* All I could see were palm trees and sunlight. Seventeen dollars bought me a ticket to watch the LA Dodgers; believing myself to be King of the World, with aristocratic entitlement I moved to a better seat behind home plate. *Was this how things were going to be from now on? Was this my job now?* Back in London, I worked as hard as I knew how to ensure that my first feature for *Kerrang!* was as good as it could be. *Why hadn't I thought of this before?* Handing over my work the next morning – 'a floppy disk, eh? Haven't seen one of these in a while. Maybe get yourself an email account?' – the magazine's deputy editor told me he'd be in touch.

For five days I heard nothing. Like a film on fast-forward, before I knew it a night's sleep was all that separated me from another day as a bookseller. As for music journalism, well, that'd been a bust. Boarding a plane at Terminal Four, I'd done my best to manage my expectations of what my new editors might have in mind for me. Even so, no amount of careful stewardship could protect me from the humiliation of being cast aside after only one article. *A two-page feature, that's all I'm worth.* The only reason the fucking thing would make it into print at all was because the group's record company had paid for me to go to California. Without that, I'd be on the spike. My only hope was that in time this technicality might afford me a glimmer of phony pride. In writing a piece that had been published by *Kerrang!* I would have achieved the one thing I had dreamed of since I was fourteen years old.

Returning home from a forlorn swim at the council pool, an urgent message awaits me. 'Thank God you're back,' says my house-mate. '*Kerrang!* called. They want you to give them a ring tonight. The deputy editor says he'll be on this number until ten o' clock. You've got ten minutes.'

'*What?*'

The voice on the trumpet asks me what I'm up to the day after next. 'Um . . .'

'Here's what it is,' he says. 'We need someone to go to New Orleans to interview Nine Inch Nails. It's a cover story. Flight leaves first thing Tuesday morning. Can you do it?'

Staring at a fork in the road, I tell the deputy editor that I am unable to accept the commission. 'I work in a bookshop,' I say. 'The only reason I was able to go to LA was because I was on holiday. I'm sorry to let you down but I can't just . . . *quit.*'

Returning the receiver to its cradle, I wonder if this is actually true. *Who says I can't?* Do I want to continue knocking out copies of *Liar's Poker* to flyboys from the trading rooms, or do I want to eat a shrimp and oyster po' boy on Oak Street? *What was wrong with what I just said?* Adrenaline surging through the channels, I ring my mum.

'It's a weekly magazine, isn't it?' she says.

'It is, yeah.'

'Right. Well, then there should be plenty of work. On weeks when there isn't, you can get day shifts from a temping agency. I'm hanging up the phone now so you can ring *Kerrang!* back.'

'Okay. Right.'

'And, darling . . .'

'Yes, Ma.'

'I love you. Congratulations. This is what you've always wanted.'

At 7 a.m. the story breaks. Opening the door of the bookshop, the deputy manager can hardly contain his surprise. 'Crikey,' he says, 'you're keen. You don't start 'til eight.' *Yeah, about that.* So I tell him. *I'm sorry but I need to be off. I need to be away.* Last night I was so panicked at the prospect of delivering this news that I stayed up all night watching the Oakland Athletics in the post-season playoffs on Channel 5. So if he doesn't mind, with his blessing I'll say my good-byes and get myself off to bed. Only trouble is, the man on earlies lacks the authority with which to unilaterally green-light my escape plan. He needs to phone head office to find out the score. *But I already know the score*, I want to tell him. *I've won.* So has he, while we're about it. With something close to affection he once told me I was the worst bookseller that ever lived. So let's have a look at the headlines, shall we? *I work for* Kerrang! *now. This time tomorrow I'm going to New Orleans. You can't stop me. Head office can't stop me. No one can stop me.*

As fast as that, my life as a music journalist begins again.

3: BEAUTIFULLY UNCONVENTIONAL

Hidden like a plague pit, the *Kerrang!* office is both a machine of moving parts and a clubhouse for the kinds of people not normally seen on the shop floor of a mainstream publication. Vibrating to the sound of loud music, its tempo is relentless. From a production meeting on a Monday morning to the point on a Friday afternoon at which the editor puts an issue to bed, each member of staff understands that, on a weekly title, deadlines arrive like waves from a restless sea. As part of a wider team of freelance writers and photographers, I take my place in a shock troop of soldiers in the field. Between us we are the daughters and sons of builders, lightermen and miners; few of us hold university degrees; all but one of us was born outside London. We are Geordies, boys from the Black Country, Humbersiders, Northern Irishmen, East Midlanders, Welshwomen, Greater Mancunians, and proud citizens of the People's Republic of South Yorkshire. With my new passport close to hand, it takes me no more than a fortnight to learn that I can be packed off anywhere in the world with as little as twenty-four hours' notice. Sometimes less.

The office becomes my second home. Popping in to pick up the latest issue, many are the times I'm still there three hours later. Heading out the door, I fall into the habit of issuing a loud good-bye; without turning round, I smile at the resonant chorus of voices returning the call. Over the course of a hundred visits, only once does the lovably psychotic features editor throw a hunting knife at me. Bearing legitimate intent, the weapon rebounds off a load-bearing support column onto the desk of a startled teenager on a week's work experience. 'For Christ's sake, that could have had her eye out!' someone screams. And that's the end of the matter: no disciplinary hearing, no report from human resources. Me and the knife are old friends, anyway. In one-on-one briefing meetings in the pub round the corner, my features editor prises it open and eases it shut. Prises it open, eases it shut.

'Why have you brought a fucking knife to work?'

'I don't know. I like the way it feels.'

Kerrang! is everything I hoped it would be. A fortnight into the job, in Essex I team up for the first time with Paul Harries, the magazine's best and most prolific photographer. A blue-collar talent who made his bones taking pictures at concerts for nothing more than pleasure, by the time of my arrival Harries' work adorns the cover of at least half of the issues in any given year. With kindness in the eyes and wit on tap, he is recognised by all as both the magazine's team captain and its shop steward. He might even be its soul. 'Welcome to the family,' he tells me. *Wow, thanks, man.* This is what it is, too, a noisy and dysfunctional family. Of the dozen or so newspapers and magazines to which I've contributed over the past twenty years, none give off the chaotic and communal vibe of *Kerrang!* I can still hear him saying these words. I can still recall how much they meant to me. *Welcome to the family.* In accepting every piece of work that comes his way Harries takes as much pride in a two-page feature at the Colchester Arts Centre as he does a world exclusive cover shoot in Beverly Hills. Watching him work, I learn everything I need to know about what it takes to prosper at my new home. Within the month, we're set for life.

With memories of working in the bookshop fresh in my mind, I make no effort to hide my delight at this overwhelming new world. Boarding a connecting flight at Philadelphia International Airport, Harries and I head to New Orleans in time for Halloween.

After two days in the Big Easy, we fly north to Baltimore. 'Finally,' he says, 'somewhere I've never actually been. Be nice to see something new.' Strolling through the city's lovely harbour-side streets, Harries suddenly remembers that, actually, he has been here before. It's coming back to him now. For the past half mile, he thought it might have been *déjà vu*. 'There's a decent bar coming up on the corner here,' he says. 'Look, there it is. Fancy a pint?'

Philadelphia, New Orleans, Baltimore – three cities in a long weekend. Is it any wonder we get confused? Is it any wonder I find it all so intoxicating? After a lifetime of cultural osmosis – *Bloom County*, Donna Tartt, *Hey Arnold!* – at twenty-nine I've reached the age at which *everything* about the United States of America is exciting. Those sad little stalls hawking flavourless pretzels are exciting. The newsstand from which I've bought a copy of *Sports Illustrated* to read on the flight home is exciting. (Along with the *New Yorker*, *Sports Illustrated* has taught me everything I need to know about writing features.) The Philly cheese steak I ate with a pint of local beer in the airport bar – bet your life *that* was exciting. After a decade of semi-permanent jetlag, Harries is long past the point of being hypnotised by the saturated colours of America's brilliant parade. 'Doesn't matter where you go,' he says, 'it's always cheese and beef.'

Waiting on our plane back to London, I read out the names of the cities displayed on the three departure monitors above our heads. Feel free to imagine me bouncing in my seat.

'Pittsburgh. Paul, have you been there?'

'Um, yeah.'

'What's it like?'

'Yeah, it's all right.'

'How about Houston? You been to Houston?'

'I . . . have been to Houston, yes.'

'And what's that like?'

'Houston? Yeah, it's not bad.'

'Look, there's a plane going to Chicago. I'd love to go there. I bet you've been there, haven't you?'

'A few times.'

'I bet it's great. Is it great?'

'Yeah, yeah, it's all right.'

Fixing himself a smile, Harries says, 'I should really write a travel book, shouldn't I? *Paul Harries' Guide to American Cities*. Page one: Atlanta – it's not bad there. Last page: Washington DC – yeah, it's all right.'

Despite there being an age difference of barely five years between us, for a time I play the role of Harries' excitable son. Seven weeks ago I was knocking out hardback copies of *Harry Potter and the Prisoner of Azkaban*; and here I am now eating seafood on the endless beaches of northern Florida. Around these parts, the engines roar into life with remarkable speed.

Returning to Heathrow, or Gatwick, invariably I'll be in the air again within a week or two. Back in LA for the third time in a month, in the cab from the airport Harries tells me that perhaps I ought to have a little think about all this travelling I'm doing. Two weeks ago I was here to speak with Bad Religion. A week later, I was asking questions of the Foo Fighters. (Without leaving Heathrow, I then boarded a plane for two nights in Sweden with The Hives.) This time it's Black Rebel Motorcycle Club who have brought me to Hollywood. Truth be told, I do feel a bit funny. Celebrating my thirtieth birthday, in April 2001 my mum arranges for a cake and a bottle of fizz to be delivered to my room at the Hyatt Hotel on Sunset Boulevard. Shovelling down cake and guzzling booze on the balcony of my room on the seventh floor, a sudden cough delivers a mouthful of vomit into the clumsy hands of gravity. *Oops*. And there it goes, heading towards the hairdos of the Pretty Young Things gathered on the terrace below. By the time the screaming starts, I'm hiding in the bathroom.

These are wonderful times. Evidently pleased with my stuff, only months after welcoming me to its ranks *Kerrang!* places me on a retainer. Working or not, each Friday I'm paid a set amount; on weeks that the freelance rate for my writing exceeds this figure, the magazine makes up the difference. For the first time in my life I'm placed on record company mailing lists; six days a week, the post-man brings me a bounty of free music. If it pleases me, I'm able to attend concerts for free seven nights a week. Because it doesn't please me, instead my name appears on guest-lists up to ten times a month. A plus one is industry standard; in larger rooms, journal-ists are given the best seats in the house. Attempting to mount a defence for this largesse, all I can say is that I know how lucky I am — not in the past tense, not upon reflection, but at the time. Typing away, sentences and paragraphs scream across the screen. With a good deal of care, I'll knock you up a cover story in twenty-four hours. If required, I can deliver in half that time. We can even call it a quarter, if you want. A case of extreme emergency requires me to fly to Helsinki and back in the space of a day. Key in the door at 2 a.m., my front-page feature is in port by start of play on the day the magazine goes to press. Thirty minutes later, my loveably psychotic features editor is on the phone.

First thing I ask: 'Fucking hell, what's wrong with it?'

'Nothing,' he says. 'It's fine. I just wanted to wake you up.'

Taking a stroll to the parade of lovely shops on Melrose Avenue in Los Angeles, a character from the London scene tells me he's concerned at the amount of custom he's giving to a cocaine seller in Islington. *Islington? Where I live?* It's all getting a bit heavy, he says. For the price of a 'Henry', just last month he ferried a kilo of product hundreds of miles up the M1 and M6. 'That's bad, isn't it,' he says. *Um, I mean, it's not good.* 'I fucking love the stuff,' he tells me. 'I just can't get enough of it. Tell you the truth, E' – that's what he calls me. E. Ian being such a mouthful and all – 'there's a big part of me that wishes I'd never had that first line.' *There's a big part of me that wishes I'd never had that first line.* Today I'm able to summon every detail of this conversation. I remember where we were. I can picture the weather. As a light spray of rain seasons the warm air of early autumn, at the top of La Cienega Boulevard the lessons I've learned over the course of a barren year in a bookshop are suddenly in danger. It's like looking at a sign that says 'Free Donuts! May cause death!' and thinking, 'I like doughnuts.'

For the first time, I'm noticing the prevalence of cocaine in the music industry. No longer the glamorous drug of choice for people I don't know, at once its apparent universality is within sniffing distance. In the guest enclosure at the Reading Festival the queue for the male cubicles is sometimes a hundred people deep. Call me cynical, but I have my doubts that this is the result of an outbreak of dysentery. At the same festival a photographer acquaintance makes no secret of the fact that, for an affordable price, he's selling wraps of coke and as many ecstasy tablets as you can swallow. I know this because I swallowed ten of them. Come the final day, in the sunshine perfect strangers are asking me to point him out in the throng of people whose names appear on the guest-list. Tomorrow is the day of the *Kerrang!* Awards. Beloved of everyone in the trade, the magazine's annual jamboree is by some distance the wildest event on the music industry's social calendar. Staged at a variety of upmarket hotels, come the end of the night the scene is akin to opening the doors of every enclosure at London Zoo. Once again, a long parade of people with apparent stomach complaints waits in line for the sit-down toilets.

Keen to get involved, it doesn't take long for me to make my acquaintance with cocaine. Out on the town with a similarly eager group of fellow music journalists, in the saloons and speakeasies of Soho I've soon perfected the technique of racking out a line of powder on the lid of a toilet seat. *Kneel, crouch, flush, inhale.* With the right measurements, the fraternal bonds of energy and laughter are strong. *We're shooting through the ceiling.* But, as it always is, my problem is one of greed. Filling my nose with too much blow leaves me in a state of cavernous unease.

Anyway, who ordered the cliché? Look at us, the whizz-bang gang from uptown using our own faces as chewing gum. Waiting at a cash machine at Oxford Circus, a young Australian woman turns round and says to me, 'Jesus Christ, fella, how gakked up are you?' *I'm gakked up just about right*, I want to tell her. *If I weren't, I'd be blowing into a paper bag.* She tells me that my eyes look like moons. So it's as obvious as that, is it? Maybe I should be taking a bit more care than this, then. There's no question that an appearance before the beak would amount to a career-ending sanction. Trying to charm my way past the granite-faced gatekeepers at John F. Kennedy Airport with a drug conviction on my permanent record is a fucking big ask.

One night our regular seller disappears without trace. Smashing our way through the five stages of grief in about twenty-five minutes, like all determined fiends none of us cares about the money he's taken with him. The problem here is the missing ingredient. We could, we suppose, just meet up for a few drinks. Who knows, perhaps a bite to eat? What about that for a plan, then? *What? Are you mad?* That's not gonna work, is it? *Think, men, think.* A bomb explodes in my brain. *Fellas, I might just have a plan.* In the hope of an introduction, I place a call to the person who in Los Angeles had told me of the trader based in Islington. As luck would have it, the man with the goods lives but a ten-minute walk from my front door. That's all it takes for me to become the quarterback for our Friday nights. That's all it takes to complicate my world. Within the hour, Stevie Sparks is on his way.

Arriving on his motorbike with a parcel of cocaine tucked into the folds of his head-to-toe leathers, 'Sparko' has to duck his head to get through the front door.

'All right, lad,' he says. 'Any chance of a brew?'

'Of course,' I reply. 'God knows what you'll do if I say no.'

Sometimes I think that this little exchange established a groove that somehow protected me from everything that was to follow. I was unthreatening, while Stevie was troublesome and wild. In the midst of terrifying benders that would occupy days, and sometimes weeks, of his time, I was always allowed to visit his home to pick up supplies. We both knew that his scene was unbecoming of a man more than a decade my senior. When at last I received the news of Sparko's suicide, in 2016, I felt I always knew he would one day lose the battle with the darkness at his core. But in details uncovered during the writing of this book, I learned that he had in fact killed himself immediately after beating his girlfriend half to death. Turns out that I didn't know him at all.

Stevie had pitched his tent on the populous and porous border that separates the music industry from the black economy. In recent memory, my new supplier was the tour manager for Primal Scream. God knows what that must have been like. (Imagine I'm telling you a hair-whitening story that has since been removed at the insistence of a lawyer.) Despite an absence of formal employment, Sparko retains the ability to materialise as if by magic in the best seats for concerts to which other regular guest-list habitants have been denied entry. Out on his rounds, he is sometimes accompanied by a sharp-tongued wildman with the social mores of a hyena. These are not smooth people.

'Right, well, you've got my number, lad,' he tells me. 'Be discreet on the phone, all right? Be careful with texts. Use words like "tickets", "t-shirts", that kind of thing. Don't be stupid. But feel free to get in touch any time you need anything. You got that? Any time you like.'

*

Aboard a bus bound for a festival near Dublin, months later I meet Primal Scream. Inching through traffic, I am the only passenger who has slept in the past two days. Believe me, it shows. Struggling to shoulder the heavy lifting in a one-sided conversation with singer Bobby Gillespie, I let slip that I have lately become friends with a skyscraper biker who claims to have once been the band's tour manager. Fearing that the story might not be true, at once I'm met with a smile worthy of a tooth-whitening commercial. Turning his head towards the seats at the back, Gillespie shouts, 'Hey lads! *Lads!* This guy knows Sparko!' The news is met with a cheer.

In the dressing room, a hard-faced member of the touring party dispenses dabs of speed piled high in a tinfoil crater. Along with the musicians, the drugs arrived in Ireland aboard an early morning flight from Glasgow. The technical term for this is smuggling. In a history of foolish deeds, not once have I ever considered crossing international borders with enough contraband to service an entire rock group. Dabbing away, no one says to me, *Look, any chance you could leave the open drug taking out of the piece?* I don't think anyone cares a shit what I write. Over the course of a sixty-minute live set, one of the musicians knocks back a seventy-five centilitre bottle of vodka. I watched him do it. He drank it neat.

In the backstage enclosure, a plague of guest-list locusts has stripped the area dry of all liquid refreshment. I'm not bothered about the booze but I could slaughter a glass of water. An hour later, a representative from the band's record company hands me a bottle of bathwater beer.

'Look what I've got,' he says.

'Wow, thank you.'

I take a sip and pull a face. 'Um. Where did you get this?'

'Well,' he says. 'It's a trick I picked up in my days as a student. It's called minesweeping. What you do is you go around pouring whatever remains in the bottles people have finished with into your own empty bottle.' He mimes the action. The spit of two-dozen strangers in one handy receptacle. 'You know, minesweeping?'

'You're joking, right?'

An affronted look.

Two hours later, I'm asked if I got a good interview out of Bobby Gillespie. *I mean, I'd have preferred it if he was alive.* He must have talked about something, though, surely? *He kept saying sorry for not being with it. He'd been hanging out in Oasis's dressing room, apparently. That's why he was four hours late.* Sitting alone on the ride back to Dublin, wondering how on earth I'll magic a feature out of *this*, a strange but likeable young man I recognise as Pete Doherty bounces into the seat beside me. Back in London, the ripples from The Libertines' noisy splash have made it all the way from their natural home in the *New Musical Express* to the pages of *Kerrang!* Released shortly afterwards, in 2002 the quartet's album, *Up the Bracket*, will be one of the last debut LPs from a London-based band to find truly mainstream traction.

I'm asked my name, and for whom I write.

'You gave us a terrible review,' Doherty says.

Realising that this is possible, I tear through the filing cabinet of my mind. Nothing doing.

'I don't think so,' I say.

'Yeah you did,' he tells me. 'I remember it. It was really cruel.'

Having knowingly caused offence to platinum-rated artists in the United States and Canada, I am by this point somewhat known for my waist-high tackles. But aboard a bus in the Republic of Ireland, I am innocent of the charges laid against me.

'Is it Pete? Right, sorry. Pete, I promise you I didn't. It wasn't me.' It was a different writer, I tell him, for whose actions I cannot reasonably be held to account. Do you know what I mean? I can't be taking brickbats for a dust-up in which I haven't thrown a punch.

Doherty responds to this news with a loveable and discomfiting handbrake turn. He's sorry, he says. *Don't worry, it's not a problem.* No, he's *really* sorry. *It's all right, honestly.* Okay, sure, but he hopes I'm not offended. *Of course not, not a bit of it.* Am I sure? *Yes, yes, totally.* Because, honestly, he really didn't mean to . . . And on we go, round and round, for ten barren miles. At the band's hotel, Doherty and Primal Scream extend an invitation for a night out. A glance at my wrist confirms that we're in the early hours of Monday morning. *Where the hell are they going?* Considering my options, I realise that I am frightened of their company. As I bid them all a good night, Pete Doherty wraps himself around me like a duvet.

After moving to the *NME*, a year or two later my friend Dan Silver was given the job of overseeing the filming of promotional material for the magazine's forthcoming awards ceremony. On the hunt for talking heads, Pete Doherty was invited to a filming session at the Carlton Club in Central London. A listless and distracted interviewee, to no one's surprise a visit to the toilet put the singer in a much more amenable mood. Under the music industry's normal rules of engagement this was hardly a problem, but with a membership that includes Theresa May and Michael Heseltine – not to mention a reception area replete with lavishly framed oil paintings of every Conservative prime minister – the Carlton is hardly the kind of joint to which one retires for a Jaegerbomb and a cheeky bump. With filming once again underway, Dan was approached by a colleague requesting an urgent word in his ear. 'Is there a problem?' 'Um . . .' In the last five minutes someone had sprayed 'QPR 4 EVER' – Queens Park Rangers, the west London football club Doherty supports – in thin strips of human blood on the wall of the gents toilet.

Back at home in Islington I discover that Bobby Gillespie lives on an adjoining street. Passing by one sunny morning, I spot the singer standing on his front lawn with a baby and a White Fang dog. The infant is named Wolf, while the dog . . . actually, I have no what the dog is called. Maybe it answers to the kind of name you might give to a baby. Expecting to be greeted as a perfect stranger, instead I'm invited in for tea. In the front room of a tasteful home, I tell my host about a night out during which I fell victim to the paranoid paralysis of cocaine purchased in bulk from our common friend Sparko. Yeah, it can be like that, he says. You're much better off taking speed.

'That I do know,' I say.

After a pleasant ten minutes, I take my leave. I never do get my cuppa.

A year before his death, up in the Old Country, my father lights up every room save for the ones in which he actually lives. Determined to plateau, it's been decades since he made an effort on behalf of people who love him. He doesn't fancy the pictures, or an early bird dinner at a new restaurant on Market Hill. He won't entertain the notion of doing anything that doesn't chime with his plans. On a cold night in autumn, I remember meeting him in town on an evening in which Barnsley were playing in the cup. Gathering my coat and scarf for the walk to the ground, I asked if he was planning to watch the game on the telly. Honestly, you'd think I'd suggested he take up smoking crystal meth. 'Oh no, it's too late for me, son.' 'It's a football match, Dad, not a rave club. It'll be finished by twenty-five to ten.' 'No, no, I'll not bother.' This towering intransigence eventually took its toll on a second wife nine years his junior. Realising she fancied just a little bit more out of life, without warning she called in the receivers.

With a measure of application, I reckon he could have saved his marriage. I hope so anyway, because on sluggish days I can feel my father's apathy yawning within me. Because Eric failed to recognise the inertia seeping into his bones, the news of an impending divorce hit him like the butt of a rifle. Alarmed by the chorus of cartoon birds circling his skull, for mate's rates his boss at Triple Engineering made space for him in one of his rental properties. As word spread around our remarkably porous hometown, others emerged to offer succour, grape and grain. But it was no good – loneliness was now upon him. For the first time in more than twenty years, Eric took up smoking. Waking in the slender hours, each night he would sit in his dressing gown on the back step of his one-person abode, a can of Polish lager and an Embassy cigarette for company.

My mother arrived on the scene like a hurricane of loving intent. Now living in Barnsley again, several times a week she and my stepfather met up with her first husband for drinks in town. In what sounds to me like an idea for a sitcom, she even harboured a plan to move him into the two rooms on the top floor of her town-centre home. This isn't as unlikely as it might sound; even when they weren't getting on, my mum and dad always got on. Age eight, I told a teacher that their planned separation was the result of them arguing in bed. It must be that, I said, because they were fine during the day. In a town such as Barnsley in the late 1960s couples married as teenagers. As children, really. When I emerged screaming into the world, my twenty-two-year-old mother was the oldest patient in the maternity ward. Cheekbones held tight by forceps – in a certain light, on a summer's day you can sometimes see the marks – it took an age to drag me out. Certain her child would die, the doctors rated my mum's chances as being a call between heads and tails. Taken to see her son in a ward filled with incubated offspring, from a distance of several hundred yards she caught sight of a baby with a head like a prize-winning aubergine. 'Please don't let that be him,' she whispered. 'Please don't let that be him.'

Not quite unwanted, my father's chat-up lines were at first rebuffed. Undeterred, he told the teenager with the resplendent eyes that on Sunday evening he would wait for an hour on the bench that sits on the brow of Ardsley Hill. He hoped she would join him. At 7 p.m. on the day of rest, she did just that. Married two years later, the Winwoods lived in a home near the Town End Park that cost less than a thousand pounds. With the support and encouragement of his new wife, in 1970 Eric allowed himself to be steered towards technical college – 'tech', he called it – at which he trained to become an estimator. Without her help, I often wonder if he would ever have taken even a single step in the direction of his wider potential.

But he couldn't stay away from licensed premises. A functioning alcoholic, in the final decade of his life I saw him get bent out of shape at the discovery that pubs in Camden Town opened their doors an hour later than in Barnsley. 'Can I get a beer at the zoo? Right, let's go there, then.' Drinking away the seventies, his favourite pub resounded with a calloused laughter my dad called 'badinage'. I like this a lot. Never 'banter', *badinage*. I reckon there's something to be said for the fact that the friends he made during this time remained by his side until the year he died. But as I learned to talk, and to walk – in that order, or so I'm told – his refusal to step back from life in the wild placed an unbearable weight on his new setup indoors. At the bank my mother would discover that her husband had withdrawn the last of the money from their joint account. Ten pound notes would take flight from her purse. I'm not sure she ever ran out of love for Eric, but she did run out patience.

Thirty years later, like Charlie Brown and Lucy van Pelt, they're back on the street. Joining my mother and father for football away days in the midlands and the south, I was struck by the sudden thought that we were – gosh – a *family* again. 'Eric, when did you become so fucking boring?' she'd ask. Evaluating the question, his face would flicker with pleasure. He *had* become boring, hadn't he. He *was* like an old man. *When did that happen?* Once more in the company of a woman contemptuous of his lethargy, at last things were about to change. Age be damned, my mum remains forever young. At 73, she's still in full-time employment. 'Ma, do you fancy going to see Green Day at Old Trafford Cricket Ground?' I'll ask her. 'Definitely. I'll pick you up at Wakefield station.' 'I've got tickets for Nick Cave in Nottingham. What do you think?' 'I'm there.' In one of the few concerts he ever attended, in 1966 my father saw The Who at the Civic Hall in Barnsley. 'Ian, they were *absolutely* terrible,' he told me again and again. 'Pete Townsend had an amplifier the size of a wardrobe. I don't know what he was on but he wasn't leaving that stage until he'd smashed his way through it.'

'Dad, that sounds amazing.'

'It was rubbish. Eric Burdon and The Animals were much better.'

In London, I took my parents to see The Pogues. Standing near the stage at the Brixton Academy, my dad asked me how it can possibly be that Shane MacGowan was still alive. Well, that's the question, isn't it, Pops? How has he managed to cling on for this long? Almost all of the singer's finest songs – 'A Pair of Brown Eyes', 'Fairytale of New York', 'Streams of Whiskey', 'A Rainy Night in Soho' – feature characters whose lives are in states of pronounced disarray. If anything, his own circumstances were even more deranged. Somehow unable to drink and drug himself to death, instead MacGowan allowed his exceptional talents to drown. *What a waste.*

'The truth of the matter is that most bands, from when they kick off to when they end [have a] seven or eight year lifespan,' the punk DJ and documentarian Don Letts once remarked. There is, I think, rather a lot to be said for this idea. 'Look at The Beatles,' he said. 'Look at The Smiths, look at Led Zeppelin [and] a lot of bands that I'm into. And of course there are exceptions, but one could argue that they had their best period in the first seven or eight years.' The Pogues couldn't even manage this. Entirely by accident, I saw the group support U2 at Wembley Stadium when I was sixteen. An unstoppable force, truly I had no idea what had just hit me. Twenty-two years later, in south London they're just another nostalgia act milking the Christmas market for next year's spends. *Is it worth it?*

Shane MacGowan made his bones as a face in the London punk scene of 1976. In its febrile environment, he made the acquaintance of Ian 'Lemmy' Kilmister, the bandleader of Motörhead. While MacGowan pursued oblivion, with perfect poise Lemmy indulged in the holy trinity of bourbon, cigarettes and amphetamine sulphate. *All good clean fun.* Heavy drinkers and dedicated drug users normally reach the point at which only three options remain: abstinence, ruin, or death. Not here. With stolid determination, Lemmy kept at it until four days past his seventieth birthday. Even then we were all a bit surprised that he'd finally died. Not because the idea itself seemed implausible, but because he'd kept the show on the road for so long that it appeared as if he might actually go on for ever.

'Lemmy and I hit it off straight away,' Ginger Wildheart, the songwriter and frontman with the English group The Wildhearts, told me. 'I toured with him twice and I found him to be a kind and, actually, a moral man. We both loved speed, so we'd take it and just talk each other's ears off for hours on end. But he had a very specific approach to drink and to drugs. He realised that he enjoyed doing them so much that he never wanted to reach the point where he'd have to stop. So he moderated his use so that he was the one who was in control. That was the point – it never controlled him.'

For the purposes of this book, Lemmy is an anomaly. *He was the one who was in control.* When it came to drugs, he drew distinctions that might just bear scrutiny. The experience of watching a lover die from an overdose instilled in him a loathing for heroin that was as pronounced as anything I've ever seen. As his status as an icon grew, it was tempting to place him in the same louche bracket as Keith Richards. Rock 'n' roll outlaws who never say die, that kind of thing. The only problem with this is that, in a certain light, Richards' stage clothes appear to have been dyed in blood.

Lemmy said yes to many things, but not to this. 'Heroin fucking ruined [Richards] for years,' he once said. 'It's all very well, that funky Keith business, but how many people do you think he influenced? All these young guys impressed by Keith and doing it as well. You've got to take some kind of fucking responsibility.' For the author of Velvet Underground track 'Heroin' he had stronger words still. 'Lou Reed should burn in fucking hell for the amount of people he's got into heroin for that song,' he said. With a pulse like a pneumatic drill, in 1988 he even declared, 'I believe that if you can do without them [drugs] then you're better off.' *Hold on, let him finish.* 'I hate to give advice because I'm fifty-three – I'm their parents' age – so they think, "What's that old cunt know?" But I do know. Believe me, I fucking know.'

I believed him. Towards the end of his life, Lemmy seemed to regard his lot with an understandable degree of melancholy. One of the problems with secular deification is that people stop listening to your new music. It's a decent gig for those who want it – certainly AC/DC have used the iconography of Angus Young as an excuse to spend forty-two years making inferior albums – but Lemmy rightly viewed his status as a twenty-first-century capstone as a threat to his job as a productive artist. Sometimes willing to trade on his public image as a hard-living Hall of Famer – at Motörhead concerts, supporters could buy t-shirts bearing his face and the words 'fifty one per cent motherfucker, forty nine per cent son of a bitch' – beneath the carapace lurked a sensitive man who wanted only for his band's songs to be heard. *His new songs.* At the Royal Garden Hotel, he once told me that if given the choice he would never again play 'Ace of Spades'. Such an omission would see him hanged for treason, of course, but I took to his thinking. I admired his wariness of comfort and nostalgia. Regardless of whether or not people paid it any mind, I liked that he still believed in his band's newest music. He was right to. Some of it is very good indeed.

In the middle years of the nineties, I once saw this with my own eyes. In the bar of a hotel near the southern tip of Regent's Park, Lemmy fell into conversation with a pair of politely dressed thirty-somethings enjoying Friday evening drinks at a nightspot near the centre of town. At the time, Motörhead were more than a decade removed from their highest-selling days – a period in which they would fill the Hammersmith Odeon for four straight nights – but not yet at the point at which their singer had become universally recognised. The couple *knew* that they *knew* him but, and please forgive us, they just couldn't say from where. Sorry.

'I play in a band called Motörhead,' he said.

'Oh *right*,' one of them answered. 'Right. Yeah, I remember Motörhead. I didn't know you guys were still together.'

Remember.

Like a high-rolling poker player with a terminal tell, the face of Ian 'Lemmy' Kilmister fell to the floor. It took him but a second to put himself back together, but I saw it. The sadness at being thought of as yesterday's man, making yesterday's music – *I saw it*. Waiting for our interview to commence, I listened in as the singer spent the next few minutes telling a pair of perfect strangers of Motörhead's plans for the upcoming year. Next month, a new album; after that, an American tour with a run up to Canada; then a European campaign, including a night here in London. They could even come and check it out, if they wanted to.

'Um, yeah, I guess that could be fun.'

I couldn't believe I was in his company. I was ten years old when I first heard Motörhead on the radio. Gate-crashing the top ten, in under three minutes the live version of their titular song changed my life for ever. Without it, I don't know that I would have fallen in love with music. I don't know that I would have thought of becoming a music writer. Two weeks earlier, its parent album, *No Sleep 'Til Hammersmith*, had entered the chart at number one. Concussed with admiration, I pestered my mum for the seven-inch, and then the LP; she even bought me one of the band's t-shirts. Much more than the messy sound of chaos and collision, I realise now that I was struck by the purity of it all. It was *amazing*. In 2020 I placed the LP at number one on a long list of essential live albums compiled for the *Telegraph*. About this, I had no hesitation. In the forty-odd years that have elapsed since I first held this wondrous item in my hands, not a month has gone by in which I haven't listened to it at least once.

With its inner sleeve festooned with Polaroid pictures, *No Sleep 'Til Hammersmith* afforded me my first glimpse into an entirely alien world. I recall the words 'I think these are Aberdeen' written below a photograph of a gathering of vacuum-packed human beings who looked to me like they belonged in some kind of asylum. Or in *prison*. I spent *hours* looking at these images and wondering, *Who are these people? How can I meet them? How do I go about becoming one of them?* 'Recorded live in England surrounded by maniacs' read the sleeve notes on the back cover. 'Dedicated to all the people who have travelled with, drunk with, fought with and screwed with us on the roads of England and Europe for five years . . . Thanks to every-one who came to see us. Thanks to Smirnoff and Carlsberg without whom lots of this would have been coherent.' Mouth agape, I'd read these words again and again. *What do they even mean?*

On a visit to Barnsley, my dad bought me a copy of the *Bomber* album from Casa Disco Records in the centre of town. Walking to the George & Dragon on a gaspingly frigid December afternoon, I took stock of the three band members pictured on the back sleeve. Lemmy. 'Fast' Eddie Clarke. 'Philthy Animal' Taylor. *'Ian, look up. Watch where you're going.'* In a room filled with sunlight, Lemmy sat behind a half-full bottle of whiskey that I knew, *I just knew*, had been opened only that day. *Who are these people?* Too young to know of the existence of the music press, I had no context for any of this stuff. For all I knew, the object in my hand may as well have fallen from space.

He takes it well, Lemmy, all of the stuff I pour into his lap the first time I meet him. Following our interview, drinking and smoking and telling jokes, in the hotel bar he gives me hours of time. Towards the end I'm helpless to prevent myself from spilling out over the side and letting him know that without him I wouldn't be here today – you know, *with him*. Trying as hard as I know how not to fool myself, I'll go so far as to say that he seemed pleased by this. Actually, I'll go so far as to say that he appeared *touched*. And thank God for that. Back then, indifference or derision from the one person who permanently changed the course of my life might well have knocked me to the canvas.

He couldn't keep it up for ever, of course, this life of his. In the end I think it was the cigarettes that did for him. It was the gaspers that diminished his voice and waged a scorched-earth campaign on his lungs. You could hear it when he talked, that aerosol-can rattle of someone thirsty for air. Advised to stop drinking, he swapped his bourbon and Coke for a tumbler of vodka and orange. Approaching the task in his hand with metronomic determination, Lemmy was the kind of drinker who never seemed to get drunk. But on the three occasions I was graced by his company, without effort he put away what to my eyes, at least back then, seemed like an astonishing amount.

Little did I know that there would come a time when I would out-drink even him.

Four years after Lemmy's death from prostate cancer, cardiac arrhythmia and congestive heart failure, I take my fiancée on a guided tour of the rock quarter of Sunset Boulevard. At the foot of the strip, the Whisky a Go Go announces a week of concerts by a selection of hair metal has-beens best known for their walks, and falls, on the wild side. In what might just be my favourite story of rock 'n' roll dysfunction, I tell her how a member of one of these groups came from a moneyed family from whom he was able to steal and pawn a Stradivarius with which to raise funds for heroin. Dragged by his father down to the shop at which the violin had been hocked, the two men got into a fistfight that might have continued to this day were it not for the sound of the priceless instrument being crushed beneath the wheels of a reversing car. 'Shut up, that didn't happen.' 'No, it did. It really did. I've got stories about all of these bands. Do you want to hear another one?'

How many times have I been here? Usually right here, too – in West Hollywood, somewhere on the three-mile stretch between Book Soup and Amoeba Music. All this way for an hour in the company of fucked-up people. The drummer who almost died after taking too many prescription drugs in his room at the Royal Garden Hotel. The platinum-rated punk rock singer who cancelled a world tour after a drunken meltdown onstage. The songwriter who learned that his band had been awarded a gold album when he was in county jail for possession of heroin and crack cocaine. The vocalist who called a bandmate from hospital to say that he thought he was dying after taking a fistful of unidentified pills. The metal guitarist who drank himself to death after a bite from a venomous spider – yes, *a venomous spider* – damaged the motor neurons in one of his arms. On these streets I have been told stories that seem to be turning my hair grey.

Taking the Boxing Day air, I realise that this is the first time in – what? – at least forty visits that I've fully enjoyed being in the company of Los Angeles. For the longest time its arterial boulevards and low-standing topography summoned unaccountable feelings of deep and warm melancholy. At first, I could never understand why. But then it came to me: it's because I don't know how to drive. Walking half a mile with a local friend to what I imagined was a nearby bar, years earlier I was seized by the arm and told, 'Ian, no one in LA walks this far.' Out here, people ride Shanks's pony only because circumstances demand it. These are the characters that wake up on cardboard, or who hold spirited conversations with invisible adversaries. Imagining their stories, I picture them as having been buckled by the hustle of the Hollywood dream. *Nobody gives a damn when you're down on your luck*. With companions like these, is it any wonder that Los Angeles makes me feel sad?

Up on Sunset I take my fiancée to the Rainbow Bar and Grill. In the days when I was learning to talk, Alice Cooper was right here, on these very premises, bending the elbow with people who were well on their way to drinking themselves to death. The singer got blasted with Jim Morrison. Jimi Hendrix handed him his first joint when he was eighteen. He knocked back Southern Comfort with Janis Joplin. (So delighted were the company who produced the spirit by Janis's very public endorsement that they sent her a fur coat.) By the time he was thirty, Super Duper Alice Cooper had known more dead people than Doris Stokes. As the seventies came calling, in the wake of *Easy Rider* American rock 'n' roll was hard at work divesting itself of its approachable boy-next-door image. If you're looking for the point at which excess for its own sake was first eulogised, this is probably it. An enclave for the truly famous, up at the Rainbow space was made in the loft for Alice Cooper and his friends to do their drinking in private.

'It was called the Roost of the Vampires,' he told me. 'We were [known as] the Hollywood Vampires because you never saw us in the daytime. Every single night, that's where we'd go. One of the things we'd do was wait to see what Keith Moon was going to wear that night. Keith would go to [the outfitters] Western Costumes – one night he would be the Queen of England, and one night he would be Hitler, or a French maid, or Zorro. And it was just so much fun. That was an era when personalities were everything, so it had a signature to it. Everybody had a distinct sound and a distinct look. And we gathered there to get away from the industry. We never talked about music. John Lennon and Harry Nilsson would argue about politics, with each one taking the opposite position to the other. I'd be sat there in the middle of them like some kind of referee. It was great.' It was great for Alice Cooper because *he* escaped with his life. He got lucky. Much more of that kind of thing 'would have killed me', he told me. 'No doubt about it, it would have killed me.'

There have been some changes at the Rainbow since last I was here. The sheltered patio at the side of the building is now called 'Lemmy's Bar'. As an immigrant in LA, the Englishman spent his free afternoons sitting at the counter drinking his Jack Daniel's and Coke, smoking his Marlboros and racking up high scores on an electronic quiz machine. He lived just a block or two away in a rent-controlled apartment stuffed with military paraphernalia. Almost four years after his death – and after the death of 'Fast' Eddie Clarke and 'Philthy Animal' Taylor, too – the trio received the nod that they were headed to the Rock and Roll Hall of Fame in Cleveland. A fat lot of good that was to them.

Along with a smattering of albums on a wall-mounted jukebox, at the Rainbow the singer's memory is honoured by a life-size statue at the rear of the bar. Accepting my offer of a dollar bill, the juke cues up the version of 'Overkill' from *No Sleep 'Til Hammersmith*. *Look out*. As the song ascends, a flight of stairs falling down a flight of stairs, from behind the bar a member of staff turns down the volume.

4: THE AMBASSADOR

With its financial chicanery and its many conflicts of interest, the music industry has always been a safe space for grifters. With a royalty rate of two per cent, in the fifties The Drifters toiled on the road for a wage of a hundred dollars a week. In a scene from his novel *Utopia Avenue* David Mitchell imagines an exchange in the 1960s between Jimmy Savile – best not go *there*, eh? – and Steve Marriott, the frontman with the Small Faces. 'How does it feel, Young Steven?' the paedophile DJ asks. 'Getting utterly, royally fleeced out of every last penny by [manager] Don Arden? Not even owning the clothes you stand up in? Don't you just want to shrivel up and die? I know I would.' In 1986, in a case brought against Malcolm McLaren by the Sex Pistols, a judge at the Royal Courts of Justice ruled that the former manager owed the group a million pounds in royalties dating back to 1979. Speaking to waiting reporters, singer John Lydon said of the verdict, 'In terms of hard cash, it means a lot – and it's all mine.' At the same court, in a case filed in 1992 against Sony, George Michael claimed that from 1987 his music earned his record label a profit of £52.45 million. The singer's share amounted to £7.35 million.

Of these four random examples, the last is the most instructive. Four decades after the American DJ Alan Freed first said the words 'rock 'n' roll' on WJW Cleveland, this once renegade industry was, by the nineties, a mainstream concern. With a sophisticated business model conferring legitimacy, George Michael was widely derided for comparing recording contracts to 'slavery'. With the singer filing suit for restraint of trade and inequality of earnings, the person on the Clapham omnibus wondered how such a lavishly wealthy individual could possibly be the victim of corporate exploitation. Leaving aside long-familiar notions that an artist should forever be grateful for his or her lot, for what it's worth – and for the litigant, it was worth four million quid in court costs alone – the dispute was about the *division* of money. It seems obvious to say this, but let's say it anyway: no part of the music industry would exist without the music itself. In the case of George Michael, more than eighty-five per cent of its profits went to the company that released it.

'Record contracts are just like – I'm gonna say the word – slavery,' was how Prince described the relationship between label and artist. Speaking to a select group of reporters from the National Association of Black Journalists in 2015, he went on to say, 'I would tell any young artist . . . don't sign.'

Don't sign. But if you do, here's what you get. In a standard contract with a major label, the debt incurred by a band is set only against royalties; even if this royalty rate is as high as twenty-five per cent – a vanishingly rare figure – the musicians alone will be required to repay all monies spent in their name. In selling more than fifteen million copies of their third album, *Dookie*, Green Day were easily able to reimburse Warner Bros. the two hundred and twenty-five thousand dollars the company had advanced them a year earlier. But until they had done so, the musicians themselves earned not a cent from sales of their blockbusting LP. (Their previous label, the independent Lookout, permitted its artists an equal share of the revenue after costs. Its deals were confirmed with only a handshake.) In what might reasonably be described as double-bookkeeping, Warner Bros. began turning a profit long before the band did. In the jargon of the business section, an 'advance' is start-up capital levied against future earnings – in other words, it's a loan. But that doesn't sound quite as enticing, does it? *Promising*

Young Punk Rock Band Signs to Major Label for a Loan of Almost a Quarter of a Million Bucks.'

The imbalance of power is startling. Overwhelmingly, record companies sign musicians in the foothills of young adulthood; keen for the validation and promise of a professional contract, the artists negotiate from a position of weakness. The simple metric of supply and demand dictates that there are far more bands than there are opportunities. Complications of interest are also problematic. In establishing the particulars of a deal, managers and industry lawyers who *should* be on the side of the artist – certainly, they're being *paid* by them – are themselves incentivised by the promise of a percentage of the money levied upfront. Increasingly, the size of an advance is the key factor in whether or not a group can remain operative. With brazenly reduced royalty rates, in the twenty-first century the debt itself will often remain unpaid.

Remember, the label establishes the deficit. In real terms, often it doesn't actually exist. With signatories reduced to a state of servitude – serfdom, even – again the record company benefits from its two sets of ledgers. The debt will be cancelled only in the case of an act being cut loose before a contract has run its stipulated course. Until then, everything is billed back. Each one of the multitude of world cities nestling so nonchalantly in the chapters of this book were visited on the musicians' dime. Whether or not they knew it – and for what it's worth, at no point was it made clear to me either – the boys and girls in the band paid for my airfare, my hotel rooms, my taxicabs, my meals and my drinks. At the Capitol Grille in Washington DC I once dined on a steak that cost seventy-two dollars. I had six vodka martinis, too. Blink 182 paid for that. They even put me up for two nights at the Four Seasons Hotel. Given the rank puerility of the album they were promoting, I'd say it was the least they could do.

A major record label might rightly point out that it does a job that no one else can manage. The bankrollers of a wildly expensive and deeply exclusive industry, any group deemed to be a priority will see mountains moved in their name. Following a free public launch party at Madison Square Garden, from the summer of 1991 Metallica's self-titled fifth LP spent *four and a half years* on the US chart. Fortified by its success, the band wasted little time translating their popularity into genuine power; as well as negotiating a greatly improved royalty rate, in 1995 they became one of a very select number of acts to own the copyright to their own back catalogue. In this, Metallica managed to circumvent one of the music industry's most galling grifts. Regardless of whether a group's relationship with a record company lasts for just one album, or for many decades, under normal circumstances the label will retain the master tapes (the copyright) of all recordings for a period of *seventy years*. Sign here, please.

'Record companies think that their duty of care stops when the term of your contract ends,' Tom Gray tells me. Tom made his bones as the guitarist and keyboardist in the internationally successful Southport band Gomez. Speaking to me in his capacity as an activist against industry chicanery, today he is the founder of the Broken Record campaign. 'Even though you're no longer signed to a label, they continue to hold the rights to your music for seventy years. Wait a minute, *wait a minute*, I did three albums with you and you get to sell them for seventy years, but your duty of care to me stopped eighteen months after I gave you that third record [of a three-album deal]? *Fuck off.*

'So why don't we put a limit on it of twenty-five years?' he asks. 'They've got that long to make as much money as they can – and then, guess what? The artist gets it back. And if it's a successful record, the artist can sell it back to them and they can pay them again.'

In furnishing me with information I should really already have known, one of the few questions I *didn't* ask Tom Gray is just how good he is at holding his breath. With the music industry once more on manoeuvres, the economic circumstances for artists are starker than they ever were. As a means of illustrating the extent to which the business has changed in our lifetimes, Tom suggests I try to explain to a young person that at their age *we* were ponying up the equivalent of thirty-five pounds for a single album. Ten to fifteen quid, that's what we paid for a compact disc. 'They'd laugh at you,' he says. 'They would fucking *laugh at you*.'

Righteous and irascible, it's difficult not to warm to Tom Gray. His point, he says, is that today many millions of listeners access music from streaming services. Subscription platforms such as Spotify (premium) and Apple Music are replacing, or have indeed *replaced*, the idea of an album as a physical object. In the United Kingdom in 2020 the three major record labels (Sony, Universal and Warner Bros.) earned more than a billion pounds from streaming. Worldwide, the figure was almost eight times this number. With major label artists constituting roughly three quarters of all music played online – larger independents also follow the same business model – the record companies have seized the opportunity to increase their share of the pie. Each time a song is played, the label and the streaming platform – and, increasingly, the two are intertwined – take fifty-five and thirty per cent of the action (respectively). Paid just fifteen per cent, the songwriters themselves can expect to earn between £0.004 and £0.009 per play. That's not a typo, by the way. Non-writing musicians are paid nothing at all.

For younger audiences streaming is fast replacing radio. With royalty rates as high as twenty quid per minute, a song aired on the wireless will earn its writer a fifty per cent cut (the label and non-writing musicians each take home a quarter). As well as this, in an arrangement known as 'equitable remuneration', these amounts are independent of the debt a band might owe to its record company. For musicians and songwriters, it's money in the bank. In the age of streaming, it's anything but. A poll in 2020 by The Ivors Academy and Musicians' Union revealed that eight out of ten music creators earn less than two hundred pounds a year from streaming services. Once again, this is not a typo. (In the United Kingdom, the average base salary for Spotify employees is £60,563 per annum.) In a tweet posted on 20 March 2021 Feargal Sharkey, the former singer with The Undertones and the erstwhile head of the umbrella organisation UK Music, wrote, 'You're going to need 7,343,157 streams per month just to make minimum wage.'

Younger readers will be surprised to learn that when dinosaurs roamed the earth it was possible for a group to earn a living without its members repeatedly hearing the words 'check one two' at a sound check in a tertiary city in Illinois. The English group Talk Talk unveiled the impossibly complicated *Spirit of Eden* on a major label two years after playing their last ever gig. Exactly three years later, in September 1991 a *different* major issued the even more bamboozling *Laughing Stock*. Combined with an expansive talent, my guess is that the status of both albums as masterpieces is attributable in part to their authors abstaining themselves from the obligations of the road. Away from the circuit, Talk Talk were able to become a *vastly* different band from the (already superior) pop turn that made their audience's acquaintance at the start of the eighties. No longer required to ask themselves whether or not a song could be played live, the musicians were at liberty to become one of the most original groups I've ever heard. I'm not suggesting this kind of setup is for everyone; what I'm saying is that it's no longer available to *anyone*. Instead, in search of ticket and merchandise revenue musicians hit the road. In the twenty-first century the only way a full-time band can forego touring is if its members are somehow able to forego the costs of living.

'[Gomez have] always had to stay on the road,' Tom Gray tells me. 'There's no longer any money in recorded music so everyone just stays on the road playing hundreds and hundreds of gigs.

My band did two hundred and forty shows in 2004 – and that was *before* the age of streaming. It didn't feel like we slept. When we became a big touring band in America – and that's just a totally different speed of life – you come off one six-week tour, and you have a week off, and then you start another six-week tour. And you just do that all year. Now that's *really* brutal . . . so you've got alcoholism and all the rest of it, which is how a lot of people cope with that . . . Music attracts a lot of outlier personalities. I got into prescription uppers and downers for a few years, especially during that heavy American touring cycle. You'd get "rock docs" on the road, people who were like American physicians who would write you a prescription for anything, so long as you paid them. For me that was about maintaining performance levels because I was exhausted. Seriously, I was shot to bits. So what can I get that's going to make me appear like I really give a fuck when I'm on a stage? Because I want to appear like I give a fuck, but I don't know if I have that in me anymore. So you just say, "What can I get?" And there's a nice doctor who'll write you a prescription for Adderall so it's, like, fine. *Fine.*'

And that was before the age of streaming. Strolling through Camden Town with my fiancée in the months before The Disease, I spy with my little eye a tour bus parked at the tradesperson's entrance of the Electric Ballroom. On a mission to furnish her life with useless information, I trace a line along the side of the bus where the corridor of coffin-like bunks separates the two communal areas at the front and rear of the top deck. I describe the plasma-screen television, Formica table and cul-de-sac settee in the always-popular back lounge. Down a ninety-degree staircase stands a surprisingly spacious kitchen area; adjacent to a second exit, at its rear you'll find a lone toilet. *Watch your step back there, mind.* Backed by my own laughter I tell her how Slash, from Guns N' Roses, once told me of the time he almost ended up on the freeway at five o' clock in the morning after becoming confused as to which of these doors was which. 'What, really?' *Yeah, really*. And this was *after* he'd given up drinking.

It's just about possible that over the course of a working life I've crossed the threshold of more twelve-berth, six-wheel, thousand-pounds-a-day vehicles than I have actual houses. I am long familiar with their unwritten constitution. Aboard the bus, the driver is king; it's his ride and he alone is responsible for the safety of its occupants. En route from city to city, there are just three inviolable rules. Solid waste shall not pass from the body to the toilet; if the curtains on a bunk are drawn, its occupant shall be disturbed only in cases of emergency; and, most importantly of all, passengers should sleep with their feet facing the direction of travel. This way, should the tour bus crash they will break their ankles rather than their necks.

'And this is where they sleep?' she asks.

'Yeah, pretty much. The odd hotel here and there, maybe. But most of the time the drives are through the night, so it makes sense – economically, certainly – for bands to bed down in their bunks.'

'For how long?'

'What, on a tour?'

'Yeah. How long are they out there for?'

'A couple of months at a time, then maybe a week or two off. Three or four months if they're really working America. Depends on how popular they are, to be honest. If you're booked into arenas you can afford to have a longer buffer between campaigns. If you're in clubs the size of the Electric Ballroom it tends to be a hand-to-mouth operation. Either way, a tour *eats* money. It's relentless.'

Looking at the one-way windows of the double-decker bus, my fiancée says, 'I think I'd go mad if I lived on that thing.'

'Yeah,' I say, 'they often do.'

I'm sharing a bus bound for Munich with a group of musicians struggling to believe their luck. As special guests to Muse, four hours earlier the Lostprophets had harvested warm applause from an audience of three thousand people at the Pepsi Music Hall in Vienna. Upon arrival at our destination their passports will be ferried to the American Embassy in Berlin for the issuance of working visas that will allow them to record in New York City. Forty-two days earlier, two passenger planes brought down the towers of the World Trade Center. A year ago, no one knew of the existence of this likeable band from a post-industrial town in South Wales.

Six months ago, *I* didn't know who they were. Dispatched to Dublin and Belfast to profile this box-fresh group from Pontypridd, I arrived in the field in need of hard information. I didn't yet know that, in the online world I was struggling to master, the lionisation of one of their songs by an influential music website had led to a major label bidding war. I had no idea that the musicians had recently returned from a showcase concert in Los Angeles that had been witnessed by every A&R person in the city. Billeted in Hollywood, they were gifted a box of pornographic DVDs by a record company executive who told them that he could arrange for them to have sex with any performer who caught their eye (the offer was declined). Seeking counsel from a music industry lawyer, the band were told that the only circumstances under which they should sign a management contract would be if a call came in from Q-Prime. Given that Q-Prime represent some of the most popular names in the rock game – Red Hot Chili Peppers, Metallica, Def Leppard – the remark was made in jest. The very next day, the call came in. Within the month, the six members had signed their names at the foot of a recording contract with Columbia Records.

I liked them immediately. Some of the music I could take or leave, but *they* were great. The children of men who worked with their hands, the Lostprophets understood that without hard graft their good fortune would count for nothing. This has always seemed obvious to me, but you'd be surprised at the number of groups who regard a recording contract as a destination rather than a staging post. Watching singer Ian Watkins crowd-surf atop the raised hands of a partisan audience at the Rosetta Bar in Belfast, I caught the scent of star quality. Friends since childhood, offstage the Welshmen laughed louder and more easily than any other group I'd ever met. As harmonious as a male voice choir, theirs was a joy that amounted to more than the discovery of a path towards a unified dream. Marbled with wonder, it also contained notes of relief that suddenly – just possibly – their choices in life, at least for now, promised more than the limited prospects of a de-industrialised hometown.

Clever, determined, cheeky and loud, I realise now that I idealised the group as poster boys for the British working class. Turntablist and keyboardist Jamie Oliver was an artist who worked with oils and canvas. In New York City I remember him telling me of a newly completed painting of a father and his adult son standing by the raised bonnet of an ageing family car. The men's faces bear enormously euphoric smiles; their hands are disproportionately large. The point, the artist explained, was that the pair had been emasculated by unemployment in a town neither of them were prepared to leave. But here they were, with spanners and spark plugs, repurposed once more. For years I was almost obsessed with this idea. So vivid is the image in my mind that it doesn't at all matter to me that I've never actually seen Jamie Oliver's painting.

Now on the bus bound for Munich, *Kerrang!*'s photographer has the berserk idea of shooting the Lostprophets from the top of their moving vehicle. It'll be easy, he tells them; the roof above the thin corridor separating their bunks features three skylights that open on a hinge. If everyone places their feet on the edges of the beds, half of the band can pop their heads out of the portal at the rear, the other half through the hole in the middle, and he'll shoot them from the hatch at the front. In order to keep an eye out for anything that might be hurtling towards us, facing forwards my job is to stand at the photographer's back.

'What do you think?'

'Yeah, okay,' say the Lostprophets. 'Why not?'

'*Why not?* Because *it's crazy is* why not.'

'Shut up, it'll be all right.'

'Guys . . .'

'Come on, it'll be a laugh.'

So up I go, a crash test dummy sent out alone into the blackness above. *Jesus Christ.* Greeting the midnight air on the border between Austria and Germany, I'm met with a sight that transforms our pigeon-brained caper into a plan with potentially deadly consequences.

'There's bridges up there,' I say.

'What? How many?'

'Well . . . loads of 'em. It looks as if they're coming at us, like, every couple of hundred yards or so.'

'Right.'

'I mean, they're practically brushing the top of the bus. Three feet above us, tops.'

'Um.'

I can see in my colleague's face that this information is not quite the sanction I would like it to be.

'Listen to me. We can't do this. We'll end up decapitated.'

'Shut up, you wimp. It'll be all right.'

'I mean, I don't think it will.'

In our world of instant gratification, the prospect of death is no match for the intoxicating spirit of fuck-it derring-do. Once again, up I go through a hatch in the ceiling. This time I have a cameraman at my back. Six music makers are out here with us. Captured in a series of energetic black and white pictures, the expressions on the faces of the Lostprophets speak of freedom, exhilaration, camaraderie and the vertiginous thrill of danger. Not once do their eyes leave the blinking eye of the camera. My job is to keep us alive. Failure to speak, or to act, will bring oblivion to us all.

'Bridge!'

Down we come, up we go.

'Duck!'

Down. Up.

'Bridge! Duck!'

Up here, the night has a visceral edge. Revving and roaring in our ears, the wind summons tears to our eyes. Making myself heard requires the bark of a roustabout.

'Bridge!'

Like metronomes, by now we have our rhythm.

'Duck!'

Actually, do you know what? This is good fun.

'Duck!'

Last year I was selling books.

'Bridge!'

The bus slows to a stop on the hard shoulder of the autobahn. Nominated to be the diplomatic channel between band and driver, I receive instructions to go downstairs and see what's up. *It's probably a puncture, right? That'll be the problem.* Only it isn't that. Parting the window blinds with my fingers, I'm greeted by the sight of our bemused driver standing feet from a parked police car. Wagging their fingers and shaking their heads, its occupants loom over him with ominous intent. Something inside me quietly dies.

Up in the back lounge, the travelling party is keen for news.

'What's going on?'

'Brace yourselves . . .'

Chaos. Terror. Six musicians, blinded by panic, see how they run. Where the fuck are they going? Like oversized parcels, two members of the Lostprophets jam themselves into their bunks. Everyone is hyperventilating. We have but seconds in which to organise ourselves, only there's nowhere to go. In search of invisibility, someone places a towel over his head. To my left I hear the sound of footsteps thundering up the stairs. *No one gets out of here alive.* Len, our driver, a Lancastrian of bracing temperament, is now among us. In a lifetime of scrapes I have never before seen a man as angry as this. If I do so in the future, it will be as a precursor to my own violent death.

'All of you. In here. *Now.*'

Ducking low, the chastened musicians crowd the lounge. And so it begins.

'You fucking idiots,' he says. '*You. Fucking. Idiots.* Do you know who I've just been talking to?' (*We do, we do. No, shut up. We don't. We definitely don't.*) 'The fucking coppers. *German* fucking coppers. Did you not fucking wonder why the fucking bus had stopped? It's because they fucking pulled me over, is why. Because you fucking set of cunts are up there' – a finger stabs the air, suicide by light socket – 'fucking about on the roof. *The fucking roof!* And do you know what they told me, them coppers? That they could arrest me. That's what. They told me that I could lose my licence, which I already fucking knew. Oh yeah, and they told me that a young girl – a fucking child – had her head knocked off just last month on a school outing doing exactly what you cunts were up there doing.'

Silence. Shame. The urgent need for the sweet release of communal laughter.

'Lads, you could have been fucking killed.'

The anger of bus driver Len has no more space in which to expand; if it doesn't abate, he will collapse and die. Correctly intuiting a sliver of light in the use of the word 'lads', Ian Watkins goes to work. To a chorus line of contrite and supportive nods, the singer says that he's sorry. That we're all sorry. We didn't think it through. To be honest with him, we didn't think – and this is not meant to be an excuse – that he'd even know we were up there. We certainly didn't mean to cause him any trouble. Having him drive the band around Europe has been great. It's been a proper laugh, it has. Hasn't it, lads? (*Yeah. Yeah, it has.*) Seriously, we didn't mean for this to happen. Honestly, Len, we didn't. It was meant to be a laugh, but obviously it was just stupid.

'And dangerous,' says our driver.

And dangerous, yes. Very dangerous. Very stupid and very dangerous. And we're very, very sorry.

A negotiation of complex and barely discernible delicacy, it is a master class in subtle amelioration. 'Look into my eyes,' says Kaa, and so forth and so on. In years to come Ian Watkins will use this powerful charm as a means of aligning others to causes of terrible darkness. Charged for his crimes, he will at last attain a level of fame of which he always dreamed. Battered by the story's awful specifics, people will ask how it was possible for one man to orchestrate a conspiracy of such horror. But on a bus bound for Munich, I saw him at work. I was never in any doubt how he did it.

'All right,' says Len, already shuffling backwards towards the entrance of the lounge. 'You're good lads, you are.'

Two years later I watch the Lostprophets perform their new single on *Top of the Pops*. Onstage inside a television studio in White City, Ian Watkins looks born to the role that is now being broadcast up and across the nation. Waiting for the band to strike up the song's opening riff, he clicks his fingers with an insouciance that seems to say, 'You bet we belong here.' At home in my little studio flat in Islington, it's difficult not to be excited on the group's behalf. *Look! Someone I know is on the telly!* Not just someone I've interviewed, but someone I actually *know*. People I *like*. Jabbing at the handset, I give the singer a ring. The single-space dial tone tells me that he's in North America. Los Angeles, as it turns out.

You've just been on Top of the Pops. *It looked amazing.*

'Did it? We only filmed it yesterday.'

In 2004 the Lostprophets' second album goes gold in the United States. In finding their way onto the stereos of half a million listeners, the band join Coldplay, Muse, Bullet for My Valentine and Arctic Monkeys as the only domestic guitar acts to have achieved this feat in the twenty-first century. Despite attracting limited attention beyond the pages of the rock press, my friends are suddenly breathing rarefied air. *Good for them.* I join them in Texas for two dates on yet another North American campaign. Speaking to ticketholders at a concert in Grand Prairie, just outside Dallas, a stream of young admirers tell me that the group's genre-hopping music is the sound of the future. At a radio festival at the Cynthia Woods Mitchell Pavilion in Houston the following day I seek the opinion of a disc jockey from the city's alternative rock station KTBZ. Speaking from a broadcast booth adjacent to a stage from which a roster of acts perform to an audience of more than sixteen thousand people, he tells me that 'this band can become as big in America as they want to be. It's really that simple.'

As their adventure unfolds, I can see the excitement ablaze in the eyes of the Lostprophets. They *are* in Kansas, Toto, as well as Milwaukee, Indianapolis, St Louis, Cincinnati, Charlotte, Pittsburgh and more. They're in dressing rooms and hotel lobbies. Good fortune accompanies them on buses and planes. Major-key music, hit singles, star quality. From sea to shining sea, everything is theirs for the taking.

Until it isn't. As the years progress, Ian Watkins begins to change. Once the band's most valuable public asset, his transformation into their gravest liability is startling to behold. Casting resentment in every direction, the outside world is viewed with bitterness and disdain; music, especially, becomes a source of profound displeasure. Quick to deride the creative and commercial achievements of all other bands, his outlook contrasts sharply with the communality of almost every other musician I know. Ablaze with envy, the success of a 'competitor' is a direct belittlement of his own standing. It is food stolen from his table. *How dare they? All of this should be mine.* My word, is he tedious.

I well recall his piercing aggravation at a generous review I'd written of a British band superior to his own. *Why had I done this?* In wounded tones, he spoke at length about what he believed to be an exercise in journalistic gullibility, or dishonesty. Falling for this lot made me either a fool or a liar, he said. *Excuse me?* I realise now this meagre incident was for me the first red flag in the sorry and sordid story of Ian Watkins. It was the first time I'd looked at him as someone I didn't recognise, and didn't much like. I wasn't the only one. As the Lostprophets splintered into two factions, defiant and deluded their singer stood alone. I remember being at a recording studio in Los Angeles in 2008 at which the band were plunging themselves into debt in a doomed attempt to complete a lavishly expensive (and eventually aborted) new album. Sitting in the sunshine on outdoor furniture with guitarist Lee Gaze, I made a joke about the frontman's late arrival for our interview.

'Just run the last one you did,' he said. 'He'll only say exactly the same stuff this time round. It'll just be him complaining about everything. You can put a picture of him crying on the cover.'

As best as they were able, the rest of the band kept faith with their project. Continuing to hustle, on the afternoons of concerts in Middle America Lee Gaze trawled city streets handing out flyers to strangers who looked like they might be in the market for a rock show. *Hi, how you doing today? I'm in a band from Wales. We're pretty good. Why don't you come and check us out?* By some distance he was the group's quietest member, so I found it difficult to picture him doing this. It was far easier to imagine Ian Watkins in this role. But while the Lostprophets' most versatile musician was putting in hard yards on the pavements of foreign cities, the singer sat alone in a lounge aboard their tour bus. Distrusted and disliked, he was kept company by an array of vicious drugs.

'There was a point at which he was making his own crystal meth,' Stuart Richardson, the band's bassist, tells me. 'By this stage I was getting grossed out by just being around him. By the whole decline of him. I remember we were on tour and our tour manager went into his bag to get something and he found all this paraphernalia – a pipe, powders, all that shit. He just threw it straight in the trash. He came to us and said, "We've got to talk to Ian." We were like, "Fuck."'

Ah, *right*. So this was the source of Ian Watkins' startling and determined decline. The most routine of rock 'n' roll horror stories had ensnared another vulnerable victim. It was drugs. *Of course* it was drugs. At an intervention backstage at the Birmingham Academy, the group had already learned that their singer had been using illegal substances in what he described as a limited way for strictly creative purposes. Explaining his motives, Watkins told his friends that he simply sought to write songs from a different perspective – 'A ludicrous idea,' according to Lee Gaze – but that the experiment had run its course. Dialling up the charm, in Los Angeles he'd convinced a qualified therapist of the same thing.

But crystal methamphetamine, now that was serious. A girlfriend in New York sent Watkins photographs of addicts who appeared to have aged decades after less than a year on the pipe. *Don't worry*, he told her. *Have you ever known anyone as vain as me?* (The answer is no. Even his email address contained the words 'mirror boy'.) *Listen to what I'm saying*, he said, *do you really think that I would let that kind of thing happen to me? Do you think I'm that stupid?* But it *did* happen to him. With his life adrift from its moorings, Ian Watkins became greasy and bloated. His teeth started falling out. Collapsing in on themselves, the Lostprophets were rotting from the head.

'I remember us playing shows in Scotland and people were booing,' says Stuart Richardson. 'I said to him, "Dude, people are booing us right now and we're the fucking headliners. They've paid to see us and they're *booing* us. And they're not fucking booing me, they're booing *you* . . ."It's the kind of thing where you've spent fifteen years doing this and so you just don't want to let it go. So you ask yourself, "Is this pride that's keeping this together? What is this?" And you realise that you're watching your friend implode and you just don't want to let him down. You don't want to let *yourself* down either. But you're being held completely at ransom the whole time. Because, sometimes, being in a band can feel like limbo, you know?'

I spoke to Watkins for the last time on 4 May 2012 at the Brixton Academy. Sweeping into the dressing room only minutes before he was due onstage, the singer barely made eye contact with bandmates that had been at the venue for hours. No one said hello. Today I know for sure what back then I only intuited. *My God, they hate him.*

By then the group's appeal was on the slide. Had the gig been staged at Wembley Arena – a room they had filled just five years earlier – the frontman would have faced the sight of eight thousand empty seats. In range of my Dictaphone, Watkins told me that the band's next tour would see them play the twenty-thousand-seat 02 Arena on 'multiple nights'. I told him he was being ridiculous. Faltering bands do not increase their audience tenfold in the space of two or three years. The singer said he'd accept my apology in the fullness of time. In a moment capable of stopping a clock, I was suddenly lost for words. I had known Ian Watkins for almost exactly twelve years. For at least half of this time he had been funny, charismatic, cocky and sharp. Not anymore. The look on his face was leery and sly.

That summer the Lostprophets toured North America. When their singer failed to appear for a show in Pittsburgh the rest of the band decided to play their set with Jamie Oliver on vocals. At the end of their shift, Ian Watkins was waiting for them on the bus. By the code of the road, the singer had done the unthinkable. People in bands do not miss shows. If they are ill, they take to the stage. If their lives are in a state of perfect ruin (and some of them are), they hit their cue. The Rolling Stones minted a maxim for this – *if you can stand, you can play*. Meeting the singer's eye, Stuart Richardson simply said, 'Nice one, dude.' Legs spread like the blades of a helicopter, Watkins shrugged and said, '*What?*' All things considered, this was probably a bit strong.

'I just grabbed him and punched him in the face for what seemed like five minutes,' Stuart tells me. 'Some of the guys came on the bus and pulled me off him, but the next day his face looked like the Elephant Man. Afterwards I felt so bad that all I could do was just keep apologising to him. But he wouldn't talk to me, which of course I understood. But I did say to him, "Look, I'm really sorry. That was super out of hand. You fucked up, but I fucked up more."

'The next day [Ian] came up to me and he was crying his eyes out,' Stuart says. 'Just bawling his eyes out. And he said, "I'm so sorry. I'm just *so* sorry." And I said, "It's okay, it's just a show." I told him again that I was sorry about what had happened afterwards. But he just kept saying it: "No, I'm sorry. I'm just so sorry." At the time I thought, "What the fuck is that all about?" Now I think it was the closest he came with us to an admission of guilt.'

In December 2012 Ian Watkins was charged with conspiracy to engage in sexual activity with two minors, and for the possession of indecent images of children and 'extreme animal pornography'. The police needed the help of experts at Government Communications Headquarters (GCHQ) to unlock his laptop. The password was IFUKKIDZ. Two anonymous co-defendants faced trial for assaulting their own children at the singer's behest. Watkins met the woman identified in court as 'B' when she was nineteen. The pair described in explicit detail the acts to which they planned to subject her ten-month-old son. At the K West Hotel in Shepherd's Bush in April 2012 the singer was filmed attempting to rape the child. In September of that year he received a picture in which the mother can be seen sexually abusing her son.

That summer, he began a correspondence with a twenty-four-year-old woman identified in court as 'P'. As well as discussing forcing her young daughter (the child's age is unspecified) to engage in sex acts with animals, the singer proposed prostituting the child to men who, he believed, would pay thousands of pounds for this kind of encounter. He persuaded P to molest her child on a Skype call. The pair met at a Travelodge in Caerphilly at which, the court believed, Watkins attempted to rape the infant. Analysis of her hair showed that she had been exposed to crystal methamphetamine.

On 26 November 2013 Ian Watkins pleaded guilty to attempted rape and sexual assault of a child under the age of thirteen. The following month at Cardiff Crown Court he was sentenced to twenty-nine years' imprisonment. Defendants B and P were sentenced to seventeen and fourteen years respectively. In his sentencing remarks (which are taken from the court record) the Honourable Mr Justice Royce said that,

'Those who have appeared in these Courts at the Bar or on the Bench over many years see and hear a large number of horrific cases. This case however breaks new ground. Any decent person looking at and listening to the material here will experience shock; revulsion; anger and incredulity. What you three did plumbed new depths of depravity. You, Watkins, achieved fame and success as the lead singer of the Lostprophets. You had many fawning fans. That gave you power. You knew you could use that power to induce young female fans to help satisfy your apparently insatiable lust and to take part in the sexual abuse of their young children. Away from the highlights of your public performances lay a dark and sinister side . . . [Your] craving was fuelled by your use of cocaine and methamphetamine which increased your sexual aggression. You spoke of not knowing to what extremes you would have gone but for your arrest. It is difficult to imagine anything much worse.' The record states that "Mr Watkins presents a high risk of causing serious sexual, physical, emotional and psychological harm to children, both male and female, and to women, specifically his female sexual partners . . ." I have no hesitation in concluding that there is a significant risk to the public, in particular to young females and children, of serious harm occasioned by the commission by you of further specified offences. That risk is high.'

This shouldn't need saying but let's say it anyway: the primary victims of Ian Watkins' crimes are the children he abused. The possession of images of child sexual exploitation also contributed to an economy of financial and fungible misery in which the singer was an active participant. But as he braced himself for decades – potentially, realistically, the rest of his life – inside Her Majesty's Prison Wakefield (known locally as 'Monster Mansion'), Watkins left behind him a number of other lives scarred and warped in terrible and profound ways.

Picture this quotidian scenario. A man from the valleys of South Wales falls into conversation with a stranger seated next to him on a plane. As a drinks trolley trundles up the aisle, he is asked about his job of work. 'Well, um, I'm kind of a musician,' he answers. The response invites an involuntary widening of the eyes. 'Oh, really? Have you played on anything I might have heard?' And there – *right there* – the conversation reaches a terrible impasse. There is every chance that the stranger *has* heard the Lostprophets. The group had hundreds of thousands of fans. In the United Kingdom, two of their albums went platinum. Even if the stranger doesn't know the music, they may well recognise the name Ian Watkins. It is at this point that the passenger will realise that she or he is packed like a battery chicken in a steel tube alongside a musician that spent years in the company of a committed paedophile.

Watkins knowingly poisoned the well of shared achievements. No one will ever again wear a Lostprophets t-shirt. Listeners will not be inclined to buy or stream any of the group's five studio albums. There will be no reunion tour. Not one of their dozens of songs will be revivified on the soundtrack to a blockbuster movie, or rocketed to iconic status by a popular television programme. All of that is now gone – and it's not coming back. In terms of the craft, the creative energy, the talent, the discipline and the sacrifice required to survive as a professional musician, the group's other members – a quintet that has *done nothing wrong* – may as well have spent fifteen years of their lives in a coma.

'What Ian did was just so disgusting and so unbelievable that we stopped giving a fuck about ourselves,' says Stuart Richardson. 'We just thought, "This is so awful, who gives a fuck what happens to us right now?" *Really*. I'm not trying to say that in some altruistic way; it was just so terrible that we left it to ourselves to figure things out. But not only did he take fifteen years away from me, but he took away my future as well. Because even though the band was starting to decline, we could have gone away for a couple of years and then come back with the hope that people might give a shit. So we thought about calling it a day for a bit, and then coming back and going on the road and playing all our greatest hits until we were dead. That was the retirement plan.

'But that's all gone now,' he tells me. 'Not only had we done fifteen years of work, but we also had twenty years of the future still to come. And you're so busy being in a band – especially with Ian in the band – that I had no energy for anything else. In other areas of my life I was moving a millimetre in every direction. I didn't really set anything else up because I'd put everything I had into Lostprophets. So when it died, I didn't have anything else.'

In my experience, people in bands are uncomfortable with being businesspeople. Unlike other industries, the prioritisation of profit – as distinct from *success* – is regarded (with some justification) as being antithetical to anyone seeking to make authentic music. Perennially ripe for exploitation, a far from discountable number of musicians are all but financially illiterate. In the case of the Lostprophets, degrees of solvency depended on the season. When the Watkins story broke, the cupboard was bare.

'We were in the middle of an album cycle,' Stuart Richardson says. 'We were getting ready to earn a ton of money playing festivals, but at that point we were pretty much spent up. We had about three months' worth of money left. So we asked, "Well, where's all our savings?" And this is a good one, this is. You'll love this. God bless her, Ian's mum was sick so he bought her a house without telling us . . . But here's the plot twist, right? He never bought a house. So where did the money go? Is it in an account somewhere? Did he give it to someone else? Did he pay someone off for blackmail? These are the places my mind can go.'

Stuart was at the dentist with his daughter when he received a call from the band's manager. Where are you? he was asked. What are you doing? *Why?* 'He said that he was trying to get to the bottom of things but that some photos had been found of Ian,' he tells me. 'I said, "Photos? What kind of photos?" And he just said, "It's bad." And right then I thought, "We're finished. That's it, we're done."'

On a conference call, the Lostprophets attempted to sift through the wreckage. Did anyone know anything? Might this be a lie? Upsetting people was kind of Watkins' deal. He would always be saying stupid things in the hope of getting a rise. He was childish, really; Stuart was always telling him to shut the fuck up. Half his time was spent extinguishing fires the frontman had started for no good reason. The dude had a fucked-up attitude. He was fucked up on drugs. Who could say, perhaps something had happened that had bitten him on the arse so hard that it would scare him straight? That would explain it, wouldn't it? *Maybe it was something like that.*

But the Lostprophets were only pretending to talk themselves back to life. Away from the chatter, Stuart Richardson knew there had been no mistake. He just knew that the worst thing in the world was about to unfold. Ian Watkins had brought shame and severance to their door. None of them would ever see or speak with him again. After receiving every piece of relevant information from the police, on 1 October 2013 the group went public with a decision that had been taken the moment the news of Ian Watkins' depravity invaded their lives. In a statement on Facebook, Stuart Richardson, Lee Gaze, Jamie Oliver, guitarist Mike Lewis and drummer Luke Johnson wrote, 'After nearly a year of coming to terms with our heartache, we finally feel ready to announce publicly what we have thought for some time. We can no longer continue making or performing music as Lostprophets.'

'As much as I couldn't believe what happened, I also *could* kind of believe it,' Stuart tells me. 'I never saw it happening – it never happened around me – but when I heard what he'd done, when I heard what it was, things just fell into place for me. I was like, "Okay, yeah, he really has done this, hasn't he."'

I can only guess as to how one might go about overcoming something as awful as this. Burn the memories, Stuart Richardson's life's work had been achieved with the help of a paedophile. At home in Florida, financial ruin was averted only by the support of his journalist wife. Looking for work, he told bands playing the small clubs in the Orlando area in which he lives that he would record their music for an affordable price at the recording studio he had built by hand. In the years before the Lostprophets achieved maximum elevation, as a producer Stuart played a key role in shaping the sound of a nascent South Wales scene that in time rose to national (and in some cases international) prominence. And here he was again, harnessing the talents of young musicians looking longingly up at the first rung of a ladder he himself had once climbed.

He still plays music. As a touring member of the band Thursday, in 2019 Stuart performed more than fifty concerts on three continents. In an attempt to reclaim a measure of the shared humanity stolen by Ian Watkins, he formed No Devotion with other members of the Lostprophets. The quintet's debut London concert, at the Islington Academy in 2014, remains one of the most striking occasions of my professional life. Playing mostly unreleased material, the response from the audience amounted to an ovation for all that the musicians had been forced to endure. *You're through to the other side now*, it seemed to say. *We want you to know that we have come here tonight to show you that we believe you bear no responsibility for the things that have happened.* (At the time of writing, the group has just completed its second album.)

Alternatively, a number of detractors took delight in claiming, without evidence, that the other members of the Lostprophets were guilty of the same crimes as Ian Watkins. On social media they wrote of their hopes that Stuart's two young daughters would themselves be raped. Year upon year, the story refused to die. A report by the Independent Police Complaints Commission revealed that, were it not for the deficiencies of South Wales Police, Watkins might have been taken into custody four years earlier than the date of his arrest. Information came to light that one of the singer's many sexual partners had tried to sound the alarm as early as 2008 but had been disbelieved, she alleged, on account of being a sex worker. 'She went on TV and told everyone that she'd spent six months trying to tell us [the Lostprophets] about it,' Stuart says. 'She said that she'd told everyone in the band multiple times. I can tell you now that I have never met her. I don't know who she is.'

I remember where I was when the story broke. Sharing drinks with a journalist friend in a draughty pub near Mornington Crescent, at first we didn't notice the chyron of life-shattering information strolling across the bottom of a muted television screen. Our phones began to trill. Fucking hell. *Fucking hell.*

'There's no way the band knew about this.'

'Not a chance.'

'Stuart would have killed him. I mean, *literally* killed him. He would have taken Ian's head and pulled it off his shoulders.'

They *didn't* know. Aware of a heedless descent into drug use, the rest of the group had tried their best to guide their singer back to shore. They had tried to continue their operation within the confines of a determined narcissism that everyone I know attributed to common causes. This is how insane the music industry can be. With so much of it about, gruelling and maddeningly dysfunctional behaviour seems almost normal. Drug addiction seems normal. None of this stuff is at all surprising. The reason the Lostprophets failed to identify the presence of something *uniquely* vile within their ranks was because Ian Watkins could take his pick of routine ruinations behind which he could so easily hide.

'Ian lived in Los Angeles and was hanging out with some real douchebags,' Stuart tells me. 'You can find douchebags wherever you go, but in LA they really are everywhere. And Ian was attracted to anyone who thought he was awesome. He would always surround himself with people who thought he was the greatest person ever. That's different from how I am; I want to surround myself with people who *don't* think I'm the greatest thing ever. I always want to earn my place at the table and be part of the conversation. But that was Ian's deal. It was always just this model or this douchebag that he was in company with, just vacuous people that he surrounded himself with. It could be any one of those who got him into drugs and then whatever else he got into. I'm sure they were happy to indulge him.'

In 2018 the youngest of Stuart Richardson's two daughters told her school therapist that she wished she was three years old again.

Asked about the possibility that she may have suffered some kind of trauma at that stage in her life, her father revealed the details of the extinction-level event that had smashed a hole in his world. Suddenly things made sense. The child therapist told him that for a time he had become 'emotionally unavailable' to the people who called him 'Dad'. Those were the words she used. In the wake of the tragedy, each day he had taken his girls to the park. But although he was there, he wasn't quite there. Even from the confines of a prison cell, it seemed that Ian Watkins had found a way of damaging children's lives. The singer had once said that he would be happy to babysit the girls, but the offer was declined. He had met them, though. Sometimes Stuart wonders if he ever left the pair alone with him. Maybe he went to the kitchen to knock up some food. Perhaps he took a call in a different room. He doesn't think so. 'Have I thought about it, though?' he asks. 'Hell, yes. Of course I have.' Apprised of the details of the story, the school therapist wondered how he'd managed to cope. Many are the times I've asked him the same thing. Truth is, he doesn't really know. Even today, years later, he still struggles to articulate, or even to *describe*, the toil of rising above the kind of shock most of us will never know. He just did, is all. Or he tried to.

'Everything had linked together a little bit,' he says. 'I was a good dad. I just wasn't showing up a hundred per cent. It didn't matter how much I tried. There was always that something else on my mind.'

Like I said, I always liked the Lostprophets. But of the six of them, Stuart is the person I like best. As a schoolboy in Pontypridd he wore pop-bottle glasses through which he somehow saw his way to David Bowie and Black Flag. He made friends with music. Despite it all, the two have never fallen out. Speaking to him on Zoom is to find myself once more in the company of an old and quietly dear friend. Same easy smile, same self-deprecating manner. Up close, though, I can see the difference in him. I can see the scars.

'What happened was, like, five years of a really long day,' he says. 'It was the longest day of my life that lasted for five years.'

In what I imagine to be quite the formative experience, as a teenager Stuart Richardson used to accompany his dad on the picket lines during the Miners' Strike. Talk about a turbulent time. With the country divided, in the summer of 1984 the BBC showed non-consecutive footage from the Orgreave coking plant near Rotherham in which it was at least implied that the violent tactics of the police were a response to the provocations of striking pitmen. (Prosecutions against the ninety-five people arrested that day were dropped. In 2012 the *Guardian* and the BBC itself revealed that dozens of officers' statements had identical opening paragraphs.) As I'm typing these words, above me hangs a framed black and white photograph of a field in South Yorkshire that was once the site of a colliery. The image was one of two-dozen shots of erstwhile pits on display at Barnsley town hall. I asked the photographer responsible for this poignant array of industrial ghosts if he'd be willing to sell me one? The bewilderment in his voice suggested I'd extended an invitation to go line dancing. 'I'd like to buy the one of Houghton Main,' I told him. 'It's where my dad and his dad used to work.'

Unlike his son, my grandfather was a lifer at the pit. At the end of the Second World War, in New York City in 1945 the revellers on Broadway mistook his strident accent for that of an Amish. *Nar. Thee. Thar.* Back in Barnsley there was never any doubt about who he was, or where he was going. Walt Winwood was headed to the coalfields. Universally recognised as the toughest gig in any mine, his job as a ripper was to dislodge by hand the rock above a seam of freshly mined coal. I never heard him complain about his work. I never heard him complain about anything. Told that one of his three sons is gay, in 1974 he said, 'Why on earth would that bother me? I *always* knew.' A gentle man, he was there with me when I was taken into hospital before my first birthday. As the doctors repaired my lungs, each day Walt walked a hilly two miles to join me on the paediatric ward. For weeks on end he sat by my side singing songs as I slept. I've heard it said that he never missed a shift. *Really? But what about the pit?* 'Oh, no, the miners were on strike.' Well, of course they were. At the start of the seventies the miners were on strike so often they brought down a government.

Struck low by Alzheimer's, in the end there was nothing but sadness. With savagely determined purpose, the disease took hold in stages. An unfunny turn at a Christmas gathering required the services of a taxi on double time to take him and my grandma home. As the Winwoods and their assorted plus ones sat in a kind of concussed silence, I watched from the window in my aunt's front room as Eric shepherded his parents into the backseat of a black and white car. Oblivious to the commotion, my granddad appeared untroubled; ablaze with upset, his wife of half a century was in a state. After watching the car drive away, I asked my dad if the pair got off okay. It was the kind of thing you say in moments of terrible quiet.

'No,' he joked. 'He knocked himself out on the ice. We've had to leave him in the garden.'

We all knew that things were about to get out of hand. The new year saw my father trudging up the steep hill to Ardsley to give his father a bath and a shave. No one had ever seen Walt in a state of anger – I doubt that even the Second World War annoyed him all that much – but Alzheimer's makes unruly patients of even the most placid people. Seated at the lip of a pea-soup bathtub, three times a week Eric struggled gamely to repel the advances of an older man frightened by the sight of a disposable razor. *Come on now, lad; come on, old pal.* Sagging under the weight of it all, over drinks in his local he told me that he dreaded this duty with a despondency that permeated every aspect of his life.

'Don't let me get to that stage, Ian,' he said. 'If you see it happening, just shoot me.'

Inevitably, Walt saw out the home stretch in a care home. Decked out in pyjamas and dressing gown, we'd find him sitting in a chair in a downstairs common room. 'Nar then, Walt' – everybody in Barnsley begins sentences with the words 'nar then' – 'look who's come to see you.' *Fucking hell, he looks like Hugh Hefner.* Fascinated by his chorus of nonsense, sometimes I'd wonder if perhaps I was in the company of a genial lunatic. Widening his eyes, he'd point at me with a lucid surprise that would pass by in under a second. The pilot light was going out.

Towards the end he couldn't even get out of bed. For years he just lay there, curved like a question mark, fast asleep. Eric would take me to see him at Christmas time. 'Eyup, pal, how we doing?' With our patriarch diminished and still, the younger generations passed the time talking about books, the Labour Party, Barnsley Football Club, London and, as always, about the night at Barnsley Civic Hall on which Pete Townshend attempted to smash his way through an amplifier the size of a wardrobe.

'Dad, that really does sound amazing.'

'It was embarrassing. Eric Burdon wouldn't have done that.'

A companionable silence. A nod to the bed. 'I mean, what's he waiting for?'

'Ian, I have a vision of me walking up these hills to this fucking place when I'm eighty.' A look of theatrical opprobrium. 'He's going to outlive me, this bastard.'

But no. Come the end, even Walt Winwood couldn't stay alive for ever. Even he couldn't outlive his eldest son.

But it was closer than it ought to have been.

5: GOD'S COMIC

In the small hours of 2 April 2011 Eric Winwood smashed his head open and bled to death.

He'd come to London with my mother to see me on the weekend before my birthday. At the end of a night out he fell over and cut himself open. Before help could reach him, or even be called, his enlarged heart expedited the blood from his body.

I used to quietly worry about how he'd get on in a life without structure. I could picture him sitting in 'Spoons at ten o' clock in the morning with a budget pint and a Pete Dexter novel for company. I didn't imagine him being pissed by noon. Decanted into a cab, I couldn't see him ferried home half asleep by a driver who had once worked underground in the pits around Barnsley. *Is this it, mate? Mate? Is this your street?* But I *could* see him sitting there quietly drinking away his days. Heartbroken beyond repair, it didn't matter that women were attracted to his gentle intelligence, and to his faint scent of benign helplessness. He was too old to be hurt again. Steering a course towards a distant horizon, he was determined to sail his ship alone. Just as well, really.

It was supposed to be the day that everything came together. Only that morning he'd taken early retirement. From the moment he arrived in the city, the obligations of gainful employment were yesterday's news. Facing forwards, the livid scars of a gruelling divorce would be allowed time to heal. It all started now. On visits to Camden, Eric was a different man; drunk on its energy, he couldn't get enough of the variety of life only inches from his eyes. As his eldest child was driven mad by a missing apostrophe, at the Elephants [sic] Head he'd be nodding his head in time to the music. Ten past midnight. 'Ian, who's this?' 'Ramones, Dad. "Sheena is a Punk Rocker". Why, do you like it?' He did, yes; as a matter of fact, for a moment there even Eric was a punk rocker. In the toilets of a pub on the Chalk Farm Road, he was once offered a line of cocaine. He had no interest in joining in the action – 'I wouldn't know what to do' – but he loved that he'd been asked. *In the city there's a thousand faces.* A part of the scene once more, I have no doubt that the last day of Eric's life was one he enjoyed more than almost any other. It's what kills me, sometimes.

I could tell from the off that he had on his shooting boots. After a few pints in the afternoon sun, I accompanied him to Sainsbury's to buy a bottle of whiskey 'for later'. When my mother went to bed we retired to the balcony of his room. Drinking Scotch, by now we were both drunk. Half an hour earlier I'd been given an album of photographs telling a story of my life. On the first page was a picture from my parents' wedding. Even in black and white I could see the sunlight dancing in the eyes of the bride. Standing beside her, Eric looked like a member of the Small Faces.

I don't really remember much of what we talked about in that last hour. But I do recall us making firm arrangements to meet the following morning, ten for ten-thirty, at the brand new early-doors pub next door. I promised I would show him the view of the Shard from the top of Primrose Hill. Still under construction, London's newest protuberance was a thing of interest to a man who started the day as a practising engineer. A sucker for capitalist architecture, I was looking forward to showing off the latest grand edition to the skyline of my adopted home city. Standing to bid him goodnight, we shared an embrace that knocked my hat backwards from my head. The last words I said to him were, 'I love you, Dad.' Believe me or not, I *did* say that. 'Same goes, pal,' he replied. As it always will be, that was good enough for me.

*

Nine hours later, Eric isn't where he said he would be. Straight away, I know something is wrong. I'll go further, I know something is *terribly* wrong. Never mind never late, my father is always early. It had been a big night, but in the warm air of a Saturday morning things are as they should be. I didn't expect to see him at his station with a pint and a smile, but I was certain he'd be there with a cup of tea and a constitution that had seen off circumstances more bracing than this. He'd be reading a paper. Smiling at my approach, he'd say the words with which he'd greeted me for as long as I've been alive. *'Eyup*, pal.'

The distance from the doors of the Holiday Inn to the table on which I place my soft drink can be made on foot without drawing breath. Shooing away a sense of panicked disquiet, I tell myself that he'll be here in a minute. *You'll see. Just give it five.* On the lock a battalion of visitors is already facing the day. In one half of a split second, I evaluate the tide of late middle-aged men drifting past the window. *Is that him? No. Is that? No. Is . . .? No. No. No.* I can still feel it – now, today, as I write this *word* – the grasping need for immediate relief.

'*Eyup*, pal. Sorry I'm late.'

Handing me the receiver, at the Holiday Inn a receptionist dials the room. No answer. Something is wrong. Something is *terribly* wrong. But this is England, and I am English, so of course I am cowed by how this might sound spoken out loud. *I need you to take me up there. I need you to let me into his room.* Listen to yourself, will you? Let's have a think about this, shall we? He's not even late. When people say ten for half-past, they mean half-past. He'll have assumed that's what *I* meant, anyway. An early riser, he'll have stepped out for a walk. He knows the area. He's a grown man. He'll be in the pub now, waiting for me.

'*Eyup*, pal.'

But of course he's not. How could he be? *Something* **terrible** *has happened.* I need to rethink my strategy. I need to improve my game. Over the years, I have somehow acquired a tone of voice that serves to persuade people in positions of power that I rightly belong in places to which they are not minded to grant me access. At backstage entrances, production gates and recording studios, I know how to get to where I'm going. *I'm here to interview the people headlining this stadium. They are expecting me.* I need to use it now. Speaking once more to the hotel receptionist, I am polite and economical. But this is no longer a negotiation. 'I need to be taken to Eric Winwood's room. Please understand what I'm telling you. This is a serious matter.'

A maid with a passkey escorts me up to the fourth floor. *A decorated splatter brightens the room.* In the time it takes the door to swing back on its hinges, the unquantifiable metrics of instinct and intuition metastasise into life-changing reality. *Oh, hiya, Dad.* Bent at the middle like a sack of grain, there he is, slumped by the bed, naked and still. *Lifeless.* Straight away I realise I'm in the company of a dead man. My father's scalp, face, hands, knuckles, fingers, nails and forearms are caked in blood. The bed is a sacrificial altar. A red handprint – how did *that* get there? – stains the wall near the toilet. The carpet is ruined. *Ah, right.* This wasn't a quick or painless end, at all. Framed in the unforgiving light of a spring morning, it looks like Eric died of St Vitus' dance.

The hotel employee at my side starts to scream. If the Holiday Inn has a protocol for opening the door on a corpse, I don't think she's following it. A scalpel of noise, it is the kind of sound an establishment such as this will do anything to avoid. Determined not to be outperformed, I join in. '*Dad!*' I shout. '*Dad! Dad! Dad!*' Even at the time, I'm aware of a sense of calmness tugging gently at my sleeve. Its work will begin as soon as I've emptied my system of all this noise.

In the meantime, if you don't mind, for the next few seconds I'll use the power of my voice as a tool with which to reanimate a next of kin. *Okay, fine. But the man is dead. He's fucking dead. I mean, look at him.*

I recall what happens next only in flashes. At the news from my lips my mother steps back from her table in the breakfast room and crouches on the floor. Next thing I know I'm on the balcony of her room. Pacing back and forth, overlooking the canal I try to contact a half-brother twenty years my junior. Using sighs and silence, the woman at the DIY megastore in Barnsley at which he works lets me know my presence on the line is a testing inconvenience.

'I mean, is it important?' she asks.

'*Yes,*' I tell her. 'It is. It really, really is.'

My next job is to break the heart of an erstwhile stepbrother who has known Eric since he was two. Suddenly remembering that this is supposed to be a birthday weekend, I make contact with the six or seven friends with whom we were supposed to go and see Barnsley play Crystal Palace this very afternoon. Multiplying at speed, in the hotel room I see two, then four, then six uniformed Metropolitan Police officers. *Okay, so the players in the day's second act are here.* Before this, I hadn't even considered that this might be a legal matter. *Well, this is interesting.* My mum steps out onto the balcony. 'Darling, the police are becoming nervous about you being on the phone,' she tells me.

This is all it takes for me to realise that the day has taken a new turn for the worse. More than an unusual but inevitable story of the death of a parent, this is now a matter for the authorities. I was the last person to see my father alive; the following morning, I was the one who found him dead. Legally speaking, this is not a winning combination. In the eyes of the police, I am now a person of interest.

'What? *Why?*'

'Love, they just are,' she says. 'They want you to come inside.'

An officer takes me to one side. Craning my neck to meet his eyes, I answer a series of questions to which the answers are already known. Other information will later be verified by the time-coded images of closed-circuit surveillance. What time did I leave my father's hotel room? *About one o' clock.* Did I then go directly to my home? *Yes.* Via which route did I reach my front door?

'And have you ever been in trouble with the police?' he asks.

Astonishingly, I have not. Despite the effort and money I have invested in breaking the law, my permanent record is as white as a wedding dress.

'No. I've never been in trouble with the police.'

A high-ranking uniformed officer enters the room. Efficient and precise, so far the coppers have carried themselves with a polite certainty of purpose. But this guy – *this fucking ace* – chucks his authority around like a stretch limo in a stock-car rally. With no time for even cursory expressions of condolence or regret, he tells me that I am to be sequestered in a separate room under police guard until a forensics team has had time 'to fully examine the crime scene'. *Crime scene? What crime scene?* Absorbing this information, my mind decides to play against type. Some years earlier, following a testy meeting with the *Kerrang!* top brass, an editor once described me as 'the Yorkshire raptor'. Where's that guy when I need him? I wish he were here now, running off his mouth with an improvised energy that startles everyone in the room, himself included. But in the face of *genuine* authority, at once I become subservient. Old Bailey, here I come.

An officer is waiting for me in a smaller room on the third floor. A forty-year-old career constable – his words – PC Kevin Onlow already knows that his job for the day is babysitting a man suspected of foul play. 'Looks like we're going to be spending a bit of time together,' he says. 'Make yourself at home,' he tells me as I take a seat on the edge of a double bed from which my legs dangle half a foot from the floor. Officer, if only I could.

At the threshold of the room, the police constable receives instructions from his officious commanding officer. Over the course of the day, I am not at liberty to leave the space in which I am now sequestered. My police guard will monitor my every move. I am permitted to use the toilet only on the understanding that he will watch over me as I urinate and, on two occasions, defecate. I am not allowed to wash my hands. I am to be prohibited from eating any food or drinking liquids of any kind, including water. I am not permitted to receive visitors. I am forbidden from accessing, touching or even looking at the screen of my mobile phone.

Inevitably, it is this final sanction that at first causes most distress. With the story of Eric's misadventure by now on the wires, my pocketsize portal is ringing like tinnitus. I wouldn't mind getting an outside line on it myself. In the course of a single morning I have become the patriarch of my father's branch of the Winwood family. I realise now that practical matters require my urgent attention. Back in the north of England, a mother is yet to be told of the death of her son; two brothers and a sister do not know that their eldest sibling no longer walks among them. I don't believe my half-brother can be expected to attend to these matters. Under normal circumstances, I'd have taken care of them myself. But we're some way from normal circumstances.

The phone strikes up its urgent chorus.

'Kevin, can I not even *look* to see who it is?'

'I'm afraid not. I am sorry.'

If I were allowed to do so, by now I would be eating lunch. Instead, police officer and suspect turn on the telly to watch Leeds United pummel Nottingham Forest 4–1 at Elland Road. We talk about music. 'Kev', as by now I'm calling him, likes Cage the Elephant. *Hang on a minute.* As it so happens I know the band's press officer. She got my cats for me, in fact. She once got me off the hook after I'd lost two hundred quid's worth of receipts on a trip to Los Angeles. I tell him I'll ask her to send him one of the band's CDs.

'Ah. No. Thanks, mate, but it's all right.'

'No, really, it's not a problem,' I say. 'She won't mind. This isn't me trying to be Billy Big Bollocks or anything.'

Not for the first time, I'm missing the point. I'm not listening to what I'm *really* being told.

'I know it's not,' he says. 'But that's not it. What it is, is that I'm not allowed to accept a gift from you. It could be misconstrued ...'

... as a bribe, Ian. It could be misconstrued as a bribe. See, here's the thing of it: I keep forgetting that this is serious. Chatting away, I keep overlooking the fact that were I to attempt to leave this room I would be physically restrained and placed under arrest for the murder of my father. PC Onlow doesn't want it to come to this, and neither does he expect that it will. But if it does, this is how the day will play out. In this room, I would do well to remember the difference between friendliness and friendship. The epitome of the British system, I am being policed with my own consent.

On the television, the afternoon film is *Galaxy Quest*.

'Back of the net.'

'Oh, I love this movie,' says PC Onlow.

'I mean, it's a classic.'

On the screen, Commander Peter Quincy Taggart is being chased by creatures made of rocks.

'This bit's funny.'

Did I kill my father?

'Yeah, it's good.'

Did I kill my dad?

It's just a thought. Kicking down doors and putting in windows – it's just a thought. *Did I kill Eric?* I can recall the goodnight hug. I can remember telling him that I loved him. But after that, things are missing. The ride in the lift down to reception, the key in the door, putting myself to bed – it's not there. *Did I kill my dad?* If you must know, I *do* have an angle. There *is* something in this for me. Reviewed in the kind of light favoured by police officers and juries, the hard facts don't look good. Cheroot in hand, even Peter Falk would struggle to pull together a two-hour TV movie out of this. Lieutenant Frank Columbo, he'd have me in cuffs before the first commercial break.

'Sir, let me ask you this. Were you aware of your father's six-figure retirement nest egg?'

'Um. I was, yes.'

'Good. That's good. And did you know of the existence of a recent generous divorce settlement in his favour?'

'I would have to say . . . that . . . I was aware of this, yes.'

'I see. And did the deceased tell you just yesterday that he had recently made a will in which you and your half-brother were named as beneficiaries?'

'I mean . . . yes, I suppose I did know that.'

'You suppose you did. Thank you, sir.'

'Yeah, but . . .'

A hand held forth in gentle reproach. 'Sir, please. May we stick to the matter at hand?'

I'm reminded of an article I once read in which a group of transient people – drifters, drug addicts, casual workers – were sent to prison for the sexual assault and murder of a senior citizen in her home in the small city of Beatrice, Nebraska. So persuasive was the evidence mounted against the six defendants that all but one of them declined to stand trial. Surrendering their freedoms (such as they were) to the care of the state, instead they copped pleas. But the case was bogus. Not one of the six people in the frame had ever met the murdered woman, or, in some cases, each other. The very idea had been planted in their troubled minds by an errant and controversial psychiatrist. In layperson's terms, the doomed sextet had been marched along a gas-lit path all the way to the Big House.

Released from prison, so wedded were the group to their status as violators and murderers that even the cleansing of their permanent records couldn't dislodge the false memories from their minds.

Did I murder my father?

No, of course I didn't. I kissed him goodnight, walked home, and found him dead just hours later. *Is that not enough?* As PC Kevin Onlow switches on the light, it occurs to me that I have no idea where I'll be sleeping tonight. We've been in here for hours, he and I. Throughout the day, at intervals of sixty or ninety minutes, my captor is summoned to the hall by a knock on the door from his commanding officer. Speaking in loose-lips-sink-ships voices, after each visit all that I know is that nothing has changed. I have no idea as to the extent of the trouble I'm in. I don't know whether or not my captor and his colleagues on the fourth floor think I'm a murderer.

Outside, it's almost dark. *Why am I still here?* By now, friends and acquaintances are gathering to raise a glass for my birthday at a pub on the Kentish Town Road. I'm expecting a fairly decent crowd. A concert at the nearby Roundhouse has attracted the attention of almost everyone in my corner of the music industry; dozens of its representatives have said they'll try and swing by beforehand. Deprived of the means of letting them know that the guest of honour is shacked up with the Metropolitan Police, I begin to fret about the confusion caused by my absence. My apparent unreliability in the eyes of others summons feelings of helplessness. For the life of me I can't find a way to properly prioritise my worries. The prospect of standing up a roomful of people from an industry not known for its commitment to commitments is somehow more stressful than a murder rap. I won't lie, it's all becoming a bit much.

Girding myself, at last I ask the question that until now has been locked and gagged in solitary confinement.

Deep breath. 'Kev, am I going to prison?' My voice, I realise, sounds a good deal closer to that of a child than I would ideally like it to be. 'Or to the cells? From here, I mean. From this hotel room.'

After ten hours in my company, PC Onlow is desperate for a cigarette. I've tried to tell him that he should just fire one up and blow the smoke out of the open window. 'I'm not going to tell anyone,' I say. 'Anyway, what are they going to do, arrest you?' But he's having none of it. There are moments from this remarkable day for which I am at a loss to account. I don't remember at what point an officer asked me to place the tips of my fingers on an ink pad, or insisted that I scrape the inside of my cheek with a cotton-tipped swab. After learning that the Super Barnsley had lost 2–1 at Selhurst Park, I don't recall what we watched on television. But I do remember how Kevin Onlow responded to my question regarding the possible restoration of my liberty.

With what looks like kindness, at last he cuts me a break. 'Ian, I don't honestly know for sure what's going to happen next,' he says. 'But I can tell you that I'd be amazed if you spent the night in the nick. I've been a copper for almost twenty years. In that time I've met people who have done things you wouldn't believe. I've known murderers.' A gravid pause. 'So this is between me and you. Right?'

'Of course.'

'If you're one of them, then you're a fucking good liar.'

At a little after 10 p.m. I exit the life of PC Kevin Onlow for ever. Transferred to yet another room, a detective sergeant hands me a cold cheeseburger and an update. After due consideration, the Metropolitan Police have decided that I probably didn't kill my father. As soon as they've taken down my statement, I will be turned loose into the London night. There is just one thing, though. Unwilling to refund my statutory rights in full, I am told that I will not be allowed to enter my home until given permission to do so at an unspecified date in the future. Until then, two uniformed officers will be stationed inside and outside the property. Again, a failure of memory. I don't recall giving my consent for the thin blue line to enter my modest and pleasant garden flat. I don't remember handing over my keys. *What are they going to be doing in there, anyway?* On top of everything else, I can certainly live without the old bill discovering the two empty bindles of cocaine lurking at the bottom of the kitchen swing-bin. I hope they don't go rooting around in there. That's what everyone asks me about, by the way. When I tell my friends what happened, as one they say, *Jesus, did you have any coke about the place?* No I didn't, thank God, but only because I've never once called it a night, or a dawn, or a middle of the following afternoon, without having first finished off every last grain.

Declining my mum's invitations to head back with her up the M1, at last I'm able to break the day's news to the people in the north that have known Eric for longer than I have. With a measure of reluctance, the police promise to feed my cats. Once more an angel of mercy, my friend Dan Silver offers board and lodgings with his young family in deepest south London for as many nights as I need. *Mate, you don't even have to ask.* For this, I count myself lucky; everyone else I know lives in tiny flats or in shared houses. Strange that in such an enormous city I really don't have anywhere else to go.

I'm sometimes asked if living so close to the scene of what turned out not to be a crime after all gives me pause. The truth of it is, it really doesn't. Living barely a quarter of a mile from the Holiday Inn's glass doors means I can entertain the notion that Eric is somehow still in the neighbourhood. I don't believe that he is, but in the spirit of making a wish at a well it's a thing I sometimes like to kick around. What I can say for sure is that I rather like that he didn't die in the same place he was born. Timing and circumstances notwithstanding, I guess I'm glad that he passed away here. Gazing across the Regent's Canal at the hotel's pale walls means that I'm prompted to think of my father several times a week. In doing so I've learned to separate what happened in there from the man to whom it happened.

My previous visit to the Holiday Inn had come seven months before Eric checked in, and then checked out. On a turbid afternoon in the middle of August, I spent half an hour asking questions of Matt Skiba in the ground-floor bar. The singer and guitarist with the fine Chicago punk rock group Alkaline Trio, Skiba's songs are often jubilantly violent vignettes of murder and bloodshed told from the point of view of the wronged party. While we spoke, upstairs on the third floor *Kerrang!*'s art director was transforming a small room into what looked like the scene of a messy and awful crime. Taking care not to jeopardise a princely deposit, it took her two hours to splatter three litres of fake blood onto polythene sheets affixed to the walls. As Skiba stood amid the gore, a photographer fired off a series of shots. Printed on A4 paper a fortnight later, the singer's devilish half-grin betrayed a ghoulish delectation. It was a fabulous idea for a double-page spread. It was such a striking premonition of what awaited Eric and me on his last visit to the capital.

In a practical sense, my father's death throws my life into chaos. In south London I start to worry (without cause, of course) that my presence is transforming the Silver family home into a strange and alien place. Temporarily bereft of a place to call my own, I haven't a clue what to do next. On Saturday night it appeared obvious that I wouldn't be able to take a long-planned holiday to New York on Tuesday. Come Monday morning, it seems like this might be the only place *left* for me to go. In need of advice, I ring the police station at Kentish Town. You should catch your plane, I'm told. There's no chance that my father's body will be released into the custody of his family in the ten days I'm away. They can't even say whether or not my home will be returned to me during this period, either.

Get yourself off, lad, seems to be the gist of things. *Send us a postcard, won't you.*

I'm a bit confused. Unwilling to let me sleep in my own bed, the Metropolitan Police *are* happy for me to leave the country. They don't even check that I am in fact bound for John F. Kennedy Airport. For all they know, I could be off to Swaziland or some other place beyond the reach of international extradition agreements. Should it later be determined that I do have blood on my hands, I can't help thinking this might come up. It certainly contrasts sharply with the punctilious detail applied to other aspects of the case. Under the supervision of a likeable but firm detective sergeant, I'm allowed five minutes in my flat in which to pack a bag. Tossing shirts and books into a squeaky-wheeled holdall, for a moment I find myself alone in a room. From beyond the threshold of its open door, with some force I hear the detective whisper to his uniformed subordinate, 'He's on his own. He's on his *own*. Get. In. There. Now.'

I have been told more than once that I've never properly confronted the circumstances of my father's death. For what it's worth, I don't believe this to be true. I have grieved as best I know how. Seeking to slip its punches, in the days and weeks that follow I distil the event into something close to a comic routine. Without this fresh coat of flippancy, the details of what I've seen, and what Eric has lost, might just be a bit too much for me. Then again, perhaps not. Out on my own on the streets of New York, my favourable mood is a source of constant surprise. With one grave exception, life ticks on as it usually does. Imagining my senses temporarily numbed by shock, I wait patiently on the arrival of a crushing sense of bereavement. Today, I'm still waiting. On the avenues of Manhattan I am aware that the event is all around me; with a kind of benign bewilderment I find myself savouring its company. *Hello darkness, my old friend.*

Billeted with friends in an apartment on West 30th Street and 7th Avenue, one morning I take the air on a four-block stroll to pick up milk and other communal supplies. Today is my actual birthday. Rising to the occasion, Manhattan has gifted me a morning of warm sunshine and whispering wind. For the longest time I entertained vague notions of one day bringing Eric to New York City. In my capacity as a discreet tour guide, I would watch over him as the two of them got on like a metropolis on fire. I'd introduce him to Bea and Freddie, the English couple who, in the teeth of what must surely have struck them as foreboding circumstances, have this week made me welcome in their home. We would have ridden the Staten Island Ferry. I would have taken him to Shea Stadium for the baseball. We'd have gone to Katz's deli and to Madison Square Garden to watch the New York Rangers. We would have had a fine old time of it, the old man and I.

The sudden thought that none of these things can now happen catches me on the blindside. For a seesawing second I feel my lip begin to drop. Standing still, now is the time for my tears. But they never, ever come.

Midway through my stay in New York, word reaches me that by the time I get back to London I will be allowed back into my home. The feeling that once more I belong *somewhere* is both an emotional and practical relief. Given its immediate proximity to the turmoil of Camden Town, my little flat stands on a street that is far quieter than it has any right to be. Two hundred yards away, the marquee of the Underworld club announces 'Camden Rocks'. Well, yes it does. A fortnight after I moved in I came upon an open-top bus at the bottom of Inverness Street upon which local icons Madness were playing a short set of their best-known hits. Attempting to avoid the wheels of passing Routemasters, as the band struck up 'Night Boat to Cairo' I joined the throng of several hundred dancing people. Initially uncertain of my new neighbourhood, at once I fell in love.

Walking home from the pictures in the first summer of The Disease, my fiancée and I pass a mural in honour of the neighbourhood's greatest twenty-first century icon. 'Camden Town,' she laughs, 'where you're never more than a hundred yards away from a picture of Amy Winehouse.' To tell you the truth, I've been here so long now that I've stopped noticing them. Perhaps it's because her striking image is a stark reminder that sometimes I'm bad at my job. Sharing drinks and cocaine at a small venue in the midst of the local market, in the autumn of 2006 my friends and I neglected to watch 'Amy' play a short set in the very small room next to the bar. I wasn't working that night, but still. Well into our stride by the time she struck up 'Rehab', for the sake of nothing I missed the opportunity to witness greatness at intimate quarters. If you're in the market for an ignoble example of just how lazy and complacent a music journalist can be, this is as good as any.

I remain grateful to her for nudging the cultural resonance of Camden into the twenty-first century. On walks around the neighbourhood with visitors from out of town, for years I have pointed out that Chalk Farm tube station is the backdrop of an album cover by Madness. I've shown them the steps at Camden Market on which The Clash appear on the front sleeve of their debut LP. The stuff of local legend, I like to think of this as cracking material. But Amy was happening right here and right now; incandescent, her impact was immediate. Friends and acquaintances from outside the capital would ask if I'd seen her out and about? *Do you know where she lives?* Permitting the notion that an accident of geography equated to a tangible connection, I'd answer that, yes, actually I did. Her talent towered over me. Billie Holiday. Janis Joplin. Aretha Franklin. Amy Winehouse. And there she was, just up the road in Camden Square.

Not long after moving into my flat, one Saturday night the neighbourhood caught fire. Receiving a text from Dan in south London – *'Camden is ablaze! Are you all right?'* – I turned over to the

BBC News Channel just in time to see the flames from the market pawing the black winter sky. Realising I could do better than this I threw on my coat and took a brisk walk to the lock. There it was, a story in three dimensions: the smoke, the smell, the police tape, the fire engines. *Wow, it really has gone up.* The following night, during an acceptance speech at the Grammys, Amy (by now fully deserving of her mononym) informed a live audience at the Staples Center in Los Angeles that 'Camden is burning'. She even mentioned the Hawley Arms, the local pub in which the clientele told the fire brigade they'd leave just as soon as they'd finished their drinks.

Watching the unsurprising story of her passing on the news, on 23 July 2011, I was struck by the sudden realisation that I'd seen this film before. Like Eric Winwood three and a half months earlier, Amy was taken from her place of death to a post-mortem at St Pancras Coroner's Court. Required by Jewish law to be buried after three days, the gang at the morgue got a wriggle on. With Eric, they were able to take their time. Sliding in like any old schmuck at the end of his luck, no one took a photo of *his* arrival. Amid a flurry of interest from news outlets and papers across the world, for Amy it really was quite the scene.

A fortnight later I was greeted by one of the coroners on the sunny streets outside St Pancras train station. Standing in the glow of an ebullient hello, for a moment I struggled to place her face in its correct context. It came to me just as it was my turn to speak.

'Blimey, you had it going on down at your place, didn't you?'

'Amy?'

'I mean, yeah.'

'It was crazy,' she said. 'I've never seen anything like it. I was in the papers and everything.'

In April, this particular coroner had shown me remarkable kindness. Back from New York, for a brief but bizarre time both Eric and I were residents of the London Borough of Camden. I didn't imagine the state intended to keep him for ever, but for a while there it seemed as if they might. In the twenty days that elapsed before my old man was loaded into the back of a hearse for his final journey up to the old country, no one in authority was able to tell me anything of value. He would be in their care until he was no longer needed; when that would be they could not or would not say. With their thumbs placed on the scale, it seemed that everyone had a tacit way of letting me know that I couldn't fight city hall. But this public servant was different. I don't know if she'd been apprised of the details of the case – was it still a case, even? – but I did know she was the only person who spoke to me without an edge. Almost in passing, over the phone she mentioned something that would forever change my memory of my dad:

'You can come down and see him,' she says. 'If you like.'

And there he is, well dressed, eyes closed. It's the first time in my life I've seen him with his mouth shut. He looks older than I remember, too, which is odd because he's exactly the same age as he was two weeks ago. I make a note to remember that Eric appears entirely untroubled by the things that have ripped him apart. Surrounded by stillness, I realise I have something to say.

'*Eyup*, pal . . .'

SIDE TWO

6: HIGH PRESSURE LOW

At the midpoint of a summer in which it briefly appeared that The Disease had gone on its holidays, I spent an agreeable hour with one third of Biffy Clyro. Above London streets bejewelled by sunshine, Simon Neil, the Ayrshire group's singer, guitarist and principal songwriter, sat at a wooden table on a rooftop terrace of a hotel on Regent's Street. Answering questions for the *Telegraph*, he spoke with even-money enthusiasm about the likelihood of a low-key tour the following spring. Had we known then that our optimism was merely an illusion, surely we would have despaired. But in the weeks before the virus headed back to shore for further helpings of British flesh, for the shortest time all of our futures appeared secure once more. One more push and we'd all be back in business. One more hill and the band would return to the road.

Having heard the news of my father's death, nine years earlier Simon gave me a ring in New York. Bobbing along with his musical voice, I was pleased but not surprised by his intervention. For one thing, he knew what I was going through. In 2006, in the same city, I had spoken to Biffy Clyro at the Midtown studio at which the group had just finished recording their fourth album, *Puzzle*. Written in the wake of the death of the singer's mother, Eleanor, the LP transformed the splintered bones of grief into a resplendent work of art.

'At the time ... I didn't think, "Right, I'm going to put this all into an album,"' he says, this time speaking to me for the purposes of this book. 'It just had to be done because I couldn't communicate in any other way. I was closing down. As you know yourself, grief-stricken moments, or the trauma of having lost someone, doesn't leave your mind at all. At any point.' Drowning not waving, with remarkable panache the singer used his own songs as a buoy with which he could keep himself afloat. A near masterpiece, it's difficult to think of a clearer example than *Puzzle* of music having played such an important role in repairing an artist's deeply unbalanced state of mind.

In response to an unavoidable question, on the trumpet in New York I told Simon Neil that I had no idea how I was doing. I said that sometimes it felt as if I was watching this happen to someone else. If you want the truth, a part of me was flattered that an increasingly successful artist had taken the trouble to speak to me directly. Reliably slow off the mark, it had taken me longer than it should have done to recognise that Biffy Clyro were plotting a course towards the title of Britain's Best Band. I certainly hadn't noticed it the first time I met them. Dispatched north for the group's first four-page feature in *Kerrang!*, in 2004, the three musicians – the trio's line-up is completed by twin brothers Ben and James Johnston, on drums and bass guitar respectively – were (I would later learn) excited at having been deemed worthy of a journalist of my skyscraping stature. Isn't that adorable? Not that they were on hand to greet me, mind. On a cold morning in Scotland, I was left alone to clamber into the musty silence of yet another tour bus in which the occupants were fast asleep. Plonking myself down in a spare bunk, I dozed my way north to a place that Eric Winwood would no doubt have known as the Granite City. Aberdeen. The following evening in Glasgow the band invited me to place six bottles of chilled water and a small pile of white towels on top of the drum riser on the stage of the Barrowland Ballroom.

'These towels here?'

'The very same.'

'And these bottles of water?'

'If you don't mind.'

I can still recall the knowing smiles on the faces of the musicians as they spoke these words. *Mind? Why would I mind?* Rightly regarded as the most raucous room in Britain, front of house the crowd at the 'Barrowlands' was primed for action. With piercing immediacy, five minutes before showtime the place was already divesting itself of its mind. Scurrying to the drum riser like a rat in the shadows, I caught sight of a lake of faces chanting 'Mon the Biff! Mon the Biff!' – come on the Biffy Clyro – with a startling and percussive unity.

'Mon. The. Biff!'

'Mon. The. Biff!'

'Mon. The. Biff!'

The noise was so overwhelming that I barely dared sneak a second look in the direction of the people making it. *Are they shouting at me? It **sounds** like they're shouting at **me**. Why are they shouting at me?* At once the quotidian task of placing everyday items onto a raised platform became a stressful matter. With my customary knack of keeping things in proportion, I wondered if this was what it felt like being a soldier in a war. *Probably it is. Probably it is.* Either way, my sixty-second cameo at the Barrowlands remains one of the most intimidating experiences of my life.

'Welcome to my world,' says Simon Neil.

Occasionally challenging, sometimes obdurate, vastly and richly talented, Biffy Clyro were not originally designed as a receptacle for mainstream applause. In their earliest days, the group's ambition extended no further than the dream of one day releasing an album with homemade artwork on a local independent label. Arriving for concerts at such distant venues as the Stornoway Sea Angling Club, at the turn of the century they were often asked if they knew any songs by Oasis? 'We fucking hate Oasis' was their answer. (In a fitting example of upward mobility, in 2020 Neil added the caveat, 'Liam and Noel [Gallagher] are lovely people now that we know them.') But while other groups copied Britpop moves from south of the border, Biffy Clyro ploughed their own lonely furrow. With thumping predictability, for too long the group's nourishing heterogeneity went unnoticed by the tastemakers of mainstream opinion.

After a measure of modest success on the independent label Beggars Banquet, 'Biffy' signed to Warner Bros. Garlanded with a major label recording budget, the trio were able to hire producer Garth 'GGGarth' Richardson (Rage Against the Machine, Red Hot Chili Peppers) and, in New York, the services of mixer Andy Wallace (Nirvana, Jeff Buckley). Recording in Vancouver, the group enlisted the services of the Seattle Symphony Orchestra. With the finishing line in sight, in Manhattan they met with the man tasked with mastering their thirteen new songs. With a curriculum vitae boasting fifteen Grammys, Howie Weinberg welcomed his Scottish guests with the words, 'Biffy Clyro? What kind of name is that? That's a terrible name for a band.'

Maybe, but after years in the lower leagues 'Biffy' knew themselves well enough to utilise every inch of their brand new canvas. Entering the British album chart at number two, *Puzzle* became the springboard for yet greater artistic and commercial success. The band's last three albums have each debuted at number one. From the Roundhouse in Camden to the Brixton Academy, from Wembley Arena to the 02 Arena, with uncommon delight I have spent fifteen years watching the trio scale the property ladder of London concert halls. Such is the extraordinary wingspan of the band's music that in 2010 the singer Matt Cardle was able to claim both the title of *X Factor* champion *and* the Christmas number one with a user-friendly version of their sumptuous song 'Many of Horror' (rechristened 'When We Collide'). Out on the road Biffy Clyro rose to headline status at festivals such as Isle of Wight, Download, Sonisphere and Leeds and Reading.

Throughout this period, the band had made tidy use of their (correct) sense of themselves as outsiders. You might even describe it as a means of self-preservation. In Glasgow, in 2009 I asked James Johnston if the trio would still be together had their station not risen above a nightly audience of only six hundred people. That was how I phrased the question, the word 'only' seated at its centre like judge and jury. The structural weakness was spotted straight away. 'Six hundred?' he answered. 'Six hundred is a pretty good crowd.' Even with the band poised to ferry their production to the load-in doors of the capacious Scottish Exhibition and Conference Centre, their bassist still regarded the applause of people gathered in smaller rooms to be a prize worth pursuing. Four years later, aboard a tour bus en route to their first headline appearance at the Leeds Festival, I recall listening in silent wonder as the three musicians expressed pleasant surprise at the news that Warner Bros. had decided to exercise their option for at least one more album. 'Well, of course they have,' I thought. 'Your last LP went to number one. The one before that went to number one. You're about to play to seventy thousand people. *Why on earth would they do anything else?*'

But I understood their caution. Polite but unilateral, Biffy Clyro are not minded to fall for the music industry's routine seductions. They're not like other bands. Many are the times I've seen the excitement on the faces of young acts gathered in the offices of major label record companies. I've watched press officers taking down their orders for candy masquerading as coffee – 'an iced gingerbread latte with a double shot of espresso and whipped cream for me, please' – before spiriting them away for cheeky lunches at nice restaurants. I've seen the delight on their faces as they open boxes of free footwear sent by skate shoe companies in the market for a spot of factory-cost advertising. At twenty-two years old, I can't blame them for believing that their suddenly elevated status will somehow last for ever. I don't blame them for thinking they're special. But it's just an illusion; they're not special, at least not yet. And in the eyes of their backers, they won't be until their music turns a profit.

So this is what I've learned. In my experience, no band has got its act together tighter than Biffy Clyro. Aged seven, their world-class rhythm section formed a friendship with Simon Neil that has survived the pockmarked terrain of the music industry. Trios are often, but not always, resolute – after incurring the slings and arrows of outrageous fortune, with a unified vision the Beastie Boys rallied for a remarkable second act – but the graceful unity of the Ayrshire musicians is beyond anything I've ever seen. Aboard tour buses or in bars, people in bands are often keen to tell me, off the record, of their union's stress points, its structural weaknesses, its discrepancies and its rivalries. Sometimes I can see them for myself. Looks of displeasure lasting less than a second. An irritated interruption during an interview. Just like the industry in which they operate, all groups are dysfunctional. But rules beg exceptions, and Biffy Clyro are mine. In the eighteen years I've spent monitoring the trio's remarkable elevation, not once have I seen the slightest hint of disunity. If a young group sought my advice as to the ideal model of a rolling rock band, I'd point them in the direction of the wind-strewn farmhouse in the Ayrshire country-side at which the twins and their childhood friend rehearse. In thrall to the immediacy of their talent, I once watched them do so. In there I witnessed a band secure in the knowledge that, beneath and beyond every one of the music industry's many external com-plications, their shared instincts remained pure and consistent. 'Those lads in there,' I'd say. 'Watch what they do. Watch closely. And try to be like them.'

Even so, the following still happened. On the night before the group began recording the grand and expansive *Opposites* album, from 2012, Ben Johnston pitched up at the studio covered in blood after a fistfight with the trio's guitar technician. The drummer's relationship with alcohol had metastasised into addiction. These were the days when even Simon Neil – 'Not normally a big drinker,' he tells me – would 'drink every night for forty or eighty dates' while out on tour. On the road, the booze is always there. It's in fridges in the dressing room. It's on the bus. A balm for the yawning hours between cities, it'll keep you company in the time between the night's final song and the strange hour at which you take yourself to bed. Step into their shoes. If your job involved bidding goodnight to rooms full of screaming people, wouldn't you fancy two or three, or six or seven, tipples come the end of the shift?

'I would say that, in our industry, excessive behaviour is just so normalised,' Simon tells me. 'And what I would also say is that the mental health [issues] that people in the business struggle with while on tour would affect even the most well-balanced people in the world. If they'd come off a tour in which they'd been drinking for forty or eighty straight nights, they too would be mentally and physically spent.'

According to this metric, by the time Simon Neil arrived in Toronto, in April 2013, for the start of a short North American campaign supporting Muse, the singer had been drinking for roughly three months. Since the start of that year Biffy Clyro had already played concerts in France, Switzerland, Germany, England, Scotland, Belgium, Netherlands, Denmark, Norway, Sweden, Finland, Wales, Northern Ireland and the Republic of Ireland. As well as this, in February that year the musicians had flown west for a smattering of gigs in Pennsylvania, Virginia, California and Washington State. By their own standards, and by those of any number of groups, such an itinerary was far from extraordinary. In years past Biffy Clyro had sailed through tours far longer than this. *Mon the Biff.*

But as the plane began its descent towards Pearson International Airport, Simon Neil felt increasingly overwhelmed by a dislocating sense of complete exhaustion. It had begun, he thinks, at The Village, the studio in Los Angeles at which the group tracked *Opposites*. With Ben Johnston reacquainting himself with sobriety, and with his twin brother taking time to reframe the pair's relationship, the singer spent two thirds of the six-month recording process with his nose pressed against the canvas of an exquisite and minutely detailed double album. Containing twenty songs, the band's work in progress demanded an extraordinary degree of forensic care from its principal author. Simon did not begrudge his bandmates their time together – 'If Ben and James are good, then we're good,' he says – but with his wife Francesca busy with her career as a schoolteacher, six thousand miles from home he began to feel vulnerable and alone. Complicating the invariably challenging balance between home life and the professional duties of the outwardly mobile professional musician was the fact that the couple were soon to embark on a second round of IVF. With its members by now in their early thirties, as all cohesive bands must Biffy Clyro were traversing the rickety rope bridge that separates the conjoined insularity of the young rock group from something that looks like adulthood.

In an incident that today seems almost comically insignificant, waiting to board his plane to Ontario Simon received a call from a crew member offering a – how best to put this? – full and frank assessment of a manager whose services the trio would in time dispense. A straw upon a camel's back, this was all it took to send him freewheeling towards despair. For three and a half hours the singer sat crying in his seat. The tears were merely the prelude to a wilder storm.

'When I got to customs and immigration [in Toronto], I just broke down,' he says. 'They had me on a gurney and they had me all tied up to machines and things. So I spoke to my wife and my dad, and to our manager at the time, and they were, like, "You need to come home. You need to come home now." And do you know what my main fear was? It was that by going home I was giving the record company and everyone else an excuse to go, "Oh well, they're not worth investing in." And looking back now . . . I tried so hard not to cancel any of those shows. And the reason that I eventually did was because my family was pleading with me. Because I was on the other side of the world and I was in the worst way I could possibly be.'

South of the border, down in Burbank, California, Warner Bros. were training their eyes on the group's upcoming appearance at the nearby Coachella Valley Music and Arts Festival. Staged over consecutive spring weekends, since its inception in 1999 'Coachella' has fast become the most prestigious festival in a country in which such happenings have been surprisingly slow to blossom. Two hours from Los Angeles, the event's proximity to the record companies of the Golden State allows the music industry's brokers the chance to see their artists play to a seven-figure audience largely unfamiliar with their material. From this, decisions will be made regarding degrees of financial investment, backing, levels of collective enthusiasm, and whether or not a group becomes a 'priority act' for the North American bureaus of major record labels. For a British act signed by a company's UK office, the value and rarity of such opportunities cannot be overstated.

A band on their game will relish such a challenge. Even on a gurney in Toronto, wired like a homemade, bomb Simon Neil was determined to take his place on a tour that would see Biffy Clyro wend their way to California via concerts at such grand rooms as Madison Square Garden and the TD Garden in Boston. Heavily medicated by a Canadian doctor, through seven concerts he did his job. More than this, he did it as well as he knew how.

'Onstage I realised that I can never stop doing this,' he says. 'I was literally living in the moment. At the Coachella show, and the Madison Square Garden shows, there were moments when I forgot about everything. And that made me make a deal in my mind that I should rebuild myself so that I can [continue to] do this wonderful thing. I was having these moments of clarity where I realised that I was doing the purest and most beautiful thing that it was possible for me to do. And it was those little rays of light that made me realise that I did need to fix myself. I realised that if I stumbled through this [brace] of shows, I wouldn't be there at the end of it. The damage that I'd do to myself would mean that I would never get this feeling onstage again. If I pushed myself too far I would never be liberated in my mind. I would associate [playing live] with horror.'

Horror. Following his band's seven-song set at Coachella, Simon Neil finally called time on Biffy Clyro's turbulent North American tour. Eight time zones east, his wife's second round of IVF had been unsuccessful; in the arid expanse of Southern California, her husband was doing himself harm. Hearing the news of his imminent return, the response from the other members of the touring party was a resounding, '*Thank God for that.*' Everyone in the camp recognised what it was that Simon, and by extension the Johnstons, were facing. This was not the kind of arduous but necessary bonding experience by which a novice band road tests their unity while shedding members unsuited to life on the road. These weren't the basic materials for a well-spun war story they'd all be laughing about in months to come. Quite the opposite – this was mental illness. Unfortunately for Biffy Clyro, not everyone saw it that way.

'I had trained myself to think that if I missed this opportunity my life was going to tip over the edge of a cliff,' Simon says. 'Looking back, I realise that it wasn't quite as black and white as that. But also looking back now, we don't do as well in America as we do elsewhere. And I can pinpoint that to that exact week that a few people at our American record company at that time thought, "Oh, I don't think he's interested." Or, "He's away home, so fuck it." Now I feel fortunate to be able to tell you we now have a different group of people around us at the label. They're more supportive and have a much better understanding of these kinds of issues. But what happened to me in Toronto, and then on that tour, is a good example of how, even as your individual identity [is under threat], you have to make a decision as to how valuable you are as a human being compared to you as a commodity, for want of a better word ... And that was the tough thing. Some people at the record company at that time are pointing at me going, "Look, he's doing a show. What's wrong with him? There's nothing wrong with him. He's doing a show." So to them it didn't make sense. They couldn't understand how I could make it this far but couldn't hang on to finish the tour.'

To this day, Biffy Clyro continue to campaign in the United States of America. Eschewing the comforts of a tour bus, they ride in a van to rooms such as the Turf Club in St Paul (350 people) and the Neptune Theatre in Seattle (800 people). The group are true to the words spoken to me in Glasgow. They do believe that a night in a club thousands of miles from home is a prize worth pursuing. Over in Burbank, the relevant people who worked at Warner Bros. (at that time) may still believe that Simon Neil is the sole author of a squandered opportunity. But they're wrong. The 'failure' of Biffy Clyro to attain the kind of commercial success enjoyed in other parts of the world is the result of an unjust and arbitrary ruling against a temporarily but deeply unwell man. The verdict lacks empathy – humanity, even – and a deficit of commercial good sense.

'This is a dream that [bands] believe in,' Simon tells me. 'It's not just someone else who's saying, "Oh, you have to do these shows or else you're fucked." You feel like your entire life is hinging on two shows, or on three gigs, on the other side of the world. And that's a really unhealthy balance to get into. Now I feel fortunate that myself, Ben and James [have been] playing music together since we were thirteen or fourteen. If they hadn't known me since I was a kid, I think either the band would have ended, it could have gone dramatically sideways for me personally, or even worse. God forbid. Because we've all had friends we've lost to depression, and it's moments like that that can cause these horrible spirals.'

Diddums, you might say. Hark at them flying all over the world with their guitars and drums, drinking every night, playing to roomfuls of strangers for foreign currency and waves of applause. *That ain't working, that's the way you do it.*

On a visit to an electronics store in New York City in 1984 Mark Knopfler overheard a conversation by a group of deliverymen and salespeople gathered at a bank of televisions at the rear of the room. Watching a video of Mötley Crüe on MTV, not without admiration the workers were discussing what it would be like to inhabit the world of the professional musician. Free money, fast women, easy living. Asking for a pen with which he could write down what was being said, Knopfler's eavesdrop became the blueprint for the Dire Straits song 'Money for Nothing'. Released as a single in the summer of 1985, the track sold more than half a million copies. Its parent LP, *Brothers in Arms*, was bought by more than thirty million people. Try as I might, I cannot decide to what, if any, extent this proves the shop workers' point.

If you want the truth of it, people in bands tend to feel the same way. In what can sometimes look like Stockholm syndrome, none of them can believe their luck. All are agreed that their means of making a living is not a 'proper job'. Running down the clock in interviews, sometimes I ask them what, if not this, they might be doing with their lives. In a response that suggests to me that it might not be very much of anything, a remarkably high number reply that they would either be dead or in prison.

Aged fifteen, in an ersatz school yearbook Simon Neil laid out his hopes for the future. He said he wanted 'to be a musician. I didn't want to be a rock star, I didn't want to be a millionaire, I wanted to play music and make a living from it. I read that again recently and thought, "Wow, there's literally nothing else that I ever wanted to do."' More so than most, it's difficult to picture Simon leading a different life. A considerate man with a beaming demeanour, to my eye he conforms to the kind of musician he describes as being someone 'who is drawn to the creative arts because something is lacking'. I don't know what this is, but for the longest time I've known it to be true that he is at his purest when playing music. At no point have I caught the remotest sense of him losing touch with what for him is the specialness of his chosen field. He doesn't believe that the means by which he draws a wage is superior to that of anyone else – and neither do most people in bands. All it is, really, is a sense of profound gratitude at being paid to do the thing that makes them truly happy. In Toronto, Simon Neil simply lost sight of the fact that, sometimes, certain things are more important than the forward momentum of a rock 'n' roll band. It's easily done.

'I know I speak for Ben and James too when I say that none of us want to talk about how we're struggling with things,' he tells me. 'Especially when people have normal struggles – whether their kids are ill, or whether they're working their asses off for twelve hours a day doing what we call a proper job.' There's that phrase again. 'Also, being in that bubble of being in music does make it hard to share your stresses and worries with friends and family at home. It trains you to have this really unhealthy trait of keeping things inside and thinking, "Oh, this is a problem for me but it's not enough of a problem to share with other people." But the reality is, if it is a big problem to you then you've got to share it because it's your life. And your friends and your family care about you.

'The thing is, the music industry doesn't let you reflect,' he tells me. 'You're always moving forward until you're not. And that's where the danger of the mental health cliff [lies]. The danger of just going over the edge and suddenly staring at a void. You need to have a way to step back.'

Sensible musicians will ask themselves this: away from the band, as a person, who exactly am I? *Am I anyone at all?* The wisest will know the answer, but some will not. In a confusion of opacity, all too often the border between a group and its members' separate lives becomes indivisible. It's a dream job, remember? Why wouldn't you want it to consume every waking second of your life? In North America Simon Neil was telling himself that his trauma was a kind of treasonous ingratitude. From Singapore to Widnes, dives and hives are log-jammed with young musicians longing for a taste of the nectar that had curdled on his tongue. *Do you not want that, pal?* Simon just needed to pull himself together, is all. Because this is what he wanted, right? Right? *Exactly this.*

It can be maddening. Barely five years after scoring a hit single on both sides of the Atlantic with the song 'Pretend We're Dead', in 1997 I watched the female Californian punk rock group L7 play on the lower rungs of a bill topped by Kiss. After travelling overnight by bus from Portugal, the musicians were operating on no more than ninety minutes' sleep. Saying hello to representatives from their record company (London) they noticed a marked reticence on the part of people who were normally ebullient and warm. Come Monday morning, they found out why. Fielding a call from their manager, L7 learned that they had been released from their contract. In music industry parlance, this unilateral severance – available to all record labels, but not to artists – is known as being 'dropped'. *Dropped. Gone.* In the sunshine of Finsbury Park the band themselves were the only people who had not been informed of one of the most devastating sanctions faced by any professional musician. Bloodied and cowed, two years later the Californians issued an album on a tiny label that failed to chart anywhere in the world. It would be a full two decades before they released another LP.

'That's what's so tough for people when there's a rejection,' says Simon Neil. 'It's a rejection of your entire identity, your entire being, your entire way of thinking. And to try and rebuild that when your foundation has been taken away, that's devastating. The record company are your support group; they're there for you and they give you everything you want – until the moment they stop answering the phone. When it comes to record companies, you have these contacts and these people who are willing to do anything for you – until they're not. Until you maybe stop being worthy in a financial sense, or in a "cool" sense, or in the sense of the contractual bottom line. And that's like the worst kind of a relationship coming to an end. You don't really find the answers – apart from you presume that you're no longer wanted. You don't get a proper explanation. You don't get a rundown of exactly what's happened.

'This industry, and this world, is so out of control,' he says. 'It feels like you're on a bucking bronco at the back of a pub. You're having the time of your life while you're holding on, while you've still got a grip of it. It's only when you fall off and pick yourself up that you realise that you've maybe bruised your hip, or your thighs; or that you're dizzy and you feel a bit sick. It's only at that point when you realise the toll that it's taken . . . Without the support of being in a band with people you love and respect, you really are going to struggle. Because every now and again you need that sounding board to remind you of the base level of who you are.'

Biffy Clyro were made of hardier stuff. Repairing his engines at home in Ayrshire, Simon Neil was up on bricks for fewer than six weeks. In accepting a course of medication from his doctor, by paring back his use of alcohol to nothing more than a stiff drink immediately before a show, and in practising meditation, on 25 May 2013 the band were able to return to the stage for a fifteen-song set at the Radio 1 Big Weekend in Londonderry/ Derry. Within the week, their operation was once more back on the road.

Speaking to Simon today, I am in no doubt that the event in Toronto was the pivot on which the trio's course was reset for the better. Recognising in their friend the kind of vulnerabilities typical of many a principal songwriter, the trio's rhythm section learned to keep a yet closer eye out for a tendency to shoulder more than might reasonably be managed. Today Ben and James Johnston so regularly ask their singer if he's *really* okay, or if he's *sure* he's not taking on a bit too much, that he's been able to convert their support into fuel for greater endeavour. In other words, *he is safe here.*

It's easy to imagine things being different. As part of a less unified whole, Biffy Clyro might well have been sunk. Not in Toronto, necessarily, or at Coachella, but soon enough. It is to Ben and James Johnston's credit that the pair have never believed, or even told themselves, that their frontman's breakdown robbed them of the chance to contend from sea to shining sea. The premise is false anyway: with their singer damaged, there would have been no grandly successful North American campaign. With their machine now built to endure, in years to come there might yet be.

'That support,' says Simon Neil. 'You can't manufacture that. It can't be cultivated. It's either there or it's not, and you won't know what kind of band you are until you reach dramatic points. Because it's easy to be united in the good times . . . But these things never reared their heads. There was never any resentment from the only other people in [my] world who know what [I'm] going through. That's why if a band has the wrong dynamic, it can be really destructive. In that kind of environment, you're alienating the handful of people who actually know what the other person is experiencing.

Bands need to be strong together, to be vulnerable together, to be angry together.

'Whatever it is,' he says, 'just make sure you do it together.'

In a way that groups rarely do, writers obsess about endings. Barely at the foot of chapter six and already I'm thinking about how I might conclude this book. Not just in general terms, either, but with what sort of paragraph, with what kind of closing sentence, even. The fact that I don't yet need to know this does little to temper the sense of excitement at what might await me at the bottom of the final page. Autonomous and unilateral, in one sense the job of being a writer is easy enough that I reckon I might be able to do it for the rest of my life. That's the plan, anyway. Alongside the joy of it all, to make this my living requires very few things that are beyond my control. I'll be good to go with a few commissions and a laptop; in an overburdened week maybe I'll need to pull one or two all-nighters. No big deal, I just tell my fiancée that waking me before noon will result in me setting fire to the flat. One thing she's never heard me say is, 'Right, that's me away to work, love. I'll see you in three and a half months.'

In my experience, musicians don't spend much time at all thinking about endings. Most of them are well aware that the decision isn't really theirs to make. A professional band requires a record label, a publisher, a manager, a promoter, a booking agent, a publicist, a road crew, transportation, equipment, studio costs, merchandisers, a producer, a mixer and God knows what else. They need a large enough audience to keep them and the people at work within their organisation fed, housed and clothed. Out on the road, they can see their crowd growing bigger, or getting smaller, or plateauing to a point at which its members can decide whether or not they're happy with their lot. A clever or expensive marketing campaign might help to attract and sustain eyes and ears; the issuance of continually good music *should* be of service. But, really, they're all headed out to sea in a sieve.

Sometimes the tenacity demanded by this weird job of work can curdle into delusional co-dependency. Described by *The Times* as 'possibly the greatest film yet made about rock 'n' roll', five minutes into an advance screening of *Anvil! The Story of Anvil* I had to ask the editor of *Kerrang!* if the whole thing was a spoof. Honestly, I just couldn't tell. The story of a Torontonian metal group who refused to quit, the picture was widely lauded as an unvarnished example of the indefatigability of the human spirit. For what it's worth, I happen to disagree. The towering obstacles Anvil faced were the result of a complete absence of talent. Their determination to prioritise a doomed lust for commercial success above anything else in their monomaniacal lives (including the needs of their families) meant that the unpatrolled border that separates determination from indiscriminate selfishness had long been breached.

Interviewing the band's two principal members in London, I was delighted to discover that Steve 'Lips' Kudlow and Robb Reiner were everything I imagined them to be. Wholly addicted to each other's narcissistic misdirection, the pair somehow managed to bring together taciturn huffiness, grandiose superiority and a pitiful sense of persecution into one nauseating whole. As it relates to the evidently dismal music to which they put their name, I would honestly say they were insane.

'If you listen to Metallica and Anvil, it's pretty obvious which is the better band,' they told me. For several long seconds my mind wouldn't allow me to believe that two grown men could be so deluded. So *stupid*. Flummoxed, I told them that they couldn't be serious. *Serious?* The pair were downright aggrieved that I didn't see things the same way. *How best to explain this?* 'Fellas, the reason you're not as popular as Metallica is because you're not as good as

Metallica.' *Yeah, that might do it.* 'I don't mean to be rude, but *that's* the story of Anvil.'

Actually, I did mean to be rude. With only ten minutes left on the clock, playing nice had harvested almost nothing. As I hoped it would, hitting the booster rocket got things moving for us all. At half past the hour, Kudlow and Reiner left the offices of *Kerrang!* shouting and swearing.

In kinder moments, I can see why a band such as Anvil continues to chase the high. At the foot of a bill that included the Scorpions, Whitesnake and Bon Jovi, in the summer of 1984 the group played four arena and stadium shows in Japan. As they took to the stage in Osaka, Fukuoka, Nagoya and Tokorozawa, they caught a glimpse of what international success looks like. It wasn't *their* success, but never mind. Standing before a sea of brunettes, they heard the roar of a vast crowd made happy by the sight of a group of musicians. It makes me happy too. From armpit clubs in Deptford to American football stadiums in Texas, I reckon I must have seen a thousand shows. Whether I care for the band or not, when the lights go dark I play my part in raising the roof. The sound is electric. The knowledge that I'm a part of it all feels like magic.

Four months before The Disease ran riot through the streets and avenues of Midtown Manhattan, I watched Slayer lay waste to Madison Square Garden. After almost forty years of active service, on 9 November 2019 the swivel-eyed quartet from Huntington Park, California, were less than a month away from dissolving their operation for good. Upon learning that the New York date of their 'Final Campaign' coincided with my own visit to the city, I emitted a scream of delight that could be heard at the far end of the street. Typing at seventy words per minute, I emailed the *Telegraph* to ask if they'd let me file a piece about the event. Another scream of delight as I read the words, 'Sure, knock yourself out.'

I wrote how,

... From the cheap seats of 'The World's Most Famous Arena' the numerous mosh pits on the floor below looked like satellite images of a dozen gathering hurricanes. As the musicians onstage smashed their way through one audio nasty after another, from hundreds of feet away I stood in silence and bid farewell to a union that has been a part of my life since I was a schoolboy. Given that the band were playing a song called 'Chemical Warfare' it was quite the poignant moment. I thought back to the first time I saw them, at the Rock City in Nottingham, a show from which I was almost ejected after accidentally landing on the stage following a crowd-surfing mishap. I recalled watching in wonder from the front row of the Hammersmith Odeon as Tom Araya sang at a microphone that dripped with an unbroken trail of viscous phlegm all the way to the stage. What price such tender memories, I wondered, as Slayer said goodbye to New York, and to me. We will not see their kind again.'

I think I'm rather pleased with that. Published to coincide with the group's final concert later that month, I can see what I was driving at. Eulogising an eternally adolescent love of chaos, this was a letter of love for a band who were about to drift into the past tense. On a crisp night in late autumn, there I was, at Madison Square Garden, sharing a space with twenty thousand others as the finest act of its kind thrashed up a storm for close to the last time.

Thinking about it now, I realise that I'd missed a bit. In a rare display of unilateralism, Slayer were calling time on their career on precisely their own terms. Along the way the group had been required to replace and then rehire their original drummer – three times, as it goes – and mourn the passing of a guitarist who drank himself to death. But with long-term surrogates in post, the band stayed the course with very little fuss. Disabusing my belief that it might somehow last for ever, in 2015 founding member Kerry King told me that the band would probably wrap things up inside of a decade. 'I don't want to be playing for teenagers when I'm in my sixties,' he said. 'Sure you don't,' I thought. Three years later, he proved me wrong.

Such outcomes are vanishingly rare. With London goosed by the prospect of a third national lockdown, the Christmas break of 2020 saw me strolling past the Holiday Inn on Jamestown Road to meet my friend and near-neighbour Chris McCormack. Generous of spirit and dependably ebullient, for the quarter of a century that I've known him the forty-seven-year-old has been a welcome addition to any gathering at which he finds himself. With a South Shields accent undiluted by decades in NW1, Chris is responsible for the booking and promotion of much of the live music that gives our part of the city its enduring character. In the hope of bringing a toffee-apple hue to his cheeks, sometimes I call him 'Mr Camden'. Under normal circumstances, each September he starts work on the Camden Rocks festival at which hundreds of bands appear on the stages of the area's dozens of clubs. From Koko to the Roundhouse, he knows them all. One evening in the first summer of The Disease he sent me a text asking if I fancied joining him for a couple of hours at the Electric Ballroom. With the venue's load-in area hurriedly but tastefully converted into an outdoor bar, I asked if I could stand him a pint. With a well-judged balance of sheepishness and charm he answered, 'Ah, there's no need, mate. They give me my drinks free here.' Well, yes, of course they do.

The original plan was to make it big. As the founding guitarist in 3 Colours Red, McCormack moved to Camden in the middle part of the nineties. From here, things moved fast. Signed to Creation Records, the label's owner Alan McGee placed adverts in the music press favourably comparing his new signatories to the Sex Pistols. Finding their place in a lively domestic rock scene that included Skunk Anansie, Feeder and Ash, in the spring of 1997 the band's debut album, *Pure*, hit the UK chart at number sixteen. Up in Ayrshire, a sixteen-year-old Simon Neil read about the group in the pages of *Kerrang!* 'I honestly thought they were the biggest band in the world,' he tells me. 'I remember reading about them and thinking, "One day, if we could only get to do what 3 Colours Red do . . ."'

But even 3 Colours Red didn't get to do it for very long. By the time their second album, *Revolt*, landed in the top twenty, its authors had become a case study in the kind of fissures and fractures that can blow a band apart. Unlike Biffy Clyro, this was a group that didn't really know itself. Chris McCormack wanted to rock, while fellow songwriter Pete Vuckovic longed to pare back the loud guitars in pursuit of what he doubtless believed to be a more 'mature' sound. This disconnect could be seen even at the time. In the video for 'Beautiful Day', the group's biggest hit, Vuckovic hogs the screen while behind him his three bandmates stare into the distance with a kind of comatose passivity. Released in 1999, the Vuckovic-penned monster ballad knocked on the door of the top ten; on TV, 3 Colours Red could be seen crowding the presenters on *Top of the Pops*. They looked just like rock 'n' roll stars. But following appearances at the Leeds and Reading festivals, by the end of that summer the whole thing was cooked.

Noticeably drunk after being up all night, in October of that year Chris appeared on VH1 to explain to Tommy Vance that 'things were kind of drifting apart'. Framed in the sickly lights of a television studio at the foot of Camden Lock, he gamely attempted to account for the group's position. 'Creation Records had put so much money into the band . . . I think we'd signed a five-album deal, or something . . . publishing and that, it really gets complicated.

I don't pretend to understand half of it.' Viewing the footage today, I can only wince with sympathy. With his first shot of fame wrapped inside of four years, at the age of twenty-six the guitarist was suddenly staring at the empty pages of the rest of his life. Two seconds ago he was throwing shapes onstage at Wembley Stadium. Now there was nothing. 'For a good six months or so, I honestly didn't know what to do with myself,' he tells me.

The group's problems mined seams other than routine 'creative differences'. McCormack describes 3 Colours Red as being 'a party band' who 'were all hammered'. Its members took cocaine and drank booze. On tour, drummer Keith Baxter was getting wasted no fewer than three times a day. As a means of mitigating the hangover from the night before, the guitarist recalls his bandmate clambering out of his bunk on the tour bus at first light and downing a bottle of red wine before heading back to bed. As is sometimes the case, by this point being on the road was the thing that kept Baxter's life as close to a sense of order as could be managed. Left to his own devices, the drummer declined to a horrifying degree. Fearing for his health, in 2008 his partner phoned for an ambulance. Accompanied on his journey to the hospital by a carrier bag filled with bottles of high-strength lager, Baxter apologised to the paramedics for wasting their time. *Lads, I'm fine; honestly, I swear there's nothing wrong with me.* But there was something wrong with him. Seen by a doctor, within fifteen minutes his system began shutting itself down. Age thirty-six, on 4 January 2008 Keith Baxter died from liver failure.

'We tried everything, but the problem with Keith was that he drank even more heavily when he wasn't on tour,' McCormack tells me. 'So the one thing that kept him slightly better was being on the road, because we tried to police him. We asked him what he was doing, so he started hiding it. But when we weren't on the road, he was a fucking mess. And even on the last couple of tours it was touch and go.' These campaigns took place after the band had briefly re-formed in 2002. 'We'd have [a stand-in drummer] in the wings who had learned all the songs, because Keith was locking himself in the toilets to have a drink. It was terrible. He was a proper first-thing-in-the-morning drinker.'

The dissolution of 3 Colours Red changed Chris McCormack's relationship to music. Flattened by the machinations of a maddening industry, not even a million dollar deal with Sire Records could breathe life into Grand Theft Audio, his subsequent band. Not yet thirty, his heart was no longer stirred by the prospect of being an equal partner in an emerging group. Instead, he took a gig playing guitar for Gary Numan. Alongside Sex Pistol Paul Cook, these days Chris plays ten or twenty concerts a year as the guitarist in The Professionals. This is the way he likes it, he tells me. Freed from the tiresome obstacles that once obscured his path, all he wants is the chance to rock.

'I'm still being a part of music,' he says. 'I'm still picking up a guitar and whacking it through an amp. I've got the fun aspect and left behind all the other stuff that drags people down. I'm not trying to be the next big thing, because that would be ridiculous. I just want to play loads of riffs. I just want to rock 'n' roll . . . Maybe back in the day I liked the idea of the band as a gang. But now I like the idea of being me and doing everything on my own terms. I see things much more clearly now. I definitely have no aspirations of being a pop star or anything like that.'

It seems to me that Chris McCormack is happy in a way that too few people who have tasted success at a young age seem able to be. It is possible. He doesn't appear *haunted* by something that happened almost half a lifetime ago. We've known each other a long time, he and I, and after changes upon changes we're both more or less the same. On a frigid winter's afternoon, like pigeons in parkas the pair of us have just been shooed away from the tables that stand on the roof terrace of the branch of Starbucks on Camden Lock. 'But we've bought drinks.' 'Sorry, sorry, you must go.' Cups of tea in hand, we take a seat on one of the small wooden platforms lining the pavements of the Chalk Farm Road. To my left is the leather goods shop Gohil's, about which Roger Waters sang on the Pink Floyd track 'Nobody Home' (a song about the dislocation of life on the road). As we speak, people emerge from the shadows requesting cigarettes, or spare change. 'Merry Christmas, don't mean to bother you . . .' But in the twenty-first century neither of us smoke. In this year of The Disease, no one is allowed to pay for anything using coins. 'Sorry, fellas.'

In the cold of Camden Town, I learn something new about Chris McCormack. *He was never like the rest of them.* 'The odds that I was even in London with a record deal were fucking minute, so I knew that I was already chancing it a bit,' he tells me. 'I knew that I was already in the one per cent. So I was always aware that you can get dropped by the record company, that you can go bust, and that life can turn like *that*. In this industry, I don't think anyone should ever feel comfortable. It spits you out. If people are buying your record and people are buying tickets, they love you. But as soon as you stop, they can fuck you off and go to the next thing. There's too many flavours of the month. On your first couple of albums, you haven't earned the right [to longevity]. You need to have four or five good albums under your belt so that you've built a good solid fanbase. Even then you can never be sure. And in 3 Colours Red I hadn't done that, so I never felt secure. I was just really thankful and grateful for what I'd already got.'

In the nineties Chris McCormack discovered that he was able to live on the £2,200 monthly interest from a publishing deal worth half a million pounds. Subsisting on Pot Noodles and bottles of Newcastle Brown Ale in his small room at 9B Oval Road, the guitarist thought, 'Well, that's it, that's me sorted.' He did 'squander a bit of [the money] on women and drugs', he tells me, but having come from a family home in the north-east in which 'I didn't have a pot to piss in', he understood the value of financial emancipation.

This kind of stability is rarer than it should be. Researching an interview with Chris and Rich Robinson, the quarrelsome brothers from the Black Crowes, I placed my nose in *Hard to Handle*, the deliciously embittered memoir by the group's former drummer Steve Gorman. Along with a litany of major and minor grievances, Gorman is especially critical of Chris Robinson's habit of striking out on his own. 'Chris seems to think that singing Black Crowes songs on occasion with a pickup band is in some way meaningful,' he writes. 'But it's dubious to suggest those shows are about anything beyond financial desperation.' *Wait, financial what?* The group's first two albums sold almost ten million copies. *How can its singer be broke?* Speaking to me for the *Telegraph*, Robinson confirmed that he was indeed potless. 'All that record sales money, that's long gone,' he said. 'We weren't taken care of in that way at all. I'm not blaming anyone, I have no regrets, but I'm not a person who's very savvy with his finances. Me, I'm still a touring musician, man. I make my money on tour.'

After speaking to a financial adviser, Chris McCormack used his publishing money to buy a flat on the Camden Road. When the time came to sell, to his surprise the property had trebled in value. Finding solvency in real estate, the guitarist mined a separate seam of revenue helping others play music at venues such as the Barfly, the Underworld and the Black Heart. For years I assumed he'd undertaken this role as a means of remaining close to the action. Not a bit of it. Jerking a thumb over his shoulder, he tells me that even as a member of 3 Colours Red he used to run a club night in one of the subterranean bars on Inverness Street. He tried managing for a while, too, but found himself distressed by the barefaced demands placed on emerging bands by a greedy industry desperate to increase its share of the pie. 'I just couldn't put them through that,' he says. In the biting cold of Camden Town, without being asked he tells me this: 'Even back in the day I thought that there should be something set up within this billion dollar music industry that protects or helps people that find success. Forget the drugs and all of that, that's by the by. I'm talking about the success itself, because that's also like a drug. It's something people crave. And it's hard for people to have amounted to that and then to have it all taken away overnight.

'Because, you know,' he adds, 'not every band can be Biffy Clyro. What they've got is priceless.'

Released in the summer of 2020 Biffy Clyro's eighth studio album, *A Celebration of Endings*, concludes with 'Cop Syrup'. A masterpiece of unbridled energy, the song marries the faintest glimmer of pop music with the kind of commotion that can be corralled only by expert hands. 'I've been saved from the darkest place,' sings Simon Neil in its berserk opening section. Then, as if from nowhere, the track pivots into a three-minute and forty-seven-second instrumental section of such sublime fragility that one wonders how on earth it can be the same group, let alone the same song. In a piece of music that swells and builds like warm and welcome rains, the second act sees the three musicians joined by a keyboardist, a flutist, *ten* violinists, four cellists and three violists. One of the most remarkable pieces of music I've ever heard, to me this towering track says, *'This, right here, **this** is the sound of **our** freedom. And look, just look what we're able to do with it.'* By banding together, by working hard and keeping faith with one another through dark times, Biffy Clyro have mastered the talent and the courage required to embark on a road as uncharted as this. Seeking to find the limits of their capacious originality, in strengthening their common convictions, and by surviving the turmoil of life in a band, this – *this* – is what they created.

'Music has saved my life,' Simon Neil tells me. 'When I'm writing songs, when I'm not worrying about anyone else, that's when I'm at my happiest. When we're playing, that's when Ben and James and I are at our happiest. There's just this disregard for the outside world and for everyone else. That's where the "fuck everybody" [lyric] comes from. I don't give *a fuck*. I'm in a moment of pure unadulterated happiness and I don't give a fuck what anyone else says. It's me saying that I'm proud of who I am. And I'm proud of what we've done.

'This is who we are.'

7: I MUST NOT THINK BAD THOUGHTS

In the wake of Eric's death there are times when I can sense that things are speeding up. In the company of a photographer and writer from the *New Musical Express*, Paul Harries and I are drinking beer on an outdoor terrace on the southern tip of the Las Vegas Strip. Baked by the screaming sunshine of late afternoon, none of us should be here. En route to a press junket in Orange County, a faulty gangway at the city's McCarran International Airport has meant a missed connection and a free pass for a night in Sin City. Until we ship out at eight tomorrow morning, our time is our own. Enriched by a bounty from Eric's estate that I insist on calling 'my winnings', I have scores of thousands of pounds to my name. Amid a forest of neon specifically designed to bamboozle the senses, suddenly I'm in a place in which a night might easily be mislaid. None of this would be happening had the day stayed its original course. But a detour to a sleepless city means that I now have the two things required to do myself real damage – the element of surprise, and *space*. It isn't much space, but in my temporarily invulnerable state tomorrow morning's alarm call is a foreign country. Once again, it's a problem for future me.

I don't know why I'm not satisfied with what I already have. Paul and I are on our way to do Green Day, a band who know our names. In temperatures so extreme that the keycard to my hotel room actually *melted*, barely two years ago he and I profiled the trio in this very city. Made aware of our interrupted journey, today Warner Bros. have hurriedly booked four rooms in a good hotel.

As is industry standard, the label will underwrite our expenses for food and drink. 'Just don't take the piss,' is all we've been told. In music business parlance, this means just about anything you want it to. Me, I take it to mean keeping my spends down to a couple of hundred dollars. At this, no one will blink. So I'll have a nice steak, half a dozen beers, and three or four whiskies at the end of the night. I'll tip twenty per cent and buy a decent cigar to smoke on the walk back to our digs. I mean, it's all good. What's not to like?

There's no question that the ball will be given a good kick. That was one of Eric's favourite euphemisms, by the way. 'Ooh, Sin City. That's the place to give the ball a kick.' Out here in the desert, it's 5 p.m. – 1 a.m. UK time. Not that anyone has an eye for the clock, you understand. We'll be heading to bed at ten o' clock, say, or dawn in the country where our body clocks reside. In the hope of locking step with time zones with which we have no right to acclimatise, Harries and I have long since learned that the key to a successful foreign campaign is to stay up as late as our eyes will allow. Given this, it's all but constitutional law that the first evening of a foreign adventure is Fun Night. F. U. N. – *Fun!* Last time we were in this town, the pair of us got richly marinated on one-dollar beers at a minor league baseball game. Despite my very English reservations, over in Boston we were once made jubilantly welcome by the regulars at a transsexual burlesque bar. I had such a rum time of it that come the end of the night I had to be retrieved from a closet packed with cleaning products I'd mistaken for a toilet. (I can still hear the tender kindness with which one of the performers had said to me, 'Oh, honey, I think we need to get you home.') Clearly, this is the clay from which memories are made. It's a fabulous way to make a living.

But it's not enough. *Why isn't it enough?* Even at the time, what follows is a collage of terrible acceleration. *Click.* The photographers are gone. *Click.* I'm two miles north of our hotel. *Click.*

In the company of the trip's other writer, suddenly I'm bouncing into strangers on the walkways on the lower floors of the STRAT SkyPod hotel. Careering across heavy carpets, my pace is at a jog; if I stop I will fall over. Listing sideways, I crash into a wall. *Click.* The platform roof of this towering structure features a selection of thrill rides and attractions. Let's go up there. *Click.* In the front seat of the X-Scream ride, from the bottom of my lungs I shout in delight as its eight-berth carriage propels us over the lip of the building towards the carpet of diamonds that is the Vegas night. *Click.* Back at our original hotel – *how did we get here?* – I'm ordering Heineken and double-fingers of Johnnie Walker Black Label. With metronomic reliability, every ten minutes I'm having another, another, another. *Come on, we have time for more – **I don't know what time it is** – let's have more. Click.* Suddenly alone, I'm approached by a working girl. With what I hope is respect, but what might in fact be little more than a mouthful of vowels, I explain that I'm not interested in paying for sex. *But.* Hang on. *Hang on.* I don't suppose she knows where I can get some cocaine from, does she? Well, yes, as it happens she certainly does. What do I need? *Three and a half grams. An eight ball. I need an eight ball.* She doesn't even blink. Sure, no problem. *Click.* We're in a car en route to a dealer's house. *Click.* In need of a cash machine, we pull up in the parking lot of a twenty-four-hour convenience store. *I'll be back in a minute.* Watching the vehicle screech away I realise I've been robbed of my wallet. *Click.* I don't know where I am. *Click.* Plotting a course to what I hope are the lights of the strip, behind me the sun is about to step on the first rung of its climb through the sky. This is not a happening deal. *Click.* Somehow, *somehow* I'm in my room. Barely forty minutes before our scheduled departure for the airport, I decide to take a nap. Just in case, I swallow a powerful prescription sleeping pill.

Click.

That's me for the next three and a half hours. The sound of Harries pounding on the door for a full ten minutes doesn't wake me. At rest like the dead, the trill of the telephone leaves me undisturbed. Greeting the day in my own sweet time, at first I don't recognise the jam I'm in. *Hang on, here it comes.* With a surge of relief that threatens to burst my diaphragm I discover that last night I had placed my passport, my debit card and twenty dollars into a bedside drawer. *Oh thank Christ. Thank God I know myself so well.* On the phone to the bank, I learn that an attempt to place a large bet with stolen plastic at the tables of the MGM Grand has already resulted in the cancellation of my American Express. Not being bankrupt is also good. *What else?* I place a call to Harries in the hope of discovering how many goals are needed to keep the score respectable. Sounding very much like the General on the trumpet to Dick Dastardly, my working partner is almost shouting as he tells me, 'Don't ever do that to me again. I thought you were fucking dead. I felt so helpless.'

Yeah, you and me both, kiddo. With terrible momentum, my life is skidding out of control. It's not yet a full-time job, but it is happening with increasing regularity. Once a month, or every two or three weeks, I'm up on my joggers, slipping my leash. *Running wild in the streets.* Cocaine to send me skyward, bourbon or vodka to bring me back down. Out of otherwise empty skies, the impulse hits me like lightning; one minute the day is as it should be, the next the bullet train is on the tracks, breaks shot, screaming towards the buffers. I don't seem to be able to protect myself. In the back seat of the car last night a voice in my mind, weak as a day-old kitten, was doing all it could to let me know that my behaviour was insane. And *dangerous.* But so what? A dominant authority had taken charge of the situation. Heedless and immovable, this guy, *this fucking guy*, just can't get enough of the disorder. With broken agency I discover that I actually rather like his bullying manner. *It hits you, like a hammer.* As I'm shouted down and knocked about, I find that I appreciate being weak. Pulse quickening at the prospect of chaos, I honestly think that I'm no longer in charge.

'The front desk wouldn't let me into your room,' Harries tell me. Prostrate on the bed, I realise that his anger is marbled with relief. *Ah, that's nice.* Treading carefully, I walk towards the light.

'Um, Pa-ul.'

Two bars of silence. 'What?'

'Do *Kerrang!* need to know about this?'

In the early days of our friendship, I couldn't believe that Harries had never taken drugs. Inevitably, we were on our way to catch a plane – Budapest? Oklahoma City? Denver? – to a place he had been but I had not.

'Really? Never?' I asked.

'No, not once.'

'What, not even, like, a joint or nothing?'

'Mate, I'm just not interested.'

'Wow! Good for you.'

'Are you taking the piss?'

'Not at all, no, I'm really not.'

From hundreds of miles away, I hear a sigh that might just contain a kernel of laughter. 'Course they fucking don't.'

Seeing as I work for the one periodical in the country from which it is apparently impossible to get the sack, I can't fully account for my overwhelming sense of panic on this front.

I'm not saying we're a gang of delinquents, but if everyone on *Kerrang!* was shown the road for behaving like an idiot, the magazine would be like the *Mary Celeste.* There can be no doubt, though, that my current predicament has raised the bar somewhat. There is a chance this could be trouble. Back in London the magazine has a new editor who is doing all he can to banish the laughter and fun that has illuminated the office for as long as I have been a part of the team. Not just this, but out here in the field I'm facing a number of logistical headaches that are coming to shore like a hurricane. Green Day are a major label stadium band in the midst of a giant press campaign. While they're in California, I'm stranded in Nevada. This is not one of those times where I can just fuck it all off in the hope that someone else will clean up my mess. Still, it's got to be worth a shot. Bracing myself, I place a call to Susan Seville, the group's Hartlepool-born American press agent. A high-rolling executive with a no-questions-asked expense account, over the years this old-school operator and I have been drunk in at least four major world cities. Recognising that my only option is – pause for applause – simply to tell the truth, for the first time I recount the specific details of my night's work.

Jesus, this sounds bad.

'Oh, Ian, what were you thinking?'

*Well, Susan, since you ask, I think you'll find I was exercising my democratic right **not** to think. All things considered, I reckon that's probably what was going on there.* 'I am so sorry,' I tell her. And I am, too. I always am.

'Look, don't worry, we'll get you on the next flight to LA. Just wait where you are. Where are you, by the way?'

'Um, I'm still at the hotel.'

'Okay.' *Not okay.* 'I'll call you back in ten minutes.'

I'm thankful that certain things are on my side. In the years when the group's stock was low I had spent a far from discountable amount of energy insisting in print that Green Day were one of modern music's great bands. I undertook this work on the front foot, without equivocation. In interviews conducted in Chicago, Milwaukee, Atlanta, San Francisco, Dublin, Las Vegas, London and Los Angeles my stories ran contrary to the wisdom of the boardrooms of America. Editors in the UK thought I was pitching things a bit high. In an affectionate kind of a way, no one doubted that the trio from Oakland were a capable unit; but in the years following the release of the mega-platinum *Dookie* album it seemed as if their commercial profile was a matter of managed decline. I don't think even I really expected the band to regain the kind of status I believed was their due. But on a visit to Hollywood in the spring of 2004 I became the first civilian in the world to hear the work-in-progress that was *American Idiot*. Seated at a stereo the size of an Aga, straight away I realised that, for one time only, I may just have got something right. After the world and its media had taken a tumble for the last true blockbuster of the rock age, at a gig at the Sheffield Arena the group's singer, Billie Joe Armstrong, dedicated one of its songs to me. Bidding him a quick hello before the show, I'd told him that I'd brought my mum along. Hearing the dedication, she succumbed to tears in the seats by the stage. So, yeah, we go back a long way, Green Day and I. Surely we're not gonna let one little whoopsie spoil all these good times, are we?

God, I feel like shit. The phone rings. All the planes to Los Angeles are full. There isn't a seat to be had for love nor money. Especially money.

'It's all right, don't worry,' I'm told. 'There's a flight that'll take you to Orange County. That's where the band are anyway. I'll send a car to pick you up. You'll be landing at John Wayne Airport . . .'

'The hell I won't.'

Despite throwing the group's press schedule into disarray, and requiring a record company to pony up twelve hundred dollars for a second flight, the line gets a laugh. *See, I'm not **really** in trouble.*

'. . . which is about twenty minutes away from where we are. Obviously you'll miss your interview slot for today, but I'll clear some space for you tomorrow. I'll move things around.'

'Susan. Thank you.'

'You do know that if this was anyone else I'd just fuck 'em off home, right? Get *Kerrang!* to reimburse us for all this bloody money.'

'Susan. Thank you.'

'Your flight isn't 'til five, by the way. It's literally the only one we could get you on.'

With six hours to kill, the short ride to the airport leaves me with half a dozen bucks. Eight hours behind the beat, I will not be permitted access to further funds until the clock in the UK has ticked past midnight. On even the sunniest days, few places are as dispiritingly homogeneous as an American airport. Standing at a sorry looking concession cart near my departure gate, the purchase of a bottle of pop and a wilted salad leaves me with nickels and dimes. At least no one nicked my paperback. In need of rehydration, like a character in a Ken Loach film, every half an hour I walk to the rest room to fill up my empty pop bottle with tap water. Inch by inch, minute by minute, I begin to feel better. *This could be worse.* Come the hour at which my fellow passengers begin to gather at the gate, I've had plenty of time in which to review my misadventures from the night before. Know what? With a coat of tragicomic emulsion, with a few splodges of '*what am I like?*', I reckon I can turn this into something that might just be funny. With a bit of practice, that'll buff up nicely, that will. And it does, too. In London I have yet to meet a single person from the music industry who doesn't find my well-groomed tale of personal misfortune to be a thing of hilarity. Finally informed of roughly a quarter of its details, even *Kerrang!* dismissed the matter with little more than a shake of the head. Even now, emails sent to Susan Seville are headlined with variations of the words, 'Help. I'm naked in the desert. Send money.'

Eight hours behind schedule, at close of business I step into the sunlit expanse of a beautiful beachfront property in Orange County. Their day's work done, its occupants have been waiting on me. At a seafood joint on a marina filled with sailboats and yachts, Susan Seville orders me the first of a series of dirty martinis. It would be wrong to say that all is forgiven; Harries' deep concern notwithstanding, I was never really in trouble in the first place. No one ever is. Barely a month later, Billie Joe Armstrong enjoyed his own moment of Las Vegas madness. Irritated by a line-of-sight LCD display at the iHeartRadio Music Festival the ferociously drunk frontman embarked on a post-watershed tirade that culminated with him smashing apart his Gibson Les Paul Junior on the stage of the MGM Grand Garden Arena. Appalled by his own behaviour, Armstrong checked himself into a rehabilitation clinic before the week was out. With the band off the road for half a year, *¡Uno!*, the album that had taken me to Orange County in the first place, suffered the ignominy of being (at the time) its authors' lowest selling LP for twenty-two years.

Warming up for headline slots at the Leeds and Reading festivals, eleven months later Green Day played a concert at the Brixton Academy. Making my way down Astoria Walk towards the door reserved for people who have no idea of the price of a ticket, my progress was spotted by Tré Cool, the group's drummer. Responding to the sound of my name, I looked up in time to see Billie Joe Armstrong join him at the ledge of a dressing-room window three floors above me.

'Hey, Ian. What's going on?'

'I've come to see a band. I don't know if they're any good or not.'

'Ah, they're okay.'

'Hey, Billie, do you remember what I said?'

'What's that?'

'I told you, man. Vegas. That town ain't nothing but trouble.'

I wonder if part of the problem is that no one really has a boss. As confused a chain of command as can be imagined, the music industry is often a coalition of uneasy and poorly defined co-dependents. It's just too easy for people *not* to take charge. A band may well defer to a manager who can be sacked on a whim. A record company will write telephone-number cheques for recording sessions that in many cases will not be heard until an LP is completed. Artists write songs on which their label owns copyright. Knowing all too well that status can fluctuate (and that failure is contagious), A&R people, press agents and marketing teams hustle hard to ensure that an album takes flight. Should it fail to do so, the decision to release a band from their contract will be taken many floors above by people in the numbers game. It's unlikely that the musicians will have ever met them, and neither have I.

When it comes to touring, booking agents and promoters plot live campaigns that last for as long as demand exists. With the powers of veto and severance at their disposal, here, too, the performers are nominally in charge. They are the employers. But, drastic interventions notwithstanding, the decision as to when an artist will be allowed to go home will be determined by other people. Until then the musicians will be required to pay a tour manager to boss them around. Above it all, permeating the air like the fog of a disorientating dream, the forward momentum of a band is stronger than anyone who plays a part in it. Conversely, so too is the doomed inertia of a group with declining fortunes. This is the reality of having a job in which no one is answerable to anyone else.

'There's often a lack of accountability,' Dr Charlie Howard tells me. 'Often managers or the record label might want to say something – particularly managers, actually – to a band, or to an artist, but they feel like they can't because they're vulnerable because they don't want to be fired. So there are often things that I notice that need to be named and called out and worked through that are often quite tricky, but I see a lot of passing those things around. "Oh, that's the label's job; that's the manager's job." And the manager will say, "Oh, I'm not doing it. It's not my job." There's kind of this vacuum, this reluctance to take responsibility for things that are tricky in relation to an artist. I've had people to say to me, "You know, Charlie, it's crazy when you're in a band. I've smashed up hotel rooms and no one's told me that that's not okay." And that's really *not* okay. But nobody is raising that with them.'

I don't wish to sound like a Whig traditionalist bemoaning the absence of natural order. Of the many hundreds of pieces to which I've put my name, the only one that was ever spiked – by the *Mirror* – was an article questioning the cosy relationship between the armed forces and popular culture. Writing about the high number of ex-service personnel sleeping in shop doorways on the streets of British cities, I'd said that 'as well as getting drunk on the applause for looking after the nation, the military might also take some time to actually look after its own'. For the nominally left-wing tabloid, this was tricky ground. After refusing to issue a personal apology, years earlier the paper's editor, Piers Morgan, had been sacked for publishing faked images of British soldiers allegedly abusing Iraqi prisoners. 'Ian, this is a good piece,' my editor's boss explained to me, 'but we can't run it. Our relationship with the services is already bad enough.' In writing the piece I was struck by the convergent patterns of mental illness between those who have worked in an environment of strict and delineated discipline and those who have made their home in a world in which structure is opaque. In both fields the blows are taken by grunts on the frontline.

'In the music business, you're in bed with a bunch of predators,' Billy Corgan, bandleader with Chicago's the Smashing Pumpkins, told me in 2020. 'The managers, the agents, the whole industry is porn . . . it was built on the assumption that you're only going to be here for a few years, so we're going to tell you what you want to hear and we're going to say what we need to say to get what we want from you. And as soon as you fall below a certain line of usefulness, we're going to get rid of you.'

Porn. A blockbuster hit in the Superior Court of Public Opinion, even by the dysfunctional standards of the nineties, the Smashing Pumpkins appeared poorly equipped to cope with

life-changing success. Loathed by large sections of a then powerful music press – '[Corgan] is a media slut [and] a corporate
whore in the lowest and most pitifully sycophantic way,' wrote
Everett True in the *Melody Maker* – their singer's unwarranted
status as one of the super-villains of the Alternative Nation made
him feel 'targeted and bullied'. I'm not surprised. Onstage the
singer took to wearing a shirt bearing the word 'Zero'. Along
with punishment beatings from self-important tastemakers, his
group endured the omnipresent danger of hard drugs. Prior to
a concert at Madison Square Garden, on 12 July 1996 drummer
Jimmy Chamberlain and touring keyboardist Jonathan Melvoin
overdosed on heroin. Only Chamberlain survived. Despite the
severity of the tragedy, the campaign in support of their number
one album, *Mellon Collie and the Infinite Sadness*, was paused for
barely a month and a half. By the penultimate week in August the
Smashing Pumpkins were back on the road. Come the middle
of September their caravan returned to New York City for two
rescheduled dates at the Garden.

The warning signs had been flashing for years. In Chicago in
2012 Billy Corgan told me that even at the start of the group's
career Jimmy Chamberlain would disappear for days on end on
errands of mischief. Recording *Siamese Dream*, their second album,
the group were required to keep their drummer away from the drug
scene in Atlanta. In 1994 Chamberlain told *Rolling Stone* that he'd
'gotten high in every city in this country and probably half the cities
in Europe'. But the events in New York were of a magnitude that
couldn't be brushed aside. In a statement announcing the drummer's departure from the band, the Smashing Pumpkins described
how, 'For nine years we have battled with Jimmy's struggles with
the insidious disease of drug and alcohol addiction. It has nearly
destroyed everything we are and stand for . . . We wish [him] the
best we have to offer.'

Today it strikes me as noteworthy that Billy Corgan raises this matter with me without being asked. Appearing on my computer screen from his home in Chicago at 9 a.m. Central Time, the fifty-three-year-old appears to have woken up in the kind of piss-and-vinegar mood for which he is sometimes known. For all it's worth, I'm not here to quarrel with the reality of his first-hand experience. Along with the ejection of one of the world's finest drummers, in New York City a member of the Smashing Pumpkins' touring party poisoned himself to death. Denied the time they needed to grieve and repair, Corgan believes that his group were rushed to resume a highly profitable live campaign before they were ready to do so. No one is better qualified to comment on this. If this is what he thinks, then this is how it happened.

'You've got this billion dollar business but there's literally no one there to help you,' he tells me. 'Jimmy left the band' – he later returned – 'and then we were on tour six weeks later. How can that psychologically be a good idea? But we were told to get back out there. "Oh, the fans will forget about you. You'll lose your stake." Meanwhile, your band has imploded.'

In mitigation, the only thing I would say is that things are not always as mercenary, or as ruthless, as this. A distinction without a difference it may be, but sometimes the problem is nothing more sinister than people not quite knowing what to do for the best. Failed by the industry's structural deficiencies, recovering musicians often take care of their own. When Jimmy Chamberlain entered a course of treatment, Dave Navarro from Jane's Addiction was his sponsor. In need of help for an addiction to crystal methamphetamine, Elton John extended the hand of experience to Rufus Wainwright. Sometimes the question is one of timing. In his compellingly gruelling memoir *Sing Backwards and Weep*, Mark Lanegan, the erstwhile singer with Seattle's Screaming Trees, rejects the notion that people in his band's organisation failed to do everything they could to uproot him from an addiction to heroin and crack cocaine. They did, he says, he just wasn't ready to accept their interventions.

In 2020 Lanegan told me how 'lots of people within and without the industry tried to help me. Especially the guys at Q-Prime, who managed me for a long time. They were aware from the beginning of my problems [so they] kind of had an idea, but not [of] the extent or the depth of my problem. But when they became aware of it, they did try many, many times to help me. But it's tough to get a grown man to change anything if there are no consequences. And the only consequences those guys were able to throw at me was that they wouldn't work with us any more. And, of course, even though it was an incredible break for my band to be managed by Q-Prime, who at the time were arguably the most powerful management company in the world, that still was not enough for me. So I chose the third option, which was, "Okay, well, I won't work with you any more."'

No consequences. An integral part of some of the most stirring music of the late twentieth century, for decades Mark Lanegan was possessed of an apparently boundless determination to do himself harm. Reduced to sleeping beneath a tarpaulin next to an overpass, when the time finally came for him to put things right it was Courtney Love, the bandleader with Hole and the widow of Kurt Cobain, who paid for a stay in a rehabilitation clinic in Southern California. As the singer prepared to return to the wild, Duff McKagan from Guns N' Roses offered him a place to live. At the nadir of his own addiction, in 1994 McKagan's pancreas swelled to the size of an American football. It then exploded. *Give up drinking or be dead within the month*, the doctors told him. With Mark Lanegan at a potentially vulnerable early stage in his own recovery, it was the bass player with what had been one of America's most ruinous bands that helped him stay well.

'He [McKagan] was a guardian angel and one of my very best friends,' is how Lanegan described the intervention to me. 'He just basically heard that I was in this recovery house in Pasadena and he came looking for me. Because Duff is an icon in Seattle, and because I was a Seattle guy, he came to see if there was anything he could do to help. Subsequently I ended up living in his house and driving his vehicles for three years. Even as I started making money again, never would he let me pay rent. He said that I was doing him a favour. But the opposite was the truth.'

The music industry has scores of happy endings to stories that would put hairs on your chest. It also boasts an equally voluminous library of tales that end in death. At the time of writing, my most recent interview was with Dave Grohl. As the drummer with Nirvana, Grohl had stood by helpless as Kurt Cobain used a shotgun to quiet the clamour from both inside and outside his head. Unsure as to whether or not he actually wished to continue making music, in founding the Foo Fighters the then twenty-five-year-old took great care to construct a working environment in which he and his colleagues felt safe. In a pioneering power play, rather than sign to a major label the group decided to license their music to record companies for only a limited period of time. As a means of controlling their public image, they made their own videos. Burnished by success, in time they built their own recording studio-come-boys' club in the San Fernando Valley. I've been there, and very nice it is too. To as large a degree as could be managed Dave Grohl worked hard to ensure that his and his group's happiness and security would no longer be put at risk by the wild vagaries of an overwhelming and unpredictable industry.

In what was an exceptional incident, even this carefully constructed environment wasn't quite enough to prevent drummer Taylor Hawkins from taking a near-fatal overdose of prescription pills in his room at the Royal Garden Hotel in London in 2001. In a recording studio on Melrose Avenue in Los Angeles the following year, I pressed him on exactly what happened that day. He called me a 'nosy bastard'. Aside from this, though, the band's exoskeleton has survived everything that has rained down upon it. After less than four years as the drummer with Nirvana, Dave Grohl has been at the helm of the Foo Fighters for almost half of his life.

'I think that some of life's best lessons are the ones that show you what *not* to do,' he told me. 'Right? So when we started the Foo Fighters, I had a long list of those.' At this, Grohl emitted a short laugh that contained a good deal of weight. 'I knew that in order to navigate what we were going through, I had to refer to a lot of those lessons. So, yeah, you know nobody in Nirvana expected [the success] to happen. Nobody expected that we would go from a club of hundred and twenty-five people to a gold record in thirty fucking days, you know. That's really difficult to process. It happened so quickly that I've always kept that in mind with the Foo Fighters. I think of the ups and I think of the downs. But I think that the thing that I'm most surprised of is that we've survived. I've seen a lot of people not make it. When I see our friends from back in the day onstage still performing music, I get emotional because I'm thankful that they've survived. I remember watching Pearl Jam five or six years ago at a festival and feeling so thankful that *they* survived. Because all I've ever wanted to do is play music and live. And so I'm very thankful that we've made it this far.'

The nineties were ruinous for people who made credible rock music. Along with Kurt Cobain, drug related misfortune claimed the lives of Stefanie Sargent (7 Year Bitch), Andrew Wood (Mother Love Bone), Kristen Pfaff (Hole) and Dwayne Goettel (Skinny Puppy). So great was the overall dysfunction that musicians in neighbouring scenes began to exercise caution. With change in the air, by the spring of 1994 the gloomy vacuum of grunge had been permeated by the equally authentic sound of brightly coloured punk rock. It wasn't that these groups were any smarter, necessarily, but they did somehow seem better prepared for what might be coming their way. When the Californian quartet The Offspring unexpectedly sold seven million copies of their third album, *Smash*, its members politely declined invitations to appear on career-defining television programmes such as the *Late Show with David Letterman* and *Saturday Night Live*. The group's record label, Epitaph, a defiant independent, supported their decisions.

'There was all this stuff where people were literally dying because of what was going on,' the band's singer, Dexter Holland, once told me. 'And so we thought, "You know, maybe it's not a good idea to all of a sudden turn up the heat to a million and a half and hog the entire spotlight." Maybe it's not a good idea, mentally, to do that.' In 2021 he told me that, 'The music industry produces casualties. That is for sure.'

Researching this book, I had a look over the articles I've written for the *Telegraph* over the past couple of years. In a hotel suite in Bloomsbury, Marc Almond told me how he was once 'horribly addicted' to 'benzodiazepine, as well as sleeping pills and valium'. On the line from the Berkshires, in Massachusetts, James Taylor recalled the days when 'essentially I was an addict for twenty years, from the age of seventeen to the age of thirty-five', a time when 'I was addicted to various types of opiates'. I wrote a piece about Tom Petty's *Wildflowers* album, the resplendent masterpiece recorded at a time when the singer was heavily in hock to heroin. I profiled Aerosmith, a band who were so out of it that they once forgot that they'd hidden an irreplaceable 'riff tape' inside a biscuit barrel. I spoke to Jeff Tweedy, from the Chicagoan group Wilco, who became a survivor of his country's opioid epidemic. I hit upon a quote from Rosemary Barrett, the sister of one-time Pink Floyd singer Roger 'Syd' Barrett, about how her sibling 'was always looking for the next big thing – and that applied to drugs . . . Most people know when to stop. Roger didn't.' I spoke to Wayne Kramer, the wunderkind guitarist from the MC5 – now the MC50 – who went to prison for selling cocaine. I wrote about AC/DC, whose singer Bon Scott drank himself to death following a night out at a venue less than half a mile from my front door. I described a 'rock doc' doling out drugs to a plane full of musicians en route to a festival in pre-Glasnost Moscow (the event itself was staged in the hope of mitigating a manager's upcoming trial for smuggling cocaine). I touched upon the doomed junkie love affair of Sid Vicious and Nancy Spungen that left both of them dead. I spoke to Chuck D, from Public Enemy, whose bandmate Flavor Flav claims to have spent *six million dollars* on drugs. I talked to Tony Iommi from Black Sabbath, a band who used to travel on private planes furnished with vacuum-packed bags of uncut blow. I wrote about how Eddie Van Halen once kept a drug seller on call ready to fly anywhere in the country when Van Halen were on tour.

In the past, if I considered the matter at all, I guess I used to think that the bloodstains on the otherwise exquisitely woven tapestry of music were mere spillages. But the closer I looked, the more I saw them as being part of the fabric. In this new light, even the unlikeliest people can be a VH1 *Behind the Music* special waiting to happen. Pick a band, any band. In the autumn of 2004 I rode in a van with Kings of Leon en route to a concert at the compact Paradise Club, opposite Fenway Park in Boston. Southern gentlemen one and all – I seem to remember them calling me 'sir' at least twice – I flew back to London thinking, 'Well, they seem pretty grounded.' Probably they were, too, but after a few years in the spotlight three quarters of the group were required to ask their singer, Caleb Followill, to enter rehab. Seated in the restaurant of London's K West Hotel, Chris Wolstenholme, from Muse, handed me his phone number so that we could go to the match together next time Barnsley played Rotherham United. He also told me that had he not given up drinking he would have died. Honestly, I'm just picking these at random. Mike Kerr, from Royal Blood, decided to forego alcohol after taking one last espresso martini in Las Vegas. 'At the time I felt that I was nipping something in the bud,' he told me in 2021. 'But it wasn't until I'd had some time being sober, and some clarity, that I realised the state I was in. I think [musicians] are good at getting used to feeling like shit, and feeling satisfied with that kind of living. [It's] the high cost of low living.' Often, the cost of the high life is equally steep.

At a garden party hosted by Faber & Faber, this book's publisher, I once had the opportunity to express my gratitude to Jarvis Cocker, from Pulp, for writing the lyrics to *This is Hardcore*, perhaps the grimmest and most fascinating account of fame and license I've ever heard. '[The] rock 'n' roll clichés [are] the things that are supposed to bring you happiness, aren't they,' Cocker told the journalist Simon Hattenstone in 2008. 'You make it, and you're bathing in champagne and you can snort as much cocaine as you want and fuck as many beautiful women as you want. Then you find you can do those things, but they don't actually make you very happy.'

The truth of this observation has been learned countless times over, not least by a member of a group with whom Pulp share a home city. Def Leppard's determination to forge a career based on the pursuit of happiness made them Sheffield's most successful export as well as victims of routine tragedy when Steve Clark died aged thirty addicted to alcohol and drugs. A blue-collar kid from Hillsborough, the guitarist had helped create *Pyromania*, released in 1983, a record that sold six million copies in the United States alone. Its successor, *Hysteria*, did even better. At the end of a subsequent fifteen-month world tour, with more money than he could sensibly spend, Clark began to disintegrate. 'Steve, you're scaring the shit out of us,' bandmate Phil Collen told his friend at a treatment centre in Minnesota. At a rehab facility in Tucson, the guitarist began a relationship with Janie Dean, a fellow patient who was being treated for heroin addiction. The pair's decision to discharge themselves did not survive the stress-tests of the outside world. On 8 January 1991 Dean found her partner dead from a fatal mixture of alcohol and prescription drugs.

'We thought we were supportive,' Collen told me in 2020. 'I thought, "Fuck, I'm just going to put him in my back room." But you can't do that to your thirty-year-old friend. You can't say that you can't see this girl any more so you're coming to live in my back room. But I actually did think about [doing that]. If it happened now we would obviously be better equipped [to deal with things]. But families let this stuff happen all the time, you know. It kind of creeps away and before you know it someone has a real issue and a real problem.'

After giving up drinking in the eighties, Phil Collen had the strength of purpose to help himself but not the powers of persuasion needed to assist his stricken bandmate. Ridden with misplaced guilt, he paid serious mind to turning his back on a group whose last album had sold more than twelve million copies. *I'll become a plumber*, he thought. I can almost imagine this. As working class as a crisps-and-salad-cream sandwich, Def Leppard's internal combustion engine was ignited on the shop floors of the former industrial expanse of the Don Valley. In the second half of the seventies, singer Joe Elliott worked at Samuel Osborn & Company, a tool-making factory where the South Yorkshire wind whistled wild through cracked and broken windows. Watching men with four decades' service clocking in and out, he thought, "'Fifty years of this bullshit? No thanks."

'My generation were the first generation after the hippies that looked at this from a tangible point of view and went, "It's okay to put two fingers up at The Man and smoke weed, but you're treading water,"' he told me. 'We were the first to go, "You're not making any progress." For us, we didn't have a white-collar mummy or daddy to bail us out. This was all on us . . . so we built our own rocket and we jetted off to other planets.'

In my callow youth I'd listen to Def Leppard ask 'Do you wanna get rocked?' and think, 'Possibly – by someone else.' But in mistaking the Brits for yet another addition to a litter of now-forgotten hairspray rockers, I somehow failed to notice the talent and graft that went into albums such as *Hysteria* and *Adrenalize*. Because I didn't much like the lyrics – I still don't, actually – I missed the point that the group's studio-as-orchestra approach to creating records bore a close relation to the exalted exactitude of Steely Dan or Earth, Wind & Fire. Turns out it was me who wasn't taking things seriously. I should have liked that they were lads from the pubs and clubs of South Yorkshire; the very same breeding ground produced the Arctic Monkeys, and I can't get enough of them. Despite myself, I'd once come away from a successful interview with Alex Turner, the group's singer, aglow with a weird and inappropriate feeling of woozy validation. *He kept calling me 'Ian'. He was somehow able to recall every one of the three letters in my name.* Sometimes I still struggle to appreciate that rock 'n' roll is the people's game, and that the success of an artist can be queried but rarely dismissed. There is a reason that people love certain groups, and if I can't see why – or, worse yet, if I decline even to *try* to see why – then my place on the page is undeserved. A diligent practitioner, Steve Clark was both his band's most talented musician *and* the architect of their sound. The only valid comparison with nihilists such as Sid Vicious or GG Allin is that all three men are now dead.

I well remember the day my fiancée told me that she had never seen an arena rock show. Clutching my breast in shock I wondered aloud how on earth such a shortcoming might even be possible in a woman thirty-five years of age. *Has she been in prison? In a coma? Is she Amish?* (It gets worse. Just last week she told me that she thought ZZ Top was an African American soul singer.) 'Never mind,' I thought. 'All that matters is that we put right this deficiency of cultural nutrition as soon as possible.' Weeks later, for our first concert together I took her to the 02 Arena to see Def Leppard. Surprised at how pleased I was that this was her introduction to my world, I explained that by the metric of a whistle 'n' bells production what she was about to see would be hard to beat. By way of an aperitif, we watched Rick Nielsen from Cheap Trick, the night's opening turn, spray plectrums like confetti while playing a guitar that had *five necks*. 'See,' I said, 'this is what I'm talking about.' From my usual perch hard by the stage, the proximity, and the sightlines, were perfect for the purposes of showing a then potentially serious new squeeze the kind of place from which I draw a living.

Onstage Def Leppard were in charge of the situation. *Obviously.* One of the jungle's biggest and most enduring beasts, this was the animal in its natural habitat. Paying his union dues on a frigid shop floor, Joe Elliott imagined himself and his friends onstage in a room that holds this many people. Once again, there was no Plan B. *In at the deep end, hang on tight.* Armed only with a microphone, the singer strode slowly along the walkway that divided the floor of the unseated section directly front of house. Known to all in the trade as an 'ego ramp', with evident delight Elliott bathed in the cheers and applause of twenty thousand people. As the band behind him struck down a song that had doubtless taken months to record, I made a note that this was not the acclaim of a youthful gathering destined to move on to fresher flesh. Many in the room were people in their adult and middle years – sorting babysitters, car-parking, dinner at a restaurant beforehand – some of whom had been by the band's side for more than three decades. At the 02 – and in arenas and stadiums across the world – the group's appeal stood in the sweet spot at which depth is the equal partner of size. The timbre of the ovation suggested that everything had been carefully constructed, and built to last.

To my right, my new girlfriend leaned in and asked, 'How do they come down from this? How do they even get to sleep?'

'At the earliest, about five hours after you do.'

Twenty-two months later I speak again to Dr Charlie Howard. Keen to avoid the accusation of pursuing vulgar lines of enquiry, towards the end of a conversation about addiction and disloca-tion, mental illness and paranoia, I venture that not everyone within the music industry is vulnerable prey. With the memory of the admirably unflappable Joe Elliott in mind, I propose that many people – *most* people? – get up on the stage, give it large, stay the course, and live their lives as the happiest people they could ever hope to be. And why wouldn't they?

At the end of two seconds' silence, my layperson's stab at clinical psychology is met with a 'hmm . . .'

'I'm not sure that they do get through it unscathed,' Dr Howard tells me. 'The more artists that I speak to the more I hear them say that *they* don't know an artist who is doing well. They just don't. And that's something that's said to me *a lot*. I think a lot of them appear to be getting through it unscathed, but I'm not sure that they actually are. Of course not everybody is getting to the point of collapse or mental breakdown – that isn't the case – but I think that most artists struggle. And if they're not struggling, it's just because they haven't yet got to that stage in their career . . . I think that there are a lot of difficulties, and I think it would be a miracle if there weren't, because it's a very extraordinary world. It's a very extraordi-nary world that artists live in.'

So what's *my* excuse? In the market for bits that I could nick, during the writing of this book I read *Inside Story* by Martin Amis. In it, the English novelist and essayist describes giving a talk at his mid-dle daughter's school. Speaking to a hall filled with teenagers, Amis advocates for his trade by telling his audience that 'the aspiration starts now, at around fifteen, and if you become a writer your life never really changes. I'm still doing it, half a century later, all day long. Writers are stalled adolescents, but contentedly stalled; they enjoy their house arrest . . .' *Bloody hell, Martin, that's good. That **is** good.* Tracing my finger along the lines on the page, I read the passage out loud to my fiancée. *See. See? This is why I can't drive.* Better yet, I reckon I can go even further than this. Not only did I decide to become a writer – at around fifteen, just like the man said – but straight away I steered my course in the direction of rock'n'roll. Out here, *everyone* is an adolescent. Talk about perfect cover. So long as I hit my deadlines, so long as I can commit myself to asking a series of questions that I make up on the spot, then I'm good to go. Doesn't matter what I do.

In fact, in a telling corollary, in the wake of Eric's death my stock seems to rise in accordance with the foolishness of my behaviour. In an industry dandruffed with powder, I'm fast becoming known as a leading light in the charge for cocaine. A *fiend*. Checking into a hotel in downtown Los Angeles, a press agent I'd met for the first time only that day said to me, 'I hear you like a bit of jazz salt. There'll definitely be some of that for us later tonight.' Two thoughts at once. *Who the hell told him that?* And, *crikey, that is good news.* But it's fine, it's all right, I'm among friends here. From the Highbury Garage to the Hollywood Palladium, in this world my behaviour is mainstream.

Even so, I'm determined to push it. In the years following the unpleasant matter at the Holiday Inn, things are starting to slip. I'm playing increasingly fast and loose with deadlines. Maintaining my refusal to submit copy with which I'm not happy, I convince myself that the issue is one of muddled priorities. Drugs, drugs, drugs, drugs, *fucking* drugs. People make allowances for me, what with one thing and another. Holding the telescope the wrong way round, as I see it there's not *that* much of a problem. Explosive episodes are followed by the resumption of a somewhat regular routine. How bad can it be? In what is surely a vainglorious conceit, I don't take needle drugs and I don't smoke crack. 'That shit's bad news,' I think, while flushing the toilet on a fistful of bloodstained Kleenex.

But there are other signs, too, that I'm perhaps not well. On a free afternoon, I walk over to the Screen on the Green in Islington to watch a film whose details I cannot recall that very evening. I was sober, so it's not that. There are days during which I feel safe only in bed, naked and warm, the passing of time marked by the conversational rhythms of talk radio. By now my hours are irregular. A giddy member of the Wide Awake Club at 3 a.m., come the middle of the afternoon I'm consumed by fatigue. What's going on here? With deadlines hammering at the door, sleep arrives in ten- or fifteen-minute recesses of blessed distraction. Waking is panic. *Why can't I do this?*

A talented section editor once told me that he'd never before encountered a writer from whom words so readily explode. 'Even in emails,' he'd said. *Explode.* I believe he meant it as a compliment; certainly it was received as such. Cleaving to the duvet in the months and years after Eric's death, I dream of writing a book like this. But how can I do this when I'm feeling brutalised by the kind of pressure that for years has been my friend? Why am I lying here, twitching and coiled, jittery as a rattlesnake? Why is the noise coming to a boil? And. Then. It. Stops. Feeling something close to elation – three, two, one – suddenly I'm back in the room. Head bowed low, I tap dance an email to my editors saying that my piece will be in port by the end of the day. By now I have enough inches to make a mile. *It's okay, you can take 'til tomorrow morning. But stop making a habit of this. Okay? Ian?* **Okay?**

There's a new number in my phone. Under a different system of laws the entrepreneurial graft of Nico, my latest drug seller, would be rewarded with a plaque and a rubber-chicken lunch at a ceremony at City Hall. Open for business until 4 a.m., seven days a week, not once has it taken him longer than a quarter of an hour to bring his goods to my door. At no point has he ever been low on supplies. Notified by a single-word text – 'outside' – like a gazelle I'm up the stairs and into the billowing nicotine biosphere of my courier's Ford Galaxy. With a face like sundried chamois leather, Nico has a liking for Sheffield United. As a matter of ceremony, without fail we exchange two or three sentences about the dependable misfortunes of our respective teams. But, really, neither of us could care less about what the other has to say. In truth, I could hold my breath in the time required of each transaction. 'See you soon, pal,' I tell him, four or more grams of product in my pocket. It's never fewer than that. And I will not desist until I've taken it all.

I am by now an antisocial drug user. Hidden away in what might just be shame, I take my medicine in the privacy of my own home. Apportioning myself a generous first line – *clack, clack, clack* goes the bankcard on the dinner plate – the opening twenty minutes of each misadventure see me floating and bouncing in the stratospheric air of rarefied elation. *This. Is. Magic.* If I could just keep my foot off the accelerator, if I could only maintain this altitude, then I'd be set for the night. Actually, I'd be set for a few nights. 'This is what I'll do this time,' I tell myself. 'This time **I'll** be the one who's in charge.' But I never am.

Establishing a pattern of rapidly diminishing returns, with too much haste the second line follows the first. After this, on a black slope mapped by skulls and crossbones, it's downhill all the way. Channel surfing, internet wormholes, shallow breathing. Switching off the lights, I turn down the volume until the television can barely be heard. *Man, it's so loud in here.* By now, I know where this is headed. Come first light – *please*, not the dawn – I'm there on the settee, every muscle tensed in panic, shrink-wrapped in sweat. Urgently needing to urinate, in my hypersensitive state the sound of waste hitting water is like a tsunami. There are days when I honestly believe that a police SWAT team is hiding in the stalks of bamboo at the side of my back garden. Every sound is an explosion. Only after I've racked out the final tiny rail of white powder – only after I've held the plate to my face and *licked* its surface clean – will I reach for the antidote.

The fifteen minutes it takes Nico to arrive allow me just enough time to run out and buy two bottles of Tennessee whiskey and four litres of Diet Coke. Breaking the seal as if diffusing a bomb, in the grey of morning I pour four fingers of hooch into a smudged pint glass. The liquid is gone in a single slug. *Aaaah.* At once, the edge is buffed off my wild electric panic. The equivalent of six or eight pints of beer in under ten minutes, the third glass finds me in the transitional stage of doing a passable impression of a functioning drunk. Slowing things down, in the company of a fourth I reply to whatever emails have come my way. If there's work in the evening, or later in the week, there's a chance I'll be able to do it. Marbled with relief, by now my state of mind is one of woozy euphoria. With help from the Jack Daniel's distillery, in barely an hour I've somehow managed to steer myself back to shore. Placing a large glass of water on the bedside cabinet, I drink a fifth, and then a sixth glass of potion. Yawning like a hippo, I'm now at the point of blacking out. Coming round the following afternoon, many are the times when I've wet the bed.

Apparently Albert Einstein never did say that the definition of insanity is to repeat a course of action in the expectation of different results. Either way, according to this metric, what I'm doing is insane. Periods of abstinence are shrinking from weeks to days. My home is in ruins. Plates are piled high, the washing up hasn't been done for weeks; the fridge looks like the Gaza Strip; the floors are obscured by dirty clothes. God alone knows what it smells like in here. I know that what I'm doing is deeply wrong. Over in Mexico the cocaine industry has made Ciudad Juárez the most dangerous city in the world. And here I am, helping to fund a trade of enormous cruelty and savage violence. Across the Atlantic, the bodies of young men are hanging from overpasses. With demented nihilism, young women are raped, tortured and killed. Entire communities are pummelled into submission. And for what? So I can set fire to the fruits of my father's labour, is for what. So I can feel terrified and diminished, is why.

Girding myself, I go to New York for Christmas. In order that a neighbour can feed the cats, it takes me three days to clean the flat. En route to visit Bea and Freddie, the couple who opened their home to me in the days following Eric's death, five miles above Newfoundland I practise the lines that I will say upon arrival at their new home in Brooklyn. *Knock knock, I've brought Quality Street. I'd love a drink, thank you.* Honestly, this is what I'm doing. Sitting in a seat that turns into a bed, I'm mouthing greetings that normally spill out of my mouth with the ease of a game show host. *What on earth is wrong with me?* I sound like I've been body-snatched. I sound like an incel. I don't know if I can hold myself together.

It's obvious that something is wrong. ('You just weren't yourself,' Bea tells me, months later. 'It was like someone different was in the room.') One morning my hands shake so badly that I spill orange juice onto the floor. Seated in restaurants, or around the family dinner table, I force my hosts to endure evenings of which I have no memory. Struggling to produce even morsels of conversation, I'm spooked when I'm drunk and goosed when I'm sober. I fail to notice that my friends are sharing looks of alarm on my behalf. On New Year's Eve I don't even clock the expressions of relief that see me out of the door and into a cab bound for the airport. At JFK, as usual my air miles buy me an upgrade. Chain-drinking whiskey in the Upper Class lounge, for a moment I forget where I am. Aboard the plane, attempting to wrestle my bag into an overhead compartment, I fall heavily from my perch. I'm lying on the floor. A flight attendant responds to my request for a large Bloody Mary and two cans of beer with the words, 'I think perhaps you've had enough for the time being, sir.'

As the clouds finally clear, the shame of my behaviour in New York keeps me away from my friends' home for four years. When I do finally return, it is with my fiancée by my side. Inviting myself to stay for the first time since I ruined their Christmas, I can sense waves of uncertainty radiating from Bea's core. *He's engaged now? To who? Some cokehead from the punk scene?* But my partner has never taken drugs, which is why I know that her presence in my life will show to my friends that things are different now. It's why I want her there, as proof. With natural light and gentle laughter my resplendent plus one helps tend to wounds that cannot be salved by apology alone. Tell you what, she's like a magician. In a quiet moment, seizing my arm – '*Ow!*' – Bea administers an unvarnished coat of sound advice. '*Don't . . . fuck this up.*'

As I drank my way back to London, four years earlier Freddie wrote me an email in which he told me he was worried about me. He was sorry, he said, for not bringing this up while I was in town, he just thought that the best course of action was to check in with me electronically so that I wouldn't feel ambushed. *But seriously, mate, have a think about things, will you? Take stock of what I'm saying, and then perhaps give me a call.* So it's as bad as this, is it? Just as well that I have three bottles of duty free bourbon and a delivery from Nico with which to quell the worry gathering within me. At the finish line of a dangerous night, slipping on spillage, I shatter my left arm on a protruding drawer. Convulsing with pain, twelve hours later I'm treated to a chorus of tuts from highly qualified professionals at University College Hospital. A series of X-rays reveal a humerus that looks like a broken breadstick. A week later, after five hours in surgery I wake to discover that a dozen or more pins have been inserted through the bone via a four-inch incision just below the shoulder. Doped to the follicles, I spend three days and nights on a noisy hospital ward.

They won't be my last.

8: EPIDEMIC

Every now and again I'll clean the flat. I'll invite friends round to watch the football. Returning from Sainsbury's with a case of Sol and two bags of Doritos, whatever booze remains in the fridge come the end of the night will be left alone until the next time things go wrong. One evening I drank half a bottle and poured the rest down the sink. I just wasn't feeling it. My father's son, on tranquil afternoons I've been known to take myself to the lovely pub at the end of the street for a pint and read. *This is nice.* But it never lasts. By 2015 I no longer require space in which to create chaos. An hour before being picked up by my singer-songwriter friend Frank Turner, at the start of a day in early summer I sink three quarters of a bottle of whiskey. It would have been more, but that's all I had. Pushed for time, I drink some of it in the shower. At first convinced that I can hold things together, in the car it transpires that I can barely speak.

With London ceding ground to a green and pleasant landscape, Frank and I are on our way to the Latitude Festival in Suffolk, at which I'm due to interview him onstage in front of more than a thousand people. From Glasgow to Yeovil, over the past few years I've been part of maybe a dozen such happenings. In clubs and theatres, Frank draws the applause while I keep things moving. Sometimes I get a laugh or two. At the end of the set he plays a few songs. We have good chemistry, he and I; financially viable, on our second such tour, in 2019, we found ourselves stationed at the kind of hotels that serve eggs royale for breakfast. A writer rarely gets the chance to see an audience: even though it isn't mine, I'm grateful for having been invited to be part of such a rewarding experience. But for our booking in Suffolk, even the prospect of being paid to *talk* isn't enough to stop me. Merely functionally drunk by the time we undertake our mid-afternoon set, in the Big Top tent at Latitude I can barely hold a thought in my head.

On the long ride home, once again I remind my friend that I'm sorry.

'Honestly, don't worry about it,' he tells me. 'You more or less held it together. Anyway, who am I to talk? I played a gig in Manchester where I was so trashed that the only thing I was able to say was, "My name is Frank Turner." I say "say" – I slurred it over and over again. I dropped my plectrum and it took me, like, five minutes to pick it up.'

From this, Frank learned a lesson I seem determined to ignore. After reports of my erratic behaviour during an interview make it back to base camp, the editor of *Kerrang!* invites me in for a chat. 'Is everything all right?' 'Sorry, I had a bit of a rough spell. I'm out of it now.' 'Okay. All right. But, listen, you can always talk to us, you know.' Instead, not long afterwards I answer the door to a furious features editor demanding to know the whereabouts of a missing cover story. Despite my insistence that it would be in his inbox five hours ago, by now the article is three days late. 'Mate, I swear, it'll be with you in the morning,' I tell him. Tragically, I actually believe this to be true. A portrait of fury and concern, my visitor is sweeping up the broken glass scattered across the kitchen floor. I'm naked from the waist down. My feet are cut. I can't say for sure, but it appears that the problem is not simply a matter of poor time management. After being given more than a dozen chances to redeem myself, my editors finally grow tired of cleaning up my mess. For the second time, I allow a dream job to disappear through the many cracks in my world.

Along with party packs of bourbon and cocaine, by now I'm taking a vast concoction of very cheap and virulently nasty legal highs sold from a basement shop on the Chalk Farm Road. Wrapped in brightly coloured sachets, each packet carries the warning that this is 'plant food not meant for human consumption'. I'm swallowing a variety of pills purchased from Dr Internet. Dispatched from India, the tablets are manufactured by a company that requests payment by money transfer from Western Union. GlaxoSmithKline they are not. Warning of the dangers of buying prescription medication online, I well recall seeing an advert at the pictures in which a young man extracts a dead rat from his own mouth. *What you order might not be what you get* was the gist. But even this grisly public service broadcast isn't enough to stop me.

With my head wreaking havoc with my circuitry, I think it's fair to say that my life is in danger. One spring afternoon I wake from a vivid dream in which I've been to hospital. Placed on a stretcher by a team of paramedics, beneath sunny skies I'm carried into the back of an ambulance. Needle in hand, a doctor at University College Hospital is required to cut a vertical line up the sleeve of my three-quarter-length navy blue Ben Sherman jacket. *Oh, doc, I love this coat.* On a gurney in a corridor, I close my eyes with something close to serenity. Coming to at home – *well, that was weird* – like a doomed character in a horror movie I discover the garment from my 'dream' has indeed been cut to the shoulder. I have no idea for how long I was in the care of the National Health Service. I couldn't tell you what procedures have been undertaken in my name. I don't recall how I got home. These scrapes of mine are fast becoming unmanageable.

By now I've attracted the attentions of a team of care workers, counsellors, therapists and psychoanalysts. On calm days I walk up to a mental health facility in Belsize Park; waiting to be called, I take my place in a waiting room populated by people for whom being terribly unwell is a full-time job. Me, I can cram a month's worth of damage into two or three days. If required, I can blow the doors off in a single afternoon. 'Ian, what do you think is *triggering* this behaviour?' I'm asked. 'With all due respect,' I say, 'the verb is only relevant in the sense that this fucking thing is like a bullet.' I appreciate the talk about trying to slow things down, about learning to spot the signs, but please believe me when I tell you that by now this thing is flying through the air at a velocity that cannot be seen by my naked eye. I think it wants to kill me.

It seems like I'm always in hospital. Driven to the edge of panic by a fellow patient screaming for hours on end, one night I flee from a ward at the Royal Free in Hampstead. Trying his best to stop me, a security guard tells me that the police will pick me up before I reach my front door. Fuck that, I'll take my chances. Still in my National Health Service pyjamas, clothes clutched to my chest, I board the last Overground train to Camden Road. I'm surprisingly light on my feet, all things considered. Until this morning I'd been under round-the-clock surveillance for three days in case I was killed by the toxins in my system. I couldn't walk without the assistance of a carer. After knocking back three-dozen bottles of spirits and many bindles of cocaine over the course of a nine-day bender, the bill for my actions was steeper than ever. Gruelling and apparently without end, the requirements of drying out for seventy-two hours constitute the lowest moments of my life. As if surfing the channels of an upended world, unable to piece together linear thought, my mind leaps erratically across a topography of unconnected moments. Scrunched under a thin blanket that somehow fails to cover even my own limited form, under these conditions I'm easy prey to the worst kind of desolation I've ever known. Panic is only ever a breath away. From a hospital bed at four o'clock in the morning, my situation seems hopeless. I just can't see a way out of this.

And then I go home. The police never came. Amid the glow of an equally disproportionate belief that everything has returned to normal, over the course of a few days I walk half a mile to the crisis team at St Pancras Hospital. Abutting the coroner's complex at which I visited my father, the people treated here are on the cusp of presenting a clear and present danger to themselves and to others. One step further and we're in the realm of 'involuntary commitment'. A section order; detention without trial. By now I'm no longer in anything like the state I was just three or four days earlier. Retelling my tale, not for the first time I'm told that my case is most unusual. 'I know,' I say. 'I wish it weren't.' 'So how do you feel today?' 'Honestly? I feel all right. I really do.' After four or five visits, I'm told that I no longer fit the criteria required to access the services of the crisis team. Not that it matters. I always come back for more.

One visit to the Royal Free lasts for a fortnight. A two-week holiday in a sixth-floor ward from which I am permitted no chance of escape, this time my circumstances are even more embarrassing than usual. With the Beast from the East blowing its hateful breath down from Haverstock Hill, every afternoon I receive a ward call from a kindly intermediary charged with escorting me over the bridge that spans the departments of physical and mental health. Each day my young visitor tells me that as yet he's been unable to secure lodgings at a halfway house in which I will stay for seven or ten nights before once more returning home. Up and across Camden and Islington, brand new patients are throwing themselves at police stations and hospitals; in states of mania, their need is greater than mine. 'Don't worry,' I say. 'I understand.' One of my many problems is the time-lag between my actions and their required response. As soon as I'm in the care of the professionals, I'm putting myself back together. We need to synchronise our watches, the system and me.

Up at the Royal Free, I'm surprised at just how quickly I acclimatise to days in which I do almost nothing. Curled up in bed, I watch the hockey from the Winter Olympics; after that, it's time for repeats of *Minder* and *The Sweeney*. With a longing that suggests I'm about to depart for a trip to paradise I await the arrival of the meals ordered each morning from a sheet of photocopied paper. Chilli con carne, chicken korma, tapioca, rice pudding. Emerging from a bewildering haze of transcontinental chatter, shortly after breakfast I'm visited by the ward sister. With kind but tired patience, she tells me that, fingers crossed, this might just be the day that I'm shipped out to the halfway house. There is a name for people like me. I am a bed-blocker. Responding with muted embarrassment, by now it's obvious that there is no longer anything immediately wrong with me. After fourteen barren nights, I'm dispatched home.

People are genuinely trying to help. Pulled taut like zip-wire, the component parts of the system do their best to prevent me from crashing to the floor. But, really, *I'm* the problem. I can't be stopped and I can't be controlled. After failing to appear for a gig at the Royal Albert Hall, my friend Dan bangs on the front door for fifteen minutes. *Just sit tight, he'll go away.* 'I'm not going away,' he shouts through the letter box. 'Ian, mate, what the *fuck* is going on?' Shaking and grey, once more I'm in an ambulance en route to hospital – this time UCL on the Euston Road. Arms outstretched, with passionate reasoning I'd tried my best to convince the medics that all was peachy. But with the flat looking as if it'd been upended by a poltergeist, they were having none of it. I'm told that if I don't go voluntarily I will be removed from my home by force. By now, I'm boring even myself. Certainly I'm beaten down. The thing about all this is, it's *exhausting*.

At University College Hospital I'm visited by a psychiatrist. Exhaling through his nose, the man by my side disagrees with my assessment that I should be sent home to begin yet another streak of unremarkable days. As permeable as Sheffield steel, he tells me that this week's misadventure is sufficiently serious as to require the direct intervention of the state. In his hands is a clipboard on which are written my by now impressive array of diagnoses. Once again, let's have a big hand for Post Traumatic Stress Disorder, Rapid Cycling Bipolar

Affective Disorder, Borderline Personality Disorder, Emotional Dysregulation Disorder and Impulse Control Disorder. *Chaos.* I think it's fair to say that some of these conditions are educated guesses made by an ever-increasing number of experts. Some are majority decisions. Today I find it unhelpful to spend too much time wondering how many of these assignations actually apply to me. But back then, though, something's clearly wrong. The liquids and powders with which I am poisoning myself to death are merely symptomatic.

Knowing this, the man by my bedside offers me a choice. Either I agree to a transfer to a psychiatric care institution, or else he'll seek a second opinion from one of his colleagues and I'll be going there anyway under a section order. Considering my options, suddenly I feel like Captain Yossarian in *Catch-22*. 'That's some catch, that Catch-22,' I'll tell him, to which the shrink will reply, 'It's the best there is.' Instead, I say, 'I mean, that's some pretty slim pickings.'

'I'm afraid so.'

A moment's silence. An express train from denial to acceptance.

'This isn't a negotiation, is it?'

'I'm afraid not.'

Sometimes I wonder if the locus for all this chaos was the *inquest* into my father's passing. It preyed on my mind more than the death itself. Its terrible spectre messed everything up. Under normal circumstances, the bereaved are able to use the funeral of a loved one as the point from which they repair their wounds as best they are able. But Eric's messy denouement required a verdict from the state as to what exactly happened on that busy day at the Holiday Inn. The prospect of giving evidence and answering questions under oath at St Pancras Coroner's Court more than three months later brought a constant hum of anxiety to my system. Like buzzing power lines, I couldn't shut it off. Turned out I was right to be worried, too; speaking in court, the coroner had no more of an idea than I did as to what caused Eric's death. It might have been the result of a drunken fall, he reasoned. Then again, the deceased's enlarged heart could have been the thing that turned an accident into a tragedy. Who could say? Just to be on the safe side, in closing I was told that 'the intervention of a third party cannot be ruled out, although this remains the least likely scenario'.

Come again? Given that I was both the last person to see Eric when he was alive and the one who found him dead, I am that third party. Even though the court thought it unlikely that I was guilty of patricide, nonetheless they were unwilling to rule it out. Rearing up in shock and anger, I did the one thing the law forbids – I addressed the coroner directly. '*No, I'm not having that*' – a look of alarm from the bench – '*this is unacceptable.*' When the official report reached me by post, the offending sentence had been removed.

From the inquest, I went to a place of comradeship and warmth. I went to *Kerrang!* As if on autopilot, I had ended up there on the Tuesday after Eric's death, too. With my bag packed for New York, I'd sat on the edge of a desk and ran through the details of my remarkable weekend. The people who worked in the office are my friends; even when the faces changed, the constancy of good eggs remained strikingly high. The magazine's headquarters was usually a place of music and laughter, and of a rugged strain of kindness; in so much as I felt safe anywhere, I felt it there. The words with which photographer Paul Harries sanctioned my entry into the fold eleven years earlier – 'welcome to the family' – still held true.

But change was on its way.

In an appointment that saw *Kerrang!* fall ill almost as fast as I did, James McMahon began his six-year tenure as editor on the same morning as Eric's inquest. Talk about a bad day. Starting as he meant to go on, within weeks our once confident and pristine periodical began to resemble a cut-and-shut job thrown together by a man determined to destroy precious things. Everyone in the music industry could tell we were in bad hands. Within and without, we all knew we were heading for the rocks. Thus far, without apology, entire pages of this book have been knowingly written as a love letter to *Kerrang!*. In this spirit, I have deliberately omitted occasions when corporate hooliganism made it difficult for its freelancers to enjoy their job of work. I've overlooked the barren spells, lasting many weeks, in which we didn't get paid. I've declined to tell the story of a time a group of senior photographers and writers – including Paul Harries and myself – took strike action to prevent the parent company from stealing our copyright (a struggle that echoed the travails of many musicians, no less). That this turmoil was the result of actions taken by people I'd never met means that these decisions have been taken in good conscience. The slights and insults had nothing to do with *Kerrang!* itself. But the appointment of McMahon to the editor's chair heralded a change in culture on *our shop floor* that led directly to the darkest and most shameful episode in the magazine's decades-long history. To overlook it would be dishonourable.

After a thirty-year period in which *Kerrang!* ran with the kind of efficiency normally seen only in Soviet propaganda films, chaos abounded. In what felt like a hostile takeover of a family firm, the air in the office turned dark and cruel; with broken spirits, dedicated workers with years of service began to leave in numbers that would have caused deep alarm in a company with fewer dysfunctions.

Interviewed for this book, my friend Eleanor Goodman, who served as production editor for part of this time, tells me that she 'knew going into that office was going to be really tough because I'd heard all about the problems in there', but did so anyway because 'I'd wanted to work at *Kerrang!* for years, since I was a teenager. It was my dream job.'

It was my dream job.

She goes on to say that 'the first week that I got there, a grown man was crying at his desk. I thought, "What is this?" I could just see immediately that everybody was suffering . . . It was a very toxic culture. I was only there for two and a half years, but it felt like much longer . . . It was really hard because I didn't have anyone who could help me change the situation. I felt that I was fighting by myself in trying to keep up morale. But every effort was thwarted.'

Through the years *Kerrang!* had fostered a matrilineal blood-line that included female editors, art directors, production editors, picture researchers, subeditors and more. In this context, the appointment of my friend Jennyfer Walker to a full-time position ought to have been the starting point for a rewarding career on a magazine renowned for gender equality. Certainly, I had no doubt that she was a bespoke fit for our unruly gang when, within an hour of making her acquaintance, I was informed that one of my recent cover features was 'boring'. *Oh aye, and who are you exactly?* Only problem was, the appearance of Jennyfer's name on the masthead coincided with *Kerrang!* becoming an unhealthy and dangerous place of work – particularly for young women.

Striking up a relationship with a colleague named Ryan Cooper, she was subjected to explosive and baseless bouts of jealousy. The decision to terminate the partnership heralded a deluge of texts calling her 'a little fucking slut', 'a lying little cunt', 'a fucking whore', 'a slag', 'a hypocritical fucking twat', and more. She received a message saying that '[I] hope you overdose on your fucking shitty [parac-etamol] tablets', and that 'I actually hope you die so I don't have to see your fucking face any more'. When she asked Cooper to stop sending her texts, he wrote, 'Fine, the next letter you do get from me will be my suicide note.' The barrage continued. 'Thanks for fucking up my life,' he said. Shortly afterwards he threatened 'to top myself tonight . . . then you'll be happy'. He told Jennyfer that 'you've made me do this'. Of what was never a very serious or particularly long-term relationship, he wrote, 'To think I ever loved you and wasted my life with you. Wish I knew you were a lying little cunt.'

After showing James McMahon the messages quoted above, Jennyfer was asked to decide whether or not the matter should be taken to Human Resources. It was explained to her that this course of action might result in her abuser losing his job. 'I thought it was terrible that they put the responsibility on me,' she tells me. 'My head was all over the place and I was struggling to even get through the day. They should have been looking after me, not forcing me to make life-changing decisions on someone else's behalf.' Concerned that Cooper might capitalise on his threats to commit suicide, Jennyfer declined to pursue the matter. She was signed off work. Taking pills prescribed to her by a doctor, in time she became addicted to Xanax. Obliged to share a workspace with her abuser, she underwent a course of therapy in which she learned to 'compartmentalise' her problems. She was blacking out in meetings. Commenting on how easy it would be to push her under a train, Ryan Cooper followed her to Tottenham Court Road station.

'Looking back, it was the most stressful period of my life,' she says. 'Not only was I dealing with the breakdown [of the relationship] but due to my now ex-boyfriend continuing his tirade of abuse at work it was affecting my dream job' – there's that phrase again: *dream job* – 'my career, and everything I'd worked for. I was taking prescription medication just so I could bear sitting two metres apart from him. I just found it impossible to get anything done. Not only did my bosses let me down by not protecting me from this workplace abuser, but they even made me feel like I was the villain in *his* story.'

In a continuing pattern of abuse, Cooper shifted his attention to a second young woman. Growing into his role as a dangerous man, he threatened to publish intimate photographs and to wait for her outside her home so he could 'hurt' her. When evidence of this harassment was discovered on emails from a work account, Eleanor Goodman alerted her superiors. In an email dated 20 February 2014 she wrote that, 'On a purely work-related level, we've had nothing but problems with Ryan for months ... Both [me] and the collective group have given him numerous warnings, numerous chances, and months of time to correct his unprofessional attitude towards his work ... it blatantly doesn't work. He doesn't respect his co-workers and just won't listen.'

Moving onto the matter of sexualised abuse and harassment, she wrote:

Firstly, on a simple level, the things he's doing are actually crimes. They're morally abhorrent, and they're the exact same things he did in the office [with Jennyfer Walker]. Secondly, he's been doing these things with the K! brand literally stamped all over them, which is pretty strongly in breach of our contractual requirements ... as a woman, this kind of morally bankrupt repulsive behaviour makes me feel literally sick. There's a difference between youthful and childish indiscretions and sustained, targeted sexual blackmail. We let it slide when it was one of our own because she 'got over it', ignoring a second occurrence of it is being complicit.

Ryan clearly needs help, he's clearly troubled, but none of these things are valid excuses. What he needs right now, is to know that treating his coworkers with contempt is not OK, and psychological abuse of women is not OK.

We pride ourselves on our inclusiveness, our gender equality – it's part of our brand identity. This behaviour has no place in the culture of K! and allowing it to persist is hypocrisy.

He's discrediting the brand, barely doing his job, and [is] a repeated harasser and I just don't want to entertain the idea of working with him any more.

'[Ryan Cooper] was doing to [the second woman] what he was doing to Jennyfer,' Eleanor tells me. 'He was psychologically abusing her. And I thought, 'This is disgusting. He's doing this again

. . . [I knew that] I didn't want to work with him. I didn't want to work with someone who behaves this way. But when I raised this concern, I was told that this was something to do with me being a woman. It had *nothing* to do with me being a woman. That has *nothing* to do with me not wanting to manage him. Whichever way you look at it, it's disgusting. It was horrible. I had to manage this person. I had to work with this person every day. I didn't want to be there. I didn't have the authority to fire him, and those who did weren't going to do so. But in any other workplace, this person would have been fired for what they did.'

Instead of being sacked, Ryan Cooper was given a promotion and a pay rise of four thousand pounds a year.

'That entire period was unimaginably toxic and miserable,' is how a long-time *Kerrang!* staff member (who has asked to remain anonymous) describes working under James McMahon. 'You never knew if you were coming or going. On one occasion, in front of everyone he called someone in the office "a rat-faced little shit". When someone [Eleanor Goodman] told him he couldn't speak to staff like that, his response was, "But look at him, he looks like a rat."

'He made me feel, and I'm not alone in this, absolutely crushed,' I'm told. 'Every day it felt like walking into somewhere in which there was no happiness, or even satisfaction, in getting things done. He would move the goalposts on everything constantly. Unable to get a job elsewhere, and with seemingly no chance of losing him, no matter how bad sales were or how appallingly he conducted himself, I honestly felt there was no escape and that I wouldn't live beyond thirty. I began taking anti-depressants to help with the fact that I would both fall asleep and wake up in floods of stressful tears every single day. But the situation was never ending. It was like putting on burn cream while you're still standing on a bonfire. Although I never found myself actually thinking about going and doing it, or planning it, for a significant time, maybe a year, I was worried that the only way out of it would be to take my own life.'

In 2017 Jennyfer Walker alleged that she was sexually assaulted by someone who still works at a major British rock festival. Despite being told repeatedly to stop, the man removed her bra in a backstage portacabin. 'Normally, in situations like that you have the response of either fight or flight,' she tells me, 'but I just froze.' Following the ordeal, she rode back on the team bus in tears to the hotel at which the *Kerrang!* contingent were staying. The next day she spoke about the assault to a friend in the industry, a woman, who persuaded her against speaking out on the grounds that 'no one would believe me'. Cowed by the imbalance of power between her and her assailant, she kept her counsel for five months.

On 28 November 2017 Jennyfer gave a statement to PC Steven Downes of Leicestershire Police Force. Believing the odds of securing a conviction were stacked against her, she decided against pressing charges. As well as background details about the accused, the document included the following information:

He grabbed me from behind, put his hands up the back of my top, and undid my bra . . . so forcibly that the clasp on the bra bent back and broke. Once my bra was undone, he reached his hands round to my front and started groping my bare boobs. I felt extremely uncomfortable and BEGGED him to do my bra back up. At that point I wish I had just turned round and smacked him in the face and run away, but I was so drunk and in shock that I didn't know what to do – my instincts completely failed me. I trusted him and thought he was my friend, and I also knew he had a long-term girlfriend, so I never thought he'd try and grope me. He's also about twenty-five or thirty years older than me, and I'd never given him ANY reason to think I liked him in that way, so was just in total shock that he would do such a thing.

Anyway, I kept asking him to 'please stop' and 'please do my bra back up because I hate my boobs being touched'. He did my bra back up eventually, and said, 'But you make me so horny' (it makes me feel sick to write that). He then grabbed my hand, and pushed it onto the crotch of his trousers, forcing me to feel his erect penis.

'I pulled my hand away, and that's when he grabbed my face and started shoving his tongue down my throat. It was extremely repulsive, and reminded me of Medusa, just forceful and aggressive and evil. I tried to pull away again, but he was too strong. I was too drunk and my reflexes just weren't working. I didn't even know what was happening, let alone how to get away from it. As I was trying to pull away I kept saying 'no, please stop' over and over. And I distinctly remember him pulling me back towards him and saying 'no, no, give me a kiss' and trying to shove his tongue down my throat some more. I suffer from anxiety and panic attacks, and the whole thing was SO traumatic . . .

While many people would vouch for his good character, I've had several friends I told about the assault say they thought he was creepy, and that they had seen him make inappropriate comments on social media to young women. He has done that to me before too, but I just passed it off as his 'humour' and I never really thought too much about it back then, as I thought he was a decent guy. I've also heard recently that he's made inappropriate comments to women in his company before, so at least some people have seen a tiny fragment of what he's like.

Anyway, I just wanted to report it to you, so you have it on record in case he does this again to another young woman.

As a result of her ordeal Jennyfer was diagnosed with post-traumatic stress disorder. Along with prescriptions for the tranquiliser Diazepam, in the care of the National Health Service she underwent therapy. In the *Kerrang!* office she was required to spend as many as sixty hours a week in the company of Ryan Cooper.

Seemingly unable to find any measure of redress, in any other year this might well have been the end of the matter. But this wasn't any other year. Responding to abuse at the hands of Harvey Weinstein, on 15 October 2017 the American actor Alyssa Milano wrote that 'if the women who have been sexually harassed or assaulted wrote "me too" as a status, we might give people a sense of the magnitude of the problem'. On Twitter James McMahon responded with the words, 'Men need to hold each other accountable for their actions.' Knowing all too well that he had declined to do any such thing – and had in fact *rewarded* a known serial predator with a promotion and a pay rise – Jennyfer Walker decided the time had come to break cover.

For a Facebook post that knocked fixtures and fittings from the walls of her corner of the music industry, on 19 October 2017 she composed a lengthy passage detailing every single relevant aspect of her experiences of years of abuse at *Kerrang!* About Ryan Cooper, she wrote of having 'heard some terrible rumours about him doing much worse than anything written here to another woman, and, if true, hopefully she finds the courage to go to the police. Yet he's never suffered the consequences of his abusive actions . . . and he's doing just fine in his career and social life. In fact, he has quite the social calendar.' (Not for much longer, he didn't. The revelations led to Cooper's exit from the music industry.) 'Let's learn from this abusive man-boy-child-thing,' she wrote, 'and hope this shit never happens again . . . I personally will NEVER be letting another abusive comment or action go unreported and unpunished again, and I hope others won't either.'

Her post (the first of two) ended with 'a small selection of the hundreds (maybe thousands) of texts he sent me as proof of my harassment'. Perhaps as a means of obviating the charge of taking quotes out of context, her own measured replies were also included. Notwithstanding the challenge of imagining the words 'I actually hope you die so I don't have to see your fucking face any more' being acceptable in *any* context, for me this was the most devastating aspect of Jennyfer's communiqués.

Days earlier, *Kerrang!* had at last got rid of James McMahon. Not before time, the workers in the office had staged a putsch that saw him on his way. Stepping into a new working environment on the morning after the first of her Facebook ground-to-air missiles, Jennyfer Walker was met with the support and commendation of the entire office. Twenty-four hours later, the woman who prompted Eleanor Goodman to write the email quoted above went public on social media with her own story of abuse at the hands of Ryan Cooper. The following day, a third person did the same. Between them the three women started a WhatsApp group to which other females in the music business were invited to submit their own experiences. From the troubling to the grievous, the submissions revealed the sexual trespass of miscreants and predators that lurked in many – indeed, surely in all – corners of the music industry. The roll of dishonour included performers, managers, booking agents, concert promoters and journalists. Reading and replying to these messages occupied every hour of Jennyfer's free time for three weeks.

I suspect that the dam has yet to burst from the pressure of all this stuff. Certainly in a historical sense, I am continually amazed that stories that already exist in the public sphere have not returned to cause havoc with the careers of wildly celebrated men. Lori Mattix claims she was fourteen when she first slept with David Bowie. Steven Tyler, the singer with Aerosmith, convinced the mother of sixteen-year-old Julia Holcomb to make him her daughter's legal guardian. Courtney Love claims to have performed oral sex on Ted Nugent when she was just twelve. In 1966 Marvin Gaye had an affair with his wife's fifteen-year-old niece. John Lennon was a wife-beater. Once again, the examples are picked at random. Such stories are everywhere.

The objectification of women under the male gaze of rock 'n' roll is a different book from this one. I am not person to write it. For readers who are interested, the endlessly consultable *Under My Thumb: Songs That Hate Women and the Women Who Love Them*, a collection of essays edited by Rhian E. Jones and Eli Davies, is a good place to start. But as the twenty-first century marches on, tales of sexual transgression, even of simple disrespect, are now being (at least) viewed in a different light. In 2020 Marilyn Manson put down the phone on my friend and colleague Dave Everley after being asked about rumours that he had mistreated women. Weeks later, the actor Evan Rachel Wood alleged that Manson had sexually abused her. Within days, the singer had been dropped by both his record label and management company. I could be wrong, but I don't imagine his career will ever recover from this.

'I can see why women didn't fancy being music journalists ten years ago because as a female writer you were put into very uncomfortable positions with male artists,' Eleanor Halls tells me. Eleanor is one of my youthful editors at the *Telegraph*. 'When I interviewed a well known rap crew, which was only two years ago – in fact, it wasn't even my interview, I was giving support to a friend who was interviewing them – there were, like, ten of them in a trailer with me and her and no one else; and it was really intimidating to have ten men being incredibly inappropriate and graphic. They weren't being physically intimidating but they were saying intimidating things. They were being hypersexual. The door was closed and they were all high, and that's just not a particularly nice environment for two people who are just trying to do their jobs and who don't really want to be told about the sexual urges of the people they're interviewing.'

I even have my own story of an unsolicited advance. In a taxicab in Paris, aged twenty-four, I was once given the impression that I was being measured up by a press agent more than fifteen years my senior. She was drunk, and (I think inadvertently) I was made to feel uncomfortable. In what was by any measure a fleeting moment, I pretended to be oblivious to what I still believe was unfolding beside me. Claiming to be exhausted from a day in which I'd spent an entire forty-five minutes asking questions of a professional musician, upon arriving at our hotel I politely declined the offer of a nightcap at the bar. The following morning at breakfast things were once more as they had been before drink had been taken the evening before. And that's it – that's all I've got. This is my one story of an unwanted approach from someone who, anyway, didn't intend to put me at unease. Writing this chapter has reminded me that when it comes to an entire section of people with whom I share column space, I live in a different world.

'After I posted my story and it went viral, I was inundated with messages from other women who'd also been through something,' Jennyfer Walker tells me. 'Their stories ranged from the trivial – a man saying something inappropriate to them, say – to the life-shattering, such as a woman who had been raped. It was men-tally draining to say the least. As woman after woman came forth with their tales of terror, I realised that pretty much *every* female I knew personally had been inappropriately touched or sexually assaulted. And barely any of them had spoken out about it before. We had all spent years brushing this behaviour off as 'no big deal'. It was just accepted that these things happen.

'To know that very few women in the industry had escaped abuse felt overwhelming, unsettling, and just *sad*,' she says. 'It was confus-ing, too. Why did this have to happen? Aren't women entitled to not be groped when they're just trying to do their job, or trying to enjoy a concert? Apparently not. Music was our safe space, and suddenly it looked like it wasn't actually safe at all.'

Over in north London, my problems are of my own making. On a sunny summer's day I am taken by an NHS driver from University

College Hospital to the Highgate Mental Health Centre. In a brightly lit reception area, a polite but firm orderly asks me to surrender my Gillette razor and the charging devices for my phone and laptop. *'Really?'* The residential ward to which I am being admitted can be entered (and exited) only by passing through two sets of double-doors that are always locked and monitored by CCTV. The sparse but somewhat functional single-occupancy room in which I will sleep stands at the far end of a short corridor along which a male nurse undertakes hourly patrols from midnight until 7 a.m. Tranquilised by Zopiclone, if I'm not asleep by the time his face appears at the round window at my bedroom door sometimes I smile and throw him a wave.

To my great surprise, I find that I'm able to make myself right at home up at Highgate. A hive of amiable inactivity, in here the real action takes place in the recreation room. Furnished with worn settees and a large television positioned behind a partially scratched pane of shatterproof glass, this violently lit communal space is the *de facto* living room for the facility's dozen or so inhabitants. They're a mixed bag of unpredictable personalities: at the time of my arrival I am one of only two patients not to have been sectioned by the state for a mandatory twenty-eight days. The other is Tom. Taller than a curtain rail, Tom is made nervous by *everything*. In a certain light his piercing intelligence allows him to recognise his illness as a ludicrous imposter. 'For God's sake, I mean, just look at the state of me,' he says. And then he laughs, and I laugh too. 'This too shall pass,' I tell him.

He and I are the only people in the joint who don't smoke. Rapidly fading out of fashion in the outside world, up at Highgate this once universal pastime remains all the rage. 'This is a Smoke-free Hospital' announces a sign outside, 'Please Do Not Smoke Anywhere in the Buildings or Grounds'. Similar warnings are affixed to the walls of every room. With passive-aggressive determination, even the toilet gives thanks to anyone declining to light up a gasper. 'Fine,' we might say. 'It's a stinking habit anyway.' But for the other residents of our happy home the urgency of such an injunction poses a Big Fucking Problem. Were we in a different kind of prison, one in which its occupants do not face the prospect of having their sentence doubled or trebled – or worse – without recourse to appeal, the inhalation of flammable materials would be permitted. But not in here. In here the business of inhaling a drug to which most are acutely addicted becomes the kind of palaver normally seen in an Ealing comedy.

Let's call it Operation Light 'Em Up. A complicated manoeuvre, OLEU requires a lookout, which for some reason tends to be me. Offering little in the way of actual recreation, the rec room features a door that leads to a courtyard so compact that even an estate agent would blush to call it 'cosy'. Attempting to neck a cigarette in a single drag, at any one time up to eighty per cent of the wing's inhabitants can be found in its far from fresh air. As their wall-eyed enabler I rather like the business of being a part of this communal illicit enterprise. As well as this, I don't much fancy discovering what some of my fellow detainees might be like if suddenly starved of nicotine. Loitering at the door to the main hallway, by means of epileptic semaphore I have only seconds in which to alert the haze of desperados to my left that a member of staff is heading their way. On my cue, like a troupe of badly drilled Morris dancers the transgressors extinguish half a packet of cigarettes at once. I sometimes wonder what might be the point of all this? The only sanction faced by any resident caught smoking is a telling off. That's it. For a second, third, fourth, or fifth infraction, it's still only a telling off. Really, you'd think that between us the jailors and captors could quietly agree that blind eyes will be turned to all but the most flagrant violations of this silly rule. Smoking in the shower, say. But apparently not. With hollow vigilance in the air, an unenviable portion of each day is spent worrying about when the next opportunity for a cigarette might arise.

'It's fucking ridiculous, is what it is.'

This is Alfie. Alf. Al. Able to recall mental institutions in much the same way that career criminals reminisce about prisons, when it comes to being incarcerated on account of being crazy this is hardly Alfred's first time at the rodeo. According to him, the Highgate Mental Health Centre is a four-star joint. He's seen worse, that he does know; that he *can* fucking tell me. His latest stay at a place on which he doesn't pay rent is the result of a noisy episode at his daughter's wedding. *What's it all about, Alfie?* Funny you should ask. There is, I notice, a measure of discrepancy regarding the seriousness of what went down on that sunny Saturday. Two doctors of psychiatry regard it as being a trespass worthy of incarceration. For his part, Al thinks of it as no big deal. Potato *potato*. Whenever the subject is broached, usually by me, a face that has seen a lifetime's worth of rain dissolves into a kind of serene neutrality.

'Ah, it don't matter,' he says.

Pulling himself back into focus, Alfie tells me that the world is due a giant disaster. (Actually, turns out he was right about that.) *A what now?* It's okay though, I'm not to worry, he knows a place down in Cornwall to which we can all retire until the whole nasty business has blown by.

'Right. Okay.'

'You don't believe me, do you?'

Careful. Diffusing a bomb. 'Um, I'm agnostic on the matter, Alfonso.'

'You'll see. You'll fucking see.'

Filling his lungs with smoke, Alfie throws a staccato nod in the direction of the young woman standing at a table placed against the wall of the rec room. 'That one's got some fucking problems,' he says. 'That I do know. That I can fucking tell you.'

'Mm.'

'Sophie there. See what she just did?'

A tall woman in her early twenties, Sophie is so alarmingly thin as to appear translucent. Floating through rooms like a trainee ghost, her physical aspect reminds me of lace at play in a springtime breeze. Usually friendly, mostly silent, sometimes vengeful, Sophie is hypnotised by food. As if it were a siren song that only she can hear, I see her look down at a cake left behind by a nervous visitor. In here, confected treats are a common and communal currency. With exquisite deliberation, an M&M adorning the icing is brought slowly up to, and into, her mouth. A beat later, once more it's in the open air. Regarded as if it were a blood diamond, with a downward glance this object of complicated beauty is secreted in the pocket of the dressing gown she wears at all times of the day. Pivoting on a bare foot, telling us that we're all full of shit, Sophie leaves the room like a scream.

Someone yawns.

'I shouldn't be reading this book,' says Tom. Silent and somehow invisible, he's spent the last hour drowning in a novel in which the characters' straits are even more dire than his own. A blurb on its front cover describes the text as 'laughter in the dark'. 'It's good, but, you know, I don't know if it's good *for me*.'

All human life is here. Late at night, I make pleasant conversation with Sid, the facility's oldest and kindliest resident. For someone who's spent all day listening to Alfie tell him (not without kindness) that the problems he has faced for most of his adult life can be remedied by him 'fucking pulling himself together', come the midnight hour Sid remains implacably placid. By the light of the late night movie, I see a man in the foothills of old age who knows that his race is surely run. Dressed smartly in comfortable trousers and a buttoned woollen cardigan, at the end of each afternoon Sid is visited by his eldest daughter. Driving up from her home in Cricklewood, sometimes she brings sweets for the house. 'Help yourselves,' she says. I mean, if only we could. With a tender touch, the child takes the hand of her father.

'It'll be all right, Dad,' she tells him. 'It really will.'

'I hope so, pet,' he says. 'I do hope so.'

A new morning sees the arrival of the latest pair of unfortunates. Bowing his head to avoid the frame of a door, Michel is a giant from the outskirts of Eindhoven. Psychotic tendencies on full display, within minutes even the staff are spooked by his presence. Adorned in last season's Charlton Athletic away kit, Alfie, too, is clearly goosed by the sudden and shocking change in temperature. This is a first. While some of the people at the Highgate Mental Health Centre are mithered by voices that no one else can discern, my guess is that Al hears only the theme tune from *Top Cat. He's the most tip top – du del de da – Top Cat!* Good tune, Alf, what's it called? *What are you? Stupid? It's called Alfie's Song. Write it down, Alfie's Song.* Okay. All right. But is it really, though? Is it still? Because I'm looking at you right now, Alfred, and I can see in your eyes that the volume has been suddenly and sharply reduced.

Move over for a damage case.

An hour later, with collar-length hair and biker-gang boots, in steps Ricky. *Ah, this is better, I know what you're all about.* Outside the mercury is pushing thirty-two degrees; as London schvitzes, Ricky cleaves to the uniform of the rocker, the roller, the right out of controller. Dressed in khaki combat trousers and a grey vest that could well stand a wash, on his back hangs a denim jacket adorned with patches bearing the vivid logos of a wide but limited array of loud bands. Because I cannot help myself, I calculate the point at which I will tell our newest arrival of my encounters with many of the performers on display. You never know, some of them might even remember my name.

'If you don't mind me asking, what are you in here for?'

A finger on a nostril. A theatrical sniff. A glug from an invisible bottle. 'Ah, you know, rock 'n' roll.'

Don't you worry about that, Ricky my son, I do indeed know. Believe you me, I've been falling for this for a *very* long time.

For no other reason than the group Gang Green once sang a couple of songs about Budweiser, as young teenagers my friends and I used to put away entire crates of the stuff. Between us we could neck twenty-four servings in about an hour. As seventeen-year-old winners of a local battle of the bands competition in Boston, Gang Green once thought it a good idea to spend their prize money on so much cocaine they were able to rack out the name of their own band. They even used the accompanying picture as the cover of their first single. Actually, do you know what? That is a pretty good idea. But today the group's members will surely be as unwedded to this moment as I am to something brazen that I might have done when I was that age. The only difference is that my youthful stupidity isn't known to strangers on a different continent. It hasn't been immortalised.

In photographs and articles, songs and stories, rock 'n' roll intemperance is afforded the illusion of permanence. At one remove, as listeners we're free to make ourselves at home on its foreign shores. We are at liberty to eulogise the wild excess of it all. If it pleases us, we can even take our own rides on the wild side. But in one way or another, the people who make the music will always move on. They don't stay here for ever, and neither should you. Because it never ends well.

'Thin Lizzy, eh?'

Ricky runs his fingers over the patch at the rear of his left shoulder. 'Fucking love 'em,' he says.

At a golf club in Richmond, Scott Gorham, the group's likeable American guitarist, once told me how he reached 'the point where you don't feel like playing . . . you're sitting on the side of the stage and you haven't had enough drugs and suddenly you're thinking, "I don't want to get up there and play. I'm not stoned enough. I don't want to do this." And when you realise you're saying this, then there's something really wrong. The whole thing has gone to shit.' I remember this day well. The club's reception area featured a painting of the Queen in oils on a large canvas. The only item on the noticeboard was a poster advertising a tour by Basil Brush. It was my birthday, and Gorham had bought me a pint. As our conversation drifted in the direction of sickness and syringes, the guitarist took stock of the other people in the room. Taking a drag of an electric cigarette, he motioned in the direction of a white double-door that was closed but not locked. 'Let's go in there,' he said. 'It'll be quieter.'

I also remember this. Standing outside a newsagent at the bus station in Barnsley, aged fourteen, I saw a billboard for the *Sheffield Star* on which were written the words 'Rock Star Taken to Hospital'. The star in question was Thin Lizzy's iconic frontman, Phil Lynott, who had but days left to live. Barely a fortnight earlier, for the first time in almost a year Scott Gorham had visited his friend at his house in Kew. By now a recovering heroin addict, the guitarist was worried that stepping once more into Lynott's determinedly excessive orbit might well be 'dangerous'. Probably it was. Seeking his friend's opinion on a batch of new songs he'd recorded in Los Angeles, he did so anyway.

'I arrived at eleven o' clock in the morning,' he told me. 'Phil answered the door dressed in a bathrobe, PJs and slippers. He was all puffed up. Because of his asthma, he could barely breathe. See, that's what happened; every time he took smack the asthma would come back at him with a vengeance.' Gorham remembers the phone ringing. Responding to its message, his friend exclaimed, 'Fucking great, that's fucking great.' In a stuffy golf club in suburban south-west London, these words are recounted in an uncannily impeccable rendition of the singer's Celtic baritone. Phil Lynott had been informed that he'd just beaten a drug rap. By way of celebration he filled a pint glass three quarters full with raw vodka. Necking the drink in a single slug, he helped himself to another. He then suggested that Gorham and drummer Brian Downey join him in revivifying their beloved Thin Lizzy, a band that had been dormant for three years.

'I'm looking at him thinking, "Are you kidding me?"' the guitarist told me. 'I'm there thinking, "You know what it takes to be out on the road, man, and you're never gonna make it out there in your condition." He must have seen the look I gave him, because then he said, "Oh, man, don't worry. I'm gonna get my shit together. I'm gonna get off of this crap, man." And he sounded so determined that I actually believed he was going to do it.'

According to Scott Gorham, Thin Lizzy began a serious relationship with heroin while recording the album *Black Rose: A Rock Legend* in Paris in 1979. The LP features the song 'Got to Give it Up', on which Phil Lynott announces 'junk don't get you far'. A superior and serious composition, it is surely one of many hundreds of tracks by a wide array of artists in which the topic of drug use sounds like a terrible idea. Without very much credit at all, I think that rock 'n' roll has covered itself rather well here. Phil Lynott, certainly, seemed wide awake to the danger in which he had placed his life. But it was no good. On 4 January 1986 one of the finest and purest songwriters of his generation died at Salisbury Infirmary of heart failure due to septicaemia and pneumonia. He was thirty-six.

'How about The Wildhearts?' Ricky wants to know. 'You like The Wildhearts?'

'Sure.'

'*Maximum* rock 'n' roll.'

So I tell him about that band, too. The first time I met Ginger Wildheart, the English quartet's richly talented principal songwriter, he was preparing to play to scores of thousands of people in Osaka and Tokyo. In the first city the temperature was so extremely hot that, mid-song, the frontman hallucinated that he was actually at home in his living room. As the group thundered their way through 'Caffeine Bomb', he looked to his left and wondered why one of his band-mates was at his front door, shining with sweat, with a guitar strapped around his waist. On the streets of Shibuya the next day the quartet insisted that I get a tattoo. Eventually able to persuade them that body art is really not my thing, I was struck by what seemed to me to be my hosts' communal instinct for living in only a single moment. Honestly, a tomcat has a clearer grasp of the consequences of its actions.

On good days, Ginger Wildheart is wonderful company. With a melodious accent from the banks of the Tyne, he is often ablaze with good humour. He's also the chief architect of many a destructive misadventure. Awaiting his presence in the lobby of the band's hotel in Osaka, I wondered what on earth was about to cross my path. After taking offence at something we'd written about them, just five years earlier The Wildhearts had used baseball bats to smash apart the *Kerrang!* office. I think it says rather a lot about the magazine that even this infraction didn't sour our relationship with the group. On the contrary, that's why I was in Japan. *Ping.* And there he was, the man himself, striding forth from the lift with a hungry-wolf smile and a musical 'hello' that spanned four bars. Imagine my confusion.

I often think back to a photograph the magazine once ran of him. With his right arm raised, the accompanying caption read 'Hands up if you've taken every drug in the world'. A recovering heroin and crack addict, certainly he's given it a go. The problem with this, though, is that too many people forget that this is the easy part. Anyone can do it. Much more difficult is the fluent and resplendent music that radiates from his core. Like Motörhead, The Wildhearts are the answer to a question posed by a visiting alien: 'Tell me, what is rock 'n' roll?' *Rock 'n' roll, you say? Well, um, it's* **this**.

'I used to love the Keith Richards stories of hedonism, and of Lemmy doing speed,' Ginger Wildheart tells me in an interview for this book. 'I used to look at bands and wonder what drugs they took. And if they looked like they didn't take drugs, probably I'd get bored of them. When I was young, that was part of the deal. That was the kind of band I wanted to be in, and [the] kind of person I ended up being. And I think the lucky thing about The Wildhearts is that we never got as famous or as successful as people consider we should have done. Because me and Danny would probably both be dead by now.'

Prior to rejoining the band for the third time, bassist Danny McCormack lost a leg. The accident occurred after the fifty-one-year-old severed his femoral artery injecting a cocktail of cocaine and amphetamines into his groin. Expedited to the Freeman Hospital in Newcastle, he watched as three of his toes turned black and fell off. Fearful of gangrene, surgeons amputated his left leg below the knee. Were it not for his wife's quick thinking, he would already be dead. 'She put a credit card over the hole and called an ambulance,' he told me in 2019. 'I'd injected there so often that [the groin] was like a sponge. They told me that in four minutes I would have died. The ambulance got there in three and a half minutes.'

These days Ginger Wildheart describes his group as 'the best band on seven legs'. He's quick with a joke, I'll give him that. Now aged fifty-seven, the singer's advancement towards the sunset of his middle years can sometimes gull me into believing that he'll be in business until the natural end of his life. But I don't know that he will be; people are around until, suddenly, they're not. With alarming regularity, on social media he writes about plummeting depression and, even, suicidal ideation. None of this is new. With The Wildhearts' world-beating debut album hovering into view, in 1993 I was dispatched to the lovely headquarters of East West Records, just off Kensington High Street, to get the skinny from the man who had written its songs. Seated around a glass table in a spacious boardroom, Danny McCormack and guitarist C. J. explained to me that Ginger hadn't been seen for days; neither man had any idea where he was, or when he might return. Fifteen years later, at the Forum in Kentish Town, I watched the band play one of the worst concerts I've ever seen. Reviewing the show, with some relish I administered the kind of admonishment that is used only in cases of emergency. What I didn't know was that Ginger Wildheart was in the grip of a terrible episode. Perhaps I should have done. It's not every night that a singer is helped offstage in the arms of his bandmates.

'I once went into a hospital for a week to find out what the fuck is wrong with me, and to be put on a ridiculous diet of pills and supervision,' he tells me. 'I remember that a friend of mine had hung himself, quite recently, and I became obsessed with what colour his face had gone as he was doing this. So I wrapped the drawstring of my pyjamas, which I shouldn't even have had, round my neck and tied it to the shower and then just watched my face go from red to purple. Tighter and tighter round my neck. Then the next thing I know I'm on a hospital bed and I'm going to be sectioned . . . it's happened a few times since then.'

Up at the Highgate Mental Health Centre, Ricky tells me that he *loves* The Wildhearts. At the sound of their name, he begins singing 'The Jackson Whites', in my estimation the quartet's finest song. *I feel the apocalypse is within my sight.*

'Tune.'

'*Fucking* tune.'

'They *are* a good group.'

'They just don't care, man.'

Here's something Ginger once told me. 'As a band The Wildhearts were destructive. And we were self-destructive. We were on an eternal mission of self-sabotage. And the destructive things we've done weren't really all that funny. It's not fun at all. I think we're a cautionary tale for young bands who want to take it to the limit.'

How best to put this? 'Ricky, you do know that one of them ended up in a mental institution, don't you? You know that *you're* in a mental institution, right?'

'Yeah, but I shouldn't really be in here. It's not like they've sectioned me or anything.'

They fucking should have done. 'As you wish.'

Actually, we're presently *away* from a mental institution. As the three members of the household not to have been involuntarily committed, it is determined that Tom, Ricky and myself should be allowed out for walks in the summer air of north London. On the afternoon of my final day at the Highgate Mental Health Centre, the three of us have each ponyed up three quid to stroll among the headstones of Highgate Cemetery. Later today, Tom is due a visit from a young woman who he hopes will one day be his wife. Ricky doesn't know who Karl Marx is. A fortnight earlier, none of us were aware of the others' existence. But yet here we are, united in a living arrangement that only a vanishingly small number of people will ever know.

Back at our digs, the three of us huddle over the latest bounty of sweet treats brought by Sid's eldest daughter. Unseen and unheard, Michel the menacing skyscraper glides into the room and blindsides Tom with a punch that puts him on the floor.

On separate occasions, I see my two friends just one more time. Sitting in the reception area of the Hoo centre up at Belsize Park, I catch sight of Tom. *Tom!* I remember him telling me that he hoped one day to experience the mental health service from the professional side of the great divide, and now he does. Good for him.

Like me, out in the wild Ricky is less fortunate. Both of us have more spin cycles to endure – perhaps a dozen for me, who knows how many for him. The last time we met, the signs weren't all that promising. Once again leaving the offices of the crisis team, I hear a voice roaring through the temperate autumn air.

'*Dude!*'

Who the fuck is this? I'm a rock journalist and even I don't know anyone who looks like that.

Um. 'Oh, hiya, Ricky.'

As I'm coming out, he's preparing to go in. Not five minutes ago a counsellor with whom I am on good terms had looked at the mad pattern of splodges on my record and asked what I thought was going on. 'I think that if this continues then I'm going to die, is what's going on,' I said. At this, he only nodded. Exhausted and afraid, emerging into the soft September day I wonder if it might be possible for me not to come back here again. Not next week, not next month, not ever. The two of me were having a pretty serious talk about that, I can tell you. *Do you reckon we might find a way to step slowly away from this ledge here? Nice and slow, like. What do you think? What do you say?*

Not quite yet. But soon.

I would like to be wrong, but I wouldn't lay odds on Ricky. For the first time in my life I've encountered someone to whom I will always be the more responsible adult. Feel free to have a think about that. Far from laughing in the face of danger, he doesn't even realise that danger exists. Bounding forwards, he tells me that he's got to report to the crisis team or else he'll be in trouble. But straight after that he's off to a weekend biker party in Suffolk at which there'll be 'coke and dope and booze and bitches'. With his words loitering in the air, straight away I understand that I've committed these four ingredients to memory. I wish he hadn't used that last word. I also know that his description would scan better were he to swap the order of the final two nouns.

'It's gonna be fucking great,' he tells me.

'Lively, I'd imagine.'

Fifteen seconds and ten yards later, I say his name for the final time.

'Dude, *what?*'

'Don't die.'

A smile at so much trifling nonsense. 'Ah, you know me,' he says.

Yes. Yes I do.

'Rock 'n' roll.'

9: TRIPLE STAGE DARKNESS

If you passed him on the streets of his adopted home city of Brighton, there's every chance you might no longer recognise Dunstan Bruce. But as one of the singers in the English anarchist punk collective Chumbawamba, he once captured the ears and the mood of a vast international audience. 'I get knocked down, but I get up again,' he sang. See, you *do* know him. Released in the summer of 1997, the song 'Tubthumping' sold more than six hundred thousand copies in the United Kingdom alone. Nestled in the top ten for eleven weeks, only Will Smith was able to keep it from the summit of the domestic singles chart. In the United States, the track's parent album, *Tubthumper*, found its way into the homes of more than three million listeners. That's triple platinum, that is. In the last quarter of a century, only one guitar-based LP from a British group – *A Rush of Blood to the Head* by Coldplay – has fared better at the American box office. And even then, not by much.

I know this because I wrote about it for the *Telegraph*. Already apprised of the story's wider details, digging deeper I was struck by a sense of genuine surprise. *Oh my God, I've only gone and found one. A band who played for high stakes and beat the system. I've **actually** found one.* For eighteen hectic months Chumbawamba rode the wildest ride in the theme park that is the music industry. When it at last screeched to a halt, they walked away without a scratch. Honestly, I've seen people *die* doing what they did. That they accomplished this feat with a *monster* of a song makes the story even sweeter. Far better than almost all of the brittle class-based anthems of the adjacent Britpop movement, these days I tend to think of 'Tubthumping' as being a companion piece to 'Common People' by Pulp. Save for one crucial difference, that is. While Jarvis Cocker's watertight study of an English obsession is told through the prism of a wealthy student at Central Saint Martins College of Art and Design in London, Chumbawamba allowed the 'lower orders' to sing their own song. It sounded magnificent.

'We had no concept of a song being a hit, or what that meant, or what success meant,' Dunstan Bruce tells me. 'What did success mean to us? It was funny to us, I suppose, because everyone hated Chumbawamba. The music press hated us. We were derided constantly . . . So we had thick skins. We had *really* thick skins. When we got told that ["Tubthumping"] was going to be a hit, we were, like, "Okay, sure, we'll be in the charts for one week and that'll be it." We never really understood the scale of what was about to happen to us. So we had no idea what to expect.'

If there's a more remarkable success story of the past twenty-five years, I honestly can't think of it. *Hang on – **what?** – Chumbawamba are in the charts? All over the world?* There's been some kind of mistake, surely. Formed in 1982, this was the kind of subversive group that took enormous pleasure in antagonising polite society. They did not want to live by its rules. Sharing a squat in Leeds, the eight members shared dole money and, sometimes, each other's bodies. They were known to the police. Throughout my teenage years I remember seeing their name on the bill of forthcoming attractions at the kind of venues at which a tetanus shot was administered at the door. Flattened in the slam pit at the Mermaid in Birmingham, or Counterpoint in Milton Keynes, it was always Chumbawamba who were due to play in the next week or two. 'What a strange name for a band,' I'd think. 'I wonder what they sound like.' Today I could find out in the time it takes me to reach the end of this sentence. Back then, the answer to my question cost at least a fiver. *What* *am I, made of money?* Reliably determined to knock out nine quid at Shades Records in London for shitty import albums by Circle Jerks and Dirty Rotten Imbeciles, Crumbsuckers and Crime, when it came to domestic players I remained resolutely sniffy. For this reason, Chumbawamba and I remained perfect strangers until the first time I heard them on the wireless. 'I get knocked down, but I get up again . . .' *What the fuck is this?*

Built like a tank, the band were an exception to the truism that all groups require at least one leader. By careful design, some members wrote music while others were responsible for the lyrics; those who played no part in the songwriting process had other jobs essential to the efficient running of a gigging band. In a manner both democratic and Unitarian, internal disputes were discarded in favour of presenting a truly united front. For this genuinely radical ideology, the group received nothing but brickbats. '[Chumbawamba are] a collection of . . . anarchist bores who have been banging on since shortly after the Peasants' Revolt about how if only people would listen to their records then we would bring down the global capitalist system,' was how the music writer Andrew Mueller described them. Almost without exception the 'respectable' end of the British music press *loathed* Chumbawamba. For this reason alone, I should have paid closer attention.

'We acted collectively and we policed each other as well,' Dunstan tells me. 'The band has always been a collective in which people have an equal say. I think that's why we were able to function through all this [success]. All eight members received exactly the same amount of money; no matter what your role was in the band, you got an eighth – or a tenth because of the managers' [cut]. Everybody got the same, so everybody's role was equally valued in the band . . . There was never anybody who was the songwriter, or who were the musicians. If you turned up at a meeting and you hadn't done what you said you were going to do, you kind of got into trouble.' He emits a laugh. 'You *were* in trouble. In the eighties that felt a bit Maoist, but in the nineties and in the early 2000s it just seemed like a very responsible way of working with a large group of people where everyone took equal ownership.'

At the end of an enjoyable hour in the company of Dunstan Bruce, I'm more persuaded than ever that the music industry was simply no match for Chumbawamba's internal structures. Better yet, the whole berserk thing seemed to happen by accident. Following a modest measure of success, by the middle years of the nineties the band appeared to be heading towards a future of steadily declining fortunes. Released in the autumn of 1995, the badly executed and poorly received *Swingin' with Raymond* LP peaked at number seventy on the British chart. Out on the road, the crowds were getting just that little bit smaller. To pay his way, Dunstan took flexible hours as a removals man. Trumpeter and co-vocalist Jude Abbott found work appearing as an extra on *Emmerdale*. Artful collectivists they may have been, but even Chumbawamba couldn't outfox the dreadful inertia of stalled momentum. Like a thousand other groups, this one appeared to be staring at two dismal options – disbandment, or incremental decay.

The band responded with a series of radical moves. After their record label One Little Indian rejected *Tubthumper* for being – yes, really – commercially unviable, for the first time Chumbawamba enlisted the services of a management team. Described by Dunstan as 'old industry types', Doug Smith and Eve Carr had in the past overseen the affairs of such groups as Girlschool and Motörhead. With the pair's help, 'Tubthumping' found its way onto the free CD attached to the weekly trade magazine the *Tip Sheet*, a publication read by every serious player in the industry. For the first time in their career Chumbawamba became the beneficiaries of the most priceless commodity in the business – *a buzz*. Sensing movement beneath their feet, out on the road the band were discovering that audiences were already taking a tumble for their brand new song. At the end of shows, perfect strangers were telling them that 'Tubthumping' should be their next single. In the corridors of power, others agreed. Courted by 'five or six' labels, after an age of internal deliberation the group eventually signed with Republic/Universal in the United States, and with the German arm of EMI for the rest of the world.

Straight away there was bother. In the nineties, any underground punk group who signed to a major label were guaranteed a mountain of grief from people in the scene keen to enforce an occasionally creditable moral code. To this end, even bands who at the time were no more ideological than a charcoal briquette – Green Day, for example – felt the heat. But Chumbawamba *were* ideological. Always up for a scrap, in 1989 the group had contributed a version of 'Heartbreak Hotel' to a compilation album called *Fuck EMI*. Yet here they were, barely seven years later, aligning themselves to the company's cause. *I tell you it was all a frame.* In defence of their decision to sign with a label that had once released 'Anarchy in the UK' by the Sex Pistols, the octet explained that by 1997 Electric and Musical Industries had at least divested itself of its links to the arms trade.

'It just seemed so hypocritical that we would sign to EMI,' Dunstan tells me. 'But we were at a point in the band's trajectory where if we didn't do something different then we might have been finished. We were bored. We had to take a risk. We had to take a leap of faith. We had to do something different.'

It was the kind of head-scratcher with which vegan revolutionaries have long tussled – ideological purity versus influence and power. For what it's worth, I tend to regard Chumbawamba's decision to test the waters of the corporate music industry as being something close to an experiment – almost an instillation, actually. In various ways, the group had spent more than a decade pressing against the boundaries of genre and presentation.

Witty and fearless, they'd invested a great deal of energy perfecting the declining art of getting up people's noses. In a stab at the Band Aid charity single 'Do They Know it's Christmas?', in 1986 they titled their debut album *Pictures of Starving Children Sell Records*. As the fictional outfit The Middle, the group wrangled an invitation to play at the birthday party of former Liberal Democrat leader David Steel. For their most startling caper, Chumbawamba even went so far as to repurpose a photograph of a young woman who had died from drinking excessive quantities of water after taking ecstasy. In its original form the poster of teenager Leah Betts lying in a hospital bed beneath the word 'sorted' became the centrepiece of a widespread anti-drug campaign. Spying alarmism in the public square, the band subverted the message by changing the word to 'distorted'. Beat that for bold.

Backed by their two major labels, the band went to work. Deciding that 'if we're going to do this, we're going to do it properly', Chumbawamba appeared on *Top of the Pops*, at a Radio 1 Roadshow, on *TFI Friday*, on TV programmes in the United States hosted by Jay Leno, the Wayan brothers, Rosie O'Donnell, Barbara Walters and many dozens more. Dunstan recalls that, 'We did plenty of stuff where you travel halfway across the world to mime to ["Tubthumping"] because EMI Japan want you to be on this quiz programme . . . and then the next day you fly to an island off the coast of Italy to do the song again.' The band undertook these tasks without being fully housetrained. On American TV they voiced their support for the death row prisoner Mumia Abu-Jamal. In Germany, singer Danbert Nobacon interrupted a television appearance from the Smashing Pumpkins by dancing across their stage naked with the word 'PUNK' scrawled across his chest. Performing 'Tubthumping' at the Brit Awards in 1998, Dunstan added the lines 'New Labour sold out the dockers, just like they sold out the rest of us'. Aggrieved that deputy prime minister and fellow attendee

John Prescott had declined to come to the aid of striking workers at the Mersey Docks and Harbour Company in Liverpool, towards the end of the drunken night vocalist Alice Nutter and Nobacon poured the dregs of a champagne bucket over his head. With this, Chumbawamba were able to put to bed quietly nagging concerns that their time in the spotlight had been just that little bit too well behaved. For his troubles Nobacon was placed under arrest.

'We loved the fact that we were in the belly of the beast,' Dunstan tells me. 'We loved the fact that we were now in a position where we had a voice. We were suddenly visible.' Following the fracas at the Brits the writer David Quantick criticised the group for attacking one of the government's few authentically working class politicians. 'If we'd have had that platform for fifteen years under Thatcher we would have done stuff about her,' Dunstan says. Caitlin Moran complained that Chumbawamba were 'not very good pop stars and they're not very good political activists, either'. Again, wrong. Alice Nutter's refusal to condemn shoplifting on the US television pro-gramme *Politically Incorrect* was the talk of a very good pop star indeed. (As well as this, in provoking a horrified reaction from host Bill Maher, the group's de facto spokesperson ably demonstrated that a smugly self-aggrandising name was not enough to save the show from being as uptight as any other.) By donating a hundred thousand dollars to the anti-corporate lobbying groups Indymedia and CorpWatch, Chumbawamba partook in activism that was both very good *and* rather expensive.

Asked if he enjoyed his time in the music industry's VIP sec-tion, Dunstan tells me that, 'I suppose the unsatisfactory answer is yes and no. Yes, the adventure was incredible. We did things we would never have done. We went to places that we would never have gone to. We travelled in comfort and we were well looked after. We were able to do things with the money that allowed us to make the kind of impact that we were never able to make before.'

But. 'But I suppose the other side of the coin was . . .' – and here Dunstan pauses, another performer snake-bitten by the extraordinary yet legitimate complaints about a job in the music industry – 'I'm really wary of complaining about what happened. What we do doesn't compare to . . .'

'Filleting chickens for a living?'

'Yeah, filleting chickens for a living. It just doesn't compare to that. But there is an aspect to it that is fucking exhausting. And there's an aspect to it where it's really fucking boring, too; where you're sitting around for hours to talk to some idiot on a pop programme and answer stupid questions about irrelevant things. You've got to find a way to turn that round to make it interesting so that there's a point to what you're doing.'

Chumbawamba were seduced by fame for about ten minutes. After getting perhaps a little bit too chummy with cocaine, Dunstan was called to account by other members in the group. Seeking to replicate the success of 'Tubthumping', the band recorded a calculated and somewhat dreadful song ('Top of the World (Ole, Ole, Ole)') that knocked on the door of the UK top twenty. But that's where it stopped. In preparing to record the successor to *Tubthumper* the decision was taken to junk demos on which they had tried too hard to replicate what, anyway, had been an accidental success. Bruce tells me that the question of whether or not the group deliberately handed EMI and Republic an unmarketable album remains a topic of live debate. For his part, the singer believes the decision to spike their own guns *was* deliberate. Either way, with a complete absence of potential hit singles, *WYSIWYG (What You See is What You Get)* remains one of the most gloriously perverse reactions to mainstream success I've ever heard.

'So this is how I think about that album,' Dunstan tells me. 'Imagine if in 1998 Eminem, an American, had come over to the UK, had had an enormous hit, toured the UK for a year, was on every TV programme you can imagine, and then his next album was a cultural and social critique of the UK, which he then released telling *us* what our country was like and what he thought of it. Of course people would be absolutely appalled. *Who the fuck does he think he is? Coming over here writing an album about our country.* But that's what we did. We spent eighteen months in the US and then we wrote an album about what a pile of shit it was. So *of course* it didn't sell. *Of course* it didn't. And what's weird about that is that we *loved* it in the States. I still go there whenever I can, and I *love* it over there.'

In a reversal of fortunes that would destroy most bands, in the United States *WYSIWYG* sold a blush over twenty thousand copies. Recognising a commercial dud when they heard one, EMI and Republic told the group not to worry because 'we're in this for the long haul'. That's what labels always say, and rarely mean. In truth, both parties surely knew that it was over. The fame belonged to 'Tubthumping' rather than the band that had written it; for all their subversive intentions, the song's likeable creators had merely squatted on its coveted real estate. Over the course of eighteen months in the glare of a piercing spotlight, Chumbawamba failed to attract *any* committed supporters to their cause. Not just this, as their profile fell the band discovered that their audience was actually *smaller* than it had been before. Remembering this, Dunstan Bruce's voice ripples with several notes of genial disbelief. 'Both [EMI and Republic] eventually sort of lost interest and it sort of petered out,' he tells me.

For once, though, there was more to it than this. In a vanishingly rare example of a mutually beneficial arrangement, the band themselves had had quite enough of being strapped to a rocket. 'We were in our mid-thirties when all this happened,' says the singer. 'And obviously there's both men and women in Chumbawamba. [Vocalist] Lou [Watts] and Alice [Nutter] in particular were at a point in their lives where they wanted to have kids. Obviously, also, we made money; we'd never had anything like that sort of money before at any point in our lives. So this was the point at which people thought, "Well, if we're going to start families, if people are going to buy houses . . ." All that day-to-day domestic real life stuff, in a way people had to do it then.'

Less than an hour after leaving my virtual meeting with Dunstan Bruce, during an episode of *Doctors* there occurred a fleeting moment of such sparkling serendipity that it would have me expelled from the National Union of Journalists were it not actually true. As two speaking actors wrestled with the kind of problem that can be remedied in barely half an hour, several noisy extras walked across the screen. For reasons I didn't quite grasp, the group were singing and shouting the chorus of a song that remains universally known almost a quarter of a century after it was first released. *I get knocked down, but I get up again . . .*

As he promised he would, Dunstan sends me a link to a working cut of a film he's been making for the past five years. Directed by Sophie Robinson, *I Get Knocked Down* retells and reframes the astonishing period in musical history during which an anarchist punk collective from the West Riding of Yorkshire briefly dined above the salt *all over the world*. My favourite moment is the sight of the reunited members of Chumbawamba cheering their younger selves on television as Ben Elton introduces them onstage at the Brit Awards. Elsewhere, the tone is less certain. In a clever device, at various points Dunstan is haunted by a human manifestation of the garish character that adorns *Tubthumper*'s front sleeve. 'You're nothing without me,' it says. 'You're fucking nothing.' But this isn't true. In the picture's closing scene, at last the taunting imposter is silenced for good.

'I'm really, really glad that we had the opportunity we did with "Tubthumping",' Dunstan tells me. 'That song has never been an albatross to me. It was a key to open the door. It was always something that we tried to use intelligently, I thought: to say stuff about things that really mattered to us . . . I remember doing interviews and saying that how we judge success is that "Tubthumping" appeared in the Rovers Return, in the Queen Vic, and that Homer Simpson sung it. To me, and to us, what could be better than that? That's rock royalty, that is, having Homer Simpson singing your song.'

In an artfully provocative article for the New York arts paper the *Village Voice*, in December 1979 the music critic Greil Marcus evaluated a list of recent rock 'n' roll casualties from the preceding ten years. Featuring a hundred and sixteen names, 'Rock Deaths in the 1970s: A Sweepstakes' asked the question: '[Since] necrophagy in rock is a tradition at least as honorable as that of the . . . greatest hits album . . . do not the dead deserve an accounting at least as irreproachable as the survivors receive with each week's edition of *Billboard*?' Allotting points for 'Past Contribution [to music]', 'Future Contribution' and 'Manner of Death', Ronnie Van Zant from Lynyrd Skynyrd (plane crash) and Jimi Hendrix (inhalation of vomit after use of sedatives, complicated by poor medical treatment) emerged as the two people with the joint highest score. The dead pool also included, among others, Gram Parsons (drugs), Keith Moon (accidental overdose of sedatives), Phil Ochs (suicide by hanging) and Terry Kath (Russian roulette). 'It shows no disrespect to those who have gone, then, to give ourselves a little pat on the back by having outlasted them; by doing so, we help keep them dead,' Marcus wrote.

In dying three years shy of his thirtieth birthday Jimi Hendrix also warrants membership in the '27 Club'. With an alumni that includes Brian Jones, Janis Joplin, Jim Morrison, Kurt Cobain, Amy Winehouse, Fredo Santana and sixty others, this hardly select gathering of musicians and performers is reckoned by a number of amateur academics to represent the age at which an artist is most likely to die of unnatural causes. I'm thankful to Jeordie Shenton, a genuine academic who is currently undertaking a Ph.D. at Goldsmith's University in substance abuse among working musicians, for providing me with this information. Over the course of two interviews, Jeordie's revelation that the veracity of 'the 27 Club has been empirically disqualified' is just about the only thing I could have figured out for myself. Obviously, it's bobbins. From a field of many thousands, it hardly seems anomalous that a number of people passed away at such a young age.

What does strike my layperson's eye as being remarkable is the markedly high number of cases in which the cause of death was the result of the misuse of drugs and alcohol. Suicide is also prevalent. Reviewing the killing fields, it's difficult to imagine, I don't know, children's television entertainers or radio presenters tapping out in this manner without a chorus line rightly deducing that the pattern is in no way normal. But in the arena of popular music, once again fatalities of this kind are factored in to the cost of doing business.

'There's no other industry like it,' Jeordie tells me. 'You just don't get this as much in the film industry. Heath Ledger and Brittany Murphy are exceptions. But in terms of substance-related deaths and suicide, the music industry is shocking. It's *shocking*. It's almost like you've got people who are attracted to the music industry who may be vulnerable to substance abuse, and then you've got the industry itself which *produces* substance abuse through socialisation. So it's a double-edged sword . . . I believe all work environments are the product of the characteristics of the people who lean towards that environment. Because musicians can be vulnerable individuals, in time the industry itself becomes vulnerable. People who may not be vulnerable [at the start of their career] end up being vulnerable.'

In time the industry itself becomes vulnerable. In an unprompted burst of statistical assistance, my studious new friend emails me a series of academic studies that make for startling reading. In 2011 Wolkewitz, et al., discovered that 'the risk of death for musicians in their twenties and thirties was two to three times higher than the UK general population'. The following year Bellis, et al., revealed that 'musicians [of all ages] experienced up to 1.7 times greater mortality compared to demographically matched UK and US general population. Of the deceased musicians, 38.7% died from substance abuse (i.e. drug or alcohol related chronic disorder, overdose or other accidents) or risk-related causes (i.e. suicide or homicide).' In 2016 Kenny and Asher, et al., discovered that 'musicians had a mortality rate twice as high as the US general population across each age group and experienced excess deaths from unnatural (i.e. accident, suicide or homicide) and liver disease . . . country, metal or rock [deaths were] associated with excess accidents, suicides and liver disease.' In an echo of the words quoted in the paragraph above, in 2017 Jeordie Shenton himself wrote that 'musicians' expected involvement in risky, impulsive and self-destructive behaviours increases with occupational stress . . . It can be argued that musicians' engagement in risky, impulsive and self-destructive behaviours is used for coping strategies, and thus their expected involvement increases with occupational stress.'

'Some people have said that [music] should be like elite sports, where if someone is using drugs then maybe they should be kicked out,' Jeordie tells me. 'Well, obviously *that's* not going to work. *A lot* of music has been based around drugs. 'The Reefer Man' ['Have You Ever Met That Funny Reefer Man'] by Cab Calloway was recorded in the thirties. So I don't think we can remove drugs from music. You're just not going to get rid of it. But what does need to change in the industry is [that] when you have musicians who have serious addiction problems, they get the support that they need. Because there's just been too many casualties where we've all just gone, "Wow, how did *they* not get the support that they *obviously* needed?" So that's one of the things that needs to happen. But I can't envision a world where music and drugs are wholly divorced.'

I wish I had shares in Zoom. On a dim afternoon in the thick of a hopeless winter, Jeordie Shenton and I strike up our band in no time at all. Speaking from an address in Suffolk at which Brian Eno once lived, my interviewee appears in the foreground of a room adorned with books and skulls. In case I'm not quite catching the drift, he's wearing a Rammstein t-shirt. It's funny, but for years entire swathes of the arts press thought it acceptable to believe, and to *say* they believed, that people who liked loud music were daft. In 2005 I spent an unhappy year at the *New Musical Express*, in whose pages a review of a heavy album made mention of 'the easily mugged *Kerrang!* crowd'. 'Oh, really?' I thought. 'So that's how it is, is it?'

Well, no, actually. Two years later, a study by the National Academy for Gifted and Talented Youth (a body of 120,000 students representing the top five per cent of academic achievement) nominated metal as the students' favourite kind of music. In making sure that I hadn't dreamed this, Yahoo! informed me that I'd once composed an article about it for the *Guardian* (rather badly, as it goes). Jeordie Shenton made himself known to me by tweeting an article from 2018 that I *do* remember writing. He'd done so as a means of providing evidence that sometimes even the most degenerate drug users can turn things around. In it, Al Jourgensen, the singer and bandleader with the Chicagoan industrial rock group Ministry, said that, 'I no longer take hard drugs, but I certainly did my time with them. I'd shoot heroin, smoke crack, take methadone – and none of those things are very smart, you know?'

Looking back over the piece, the circumstances of the interview drifted back into focus. Taking a timeout from the tumult of London, I was up in the box room of my mum's home near Barnsley town centre. On the far end of the line, Al Jourgensen was somewhere in Germany. He didn't know where, exactly, but it was backstage at yet another 'sausage fest' on that summer's European festival circuit. 'It's pretty rough,' he told me. At least he could be assured that it was as nothing when compared to the travails of his turbulent past.

A touring musician with a habit is plunged into a world of tenuous 'connections', anxious hustle and the very real threat of being required to perform while in the throes of withdrawal. On the line from Germany, Jourgensen told me that, 'Taking as many drugs as I did is dangerous. I realised that if I wanted to end up killing myself, this was probably the way to do it. I'd been taking heroin for fifteen years, which is long enough, you know. I just realised that the time had come to clean myself up. I'd been in too many scrapes, and too many bad situations, and it was time for a change.'

The first time I met Al Jourgensen, in London, apropos of very little he gave me a four hundred and fifty dollar professional Chicago Blackhawks ice hockey jersey – number 55, Sergei Krivokrasov – that I still have. As befits the leader of a group who once released an album called *Dark Side of the Spoon* (on a major label, no less), the well-upholstered garment, several sizes too large, features a variety of suspicious looking burns on the sleeves and on the lower half of its midriff. Prior to our interview, my lovably psychotic features editor had told me to 'stay with Al all night. Hopefully you'll end up in a crack den.' Instead, we went for a curry. Bracing myself, I asked if he was able to confirm the story that he'd had a toe amputated following a mishap with a syringe. Swear to God, he was halfway to removing his socks before I'd even finished framing the question. Entirely smitten, I thought him the most likeable outlaw I'd ever met.

Things are not always so enjoyable. Sitting in a dimly lit dressing room at the lovely Riviera Theatre in Chicago, I was once surprised to have my interview with Slash and Duff McKagan, from Velvet

Revolver, interrupted by a brief appearance from singer Scott Weiland. I use the word surprised because I'd already been told at least five times that my encounter with the group would not, repeat not, feature a contribution from Weiland himself. *All right, fine, I get it.* Given the frontman's turbulent history of drug misuse and arrest, this wasn't quite the surprise it might otherwise have been. It wasn't all that much of a sanction either. Far from the most famous member of what others were already calling a 'supergroup', his absence from my story could be employed as a dramatic device. It was something with which I could have a bit of fun, even. Seeing my tentative smile, at the Riviera Weiland extended the fore and middle fingers of his right hand. *Boof.* Bringing the extended digits up to the gentle gradient of a sly grin, he mimed the action of blowing away smoke from the barrel of a gun.

In the early years of the twenty-first century, Duff McKagan saved Scott Weiland's life by taking him to a cabin high in the Cascade mountain range in Washington State. 'Me and Scott went through so much,' McKagan told me in 2019. 'I shot him in the ass to wean him off heroin. I personally did that – for a month. He got his family back; he had his victory. He came to me for help 'cos he wanted to get sober the way I got sober. I was, like, "Okay, then we're going. It's gonna be a tough month but we'll get through it."'

The success was somewhat short-lived. By the time Scott Weiland did agree to speak with me he was back on the booze. Promoting Velvet Revolver's second album, *Libertad*, from 2007, at the Mandarin Hotel in Knightsbridge, I asked him why he was drinking a bottle of Stella Artois. *It's fine*, he told me, *it's just a beer.* Indiscreet and charismatic, I remember liking him much more than I did in Chicago. All the same, it didn't take a behavioural scientist to see that he was headed for trouble. On the road in the United States with his band the Wildabouts, on 3 December 2015 the singer was found dead aboard a tour bus in Bloomington, Minnesota. As well as cocaine and what is believed to be marijuana, police found pre-scription medication including Xanax, Buprenorphine, Ziprasidone, Viagra and sleeping pills. A medical examiner later determined that the forty-eight-year-old's death was the result of an accidental over-dose of cocaine, alcohol and methylenedioxyamphetamine (MDA). The report also noted the presence of atherosclerotic cardiovascular disease, a history of asthma and decades of substance abuse.

Four years later, at the London headquarters of Universal Music in King's Cross, Duff McKagan told me that he was '. . . still wres-tling with Scott's death. I've lost so many friends,' he said. 'But with this one I was struggling with survivor's guilt, I guess you'd call it. Once he went back to drugs, the game was up. "You go back to drugs, you're gonna die" – I told him that. I said, "You know where this is gonna go, Scott." But he said, "No, no, man, I got this." And then he was gone. I've got to be honest, I didn't know where to place that in my life.'

I've lost so many friends. Duff McKagan once shared a flight with Kurt Cobain and a stage with Chris Cornell. Talk about tower-ing company. In March 1992, a deliberately low-key concert by Cornell's band Soundgarden at the Underworld, in Camden Town, was the first concert I ever attended as a music journalist. The look of serene absorption on the singer's face told me that I was watching an entire genre of music change for the better. Out went pop music played (slightly) loud by guys who looked like porn actresses, and in came something heavier, smarter and darker. Decades later, I spoke to Cornell in person for the first and only time. Vaguely concerned that I was about to be granted an audience with a man who might just be as impenetrably intense as some of his songs, instead I found him to be playful company. In a rare breach of protocol, I asked that he sign the front sleeve of an album I'd cherished for more than twenty-five years. He even drew me a little doodle. 'Blimey,' I thought, 'what a very lovely man.' Two years later, he killed himself.

Like a hundred others, Cornell told me he was in recovery. It was heavy booze that was doing for him, he explained, whereas, 'Drugs for me were never the key thing. They were towards the end of [my alcoholism] but they were never the first thing. If I woke up in the morning with a terrible hangover – maybe with a show to do – then drugs were a way of getting me through that hangover. But for me it was primarily about the drink. Although having said that, there is a high level of self-deception that goes along with people who take a lot of drugs or who drink to excess . . . I didn't consider myself to be part of that group [of people such as Kurt Cobain and Layne Staley]. That's what I mean by self-deception. But at the same time, I didn't give a shit. Alcohol is a depressant, so of course I got depressed. I understood that. But meth and heroin, I knew what that was, too, and I also knew that the result of those drugs was that people would die. Drinking, I thought, was different.'

Duff McKagan remembers Chris Cornell from the time their wives were pregnant with their respective daughters. In the wake of the singer's passing, a well-judged moment in Guns N' Roses' live set from 2017 saw the group play a version of the Soundgarden song 'Black Hole Sun'. *No one sings like you anymore.* Two years later, McKagan memorialised Cornell and Scott Weiland on the song 'Feel', from his solo album *Tenderness.* 'When the lights go down . . . all you hold dear remains,' he sang. In London he told me, 'I knew that Chris struggled with depression and stuff, and I hate that he's gone. But he's also still here. The fact that we're talking about him means that he's still here.'

Maybe. On record and film, the dead can appear piercingly alive. At times they can even seem omnipresent. Late at night, Sky Documentaries regularly airs the feature *Cobain: Montage Of Heck,* on which the singer's daughter, Frances Bean Cobain, is credited as executive producer. Following the picture's release in 2015 Ms Cobain, then aged twenty-three, noted that over the course of the film's second half (during which its subject's descent into drug addiction and despair is minutely itemised) she came to hate her father. I'm not surprised. Barely two when he committed suicide, she has no personal memories of a man about whom many millions of people have an opinion.

A year after Nirvana unveiled *Nevermind*, out of nowhere Stone Temple Pilots sold more than eight million copies of their debut album *Core*. Twenty-one years later, following the death of original singer Scott Weiland, the San Diegan group recruited Chester Bennington to be their frontman. As the vocalist with Linkin Park, in 2001 Bennington exploded onto the scene with *Hybrid Theory*, an LP that found its way into the bedrooms of twenty million listeners. In what today seems like a bizarrely prophetic dead pool, in 2017 he too ended his own life. Despite telling the readers of *Kerrang!* that 'I have a lot of bad neighbourhoods in my head', the tragedy was met with evident astonishment. Was anyone really paying attention?

Prior to the release of Linkin Park's second album, *Meteora* from 2003, I interviewed Bennington in Hamburg. Thirty-six hours earlier I'd been in California; by the time I got to Germany I was so bushed that I took a nap on the sticky floor of the venue in which the group had just performed. In the presence of my Dictaphone, the following day I remember being somewhat put out that Linkin Park were not as forthcoming as I believed they should have been. Or maybe I was merely *looking* for an excuse to be put out – back then, sometimes I could be like that. I realise now that it hadn't occurred to me that the group might just be wary of yet another insistent stranger waiting in line for a piece of the action. One of the most startling things about becoming a hot property is that suddenly everybody wants a slice of you. Everyone has an angle. Courting exposure, record companies aren't minded to discuss with their signatories the shock of transitioning from being ignored to obsessed over in an instant. The next time we met – in Concord,

California, in 2014 – Chester Bennington was much better at this part of his job. It's almost possible that I was better at mine, too. Riding back over the Bay Bridge to my hotel in San Francisco, I commented to the band's PR how the singer seemed much happier than I'd imagined he would be. Evidently not.

The figures are shocking. A report in 2018 by the Canadian East Coast Music Association revealed that twenty per cent of surveyed musicians had contemplated suicide in the month that they were consulted. Twenty-six per cent had attempted to kill themselves at some point (the national average is just over three per cent). In the same year the Music Industry Research Department revealed that almost twelve per cent of musicians 'reported having "thoughts that you would be better off dead or hurting yourself in some way" in at least several days in the last two weeks'. A survey from 2016 by the New Zealand Music Foundation found that 'when asked whether they had experienced suicidal thoughts almost six in ten [artists] experienced feeling that life wasn't worth living . . . and a similar proportion had thought about taking their own life'. In 'Life Expectancy and Cause of Death in Popular Musicians', in 2016 Kenny and Asher, et al., found that 'popular musicians died earlier and in greater proportions from violent deaths . . . compared with the general population'.

'No one ever does a mental health risk assessment on musicians,' Jeordie Shenton tells me. 'What duty of care does a manager have for their artist? Do they just ignore it because it's all about money, or do they go, "No, we have to stop this tour because we need to help the musician"? It's the same thing with [suicide]. If we're going to talk about a duty of care then perhaps we need to talk about mental health risk assessments . . . that kind of makes sense, doesn't it? Because suicidality is measured in three ways. You have suicide ideation, which is thoughts about feeling low during which someone might feel suicidal; there's planning, which means *actively* planning; and then there's the attempt, which is the implementation. I think an important thing that we need to highlight is that it's not just the rate of [actual] suicides, it's also the number of people who attempted suicide, planned suicide, or who at least had some kind of suicidal ideation. If you took those into account, the figure would be even *worse* than we imagine.'

Barely five months into my time at *Kerrang!* I was sent to Cape Town to interview the British band Feeder. On our day off we charted a boat to take us out to see the great white sharks patrolling the all-you-can-eat buffet that is Seal Island. With the warm sun of the South African summer bidding our party a gentle good morning, my mood of perfect serenity was holed below the waterline by the piercingly rancid stench of sixty-four thousand Cape fur seals. Seeking sanctuary while vomiting profusely I collapsed in a foetal position on a bed in one of the boat's two cabins. So complete was my nausea for the next six hours that I wouldn't have cared if a great white had clambered onboard for a selfie. I doubt I would even have noticed. Certainly, I barely registered the presence of Jon Lee, the group's funny and universally popular drummer, who kept popping below deck to check that I was still alive.

When Lee hanged himself at his home in Miami the following year (2002) he became the first person I'd ever met who had ended his own life. Rocked by the tragedy, each night Feeder's singer and guitarist Grant Nicholas went to the Lord Stanley pub at the top of Camden Square and got plastered. By day he wrote and recorded songs that were suddenly spilling out of him. Two years later, seated on the floor of a tasteful sushi restaurant in Tokyo, Nicholas reflected on the band having lost a third of its personnel. 'Why did he have to do it?' he wondered. 'That's what I find myself thinking. I just think, "Oh, Jon, you bloody silly sod."' One of the things about being in a band with someone who commits suicide is that you'll be required to answer questions on the subject for the rest of your life. Fifteen years later, in a career-spanning interview, I asked him to talk once more about the death of his friend.

'It's such a difficult thing,' Nicholas told me. 'I think sometimes it's the people you least expect to be going through something that are doing so. Obviously I've lived with what happened since [2002], and I still think about Jon a lot. He's kind of constantly around me in some way. I still think about [what happened] and sometimes I'm okay with it, and other times it's very hard. But the signs weren't there. At the time, Jon was living in America so I didn't really know that side of his life. I just didn't. I knew Jon really well, and we could argue like cat and dog, but because we were so close the next day it'd be forgotten. But I think the constant travelling back and forth between here and America to see his kids – and at the time I didn't have kids – was hard for him. I think he felt pressure to be around for his kids, to make money for them from the band, and I think he found that really hard. But he was never really down, so there were no obvious signs. Being in a band is not easy sometimes, but even now I don't see any signs that led to it happening. Of course there's so much in the press now about people who suffer from depression, especially in the music world, and we know that you can have all the money in the world and still be troubled. Sometimes it's just there inside you. But there is a part of me that thinks that Jon had something in his mind that meant that he did that, full hog. But there's another part of me that wonders if he really did want to do it. Does that make sense?

'I mean, this is so hard for me to talk about,' he told me. 'But Jon called me before he did it, and I didn't take the call. If I'd spoken to him, could I have changed what happened? I don't know. And that's something that bugs the hell out of me even now ... because suicide is a very selfish act. I won't lie about that. I know how I felt, but imagine being Jon's kids, or his mum and dad. It absolutely broke his mum. She was never the same again.'

*

On 10 May 2018 Scott Hutchison, the singer and guitarist with the Scottish band Frightened Rabbit, was found dead in the Port Edgar region of South Queensbury, near Edinburgh. Prior to leaving a hotel in the area, Hutchison had tweeted, 'Be so good to everyone you love. It's not a given. I'm so annoyed that it's not. I didn't live by the standard and it kills me. Please, hug your loved ones. I'm away now. Thanks.' Following the news of his passing, on social media Scottish First Minister Nicola Sturgeon wrote, 'Heartbreaking news. My thoughts are with Scott's family, friends and fans. A remarkable and much loved talent.' Tributes were paid by the comedian Sarah Silverman, Frank Turner, Paramore singer Hayley Williams, the Minnesotan band The Hold Steady, Gary Lightbody of Snow Patrol and more.

Grant Hutchison, the singer's younger brother and the drummer with Frightened Rabbit, had known for a while that his sibling's mental health was in a state of increasing disrepair. He also recognised that a dependency on alcohol was making things worse. The suicide brought an end to the group's fifteen-year career.

Speaking on the phone from his home in Scotland, Grant tells me that when it comes to vulnerable people 'the music industry is not safe at all'. Of this, he is without doubt. When his group signed to Atlantic Records, a major label, 'even then there wasn't enough help' for its most troubled member. As with almost all bands, by this point a pattern had long been established: 'When you go back to the start of a career for a young person who's exposed to everything – booze in dressing rooms, touring with other bands they look up to who are indulging or over-indulging – one of the things that I think is probably the most dangerous is that it's not regarded as *being* over-indulgent,' he says. 'It's normal practice ... Straight away you're thrown into a culture of alcohol and substances being a part of your working life. Some of the things that I've done, that we've done, that anyone in a band has done when on tour – which is a working environment, remember – you would be fired for in any other job. You don't drink in any other line of work. Even if you work in a bar, you tend not to drink when you're at work.'

Frightened Rabbit's album-orientated music allowed them to follow a somewhat old fashioned career path. After recording three LPs for the English independent label FatCat Records, in 2013 the quintet moved to Atlantic. With corporate muscle at their elbow, their songs were heard on television shows such as *Grey's Anatomy*, *One Tree Hill* and *90210*. They were invited to appear live on American chat shows such as *The Late Show with Stephen Colbert* and *The Late Late Show with James Corden*. Exposure like this, Grant Hutchison explained to the music journalist John Lewis, 'means that we don't just get lovelorn, beardy guys at our gigs'.

But it also meant that Frightened Rabbit were prone to the mixed fortunes of high demand. It hardly matters that to my stranger's ear Grant Hutchison sounds like the kind of man who has his affairs in order, and who possibly always did. Life on the road has ways of distorting the reality of even the most stable people. Without being asked, the drummer reflects on the disconnect between being 'on tour [where] someone plans your day for you the whole time [and where] you're sort of babysat' and a life at home in which 'there's nothing in the schedule and you're feeling a little bit blank'. The disparity was something with which he struggled, he tells me, as did his brother. For Scott Hutchison, both terrains were places of danger. Away from Frightened Rabbit, the singer was in 'a pretty abusive relationship' that served as 'a massive trigger for his poor mental health and his depression and anxiety'. Alcohol 'was also definitely a big part of it'.

At the end of two separate but consecutive US tours, in the autumn of 2013 the band were invited to appear on *The Late Show with David Letterman*. Feeling fragile and exhausted, Scott

Hutchison wanted to cancel the booking. Left alone to make a judgement on how best to proceed, the group decided that a spot on a trendsetting American television programme was not the kind of opportunity that should be allowed to slip by. Hundreds of acts would 'give anything to be on Letterman', they reasoned, and, anyway, what might Atlantic Records make of signatories that couldn't be bothered to play for barely four minutes on network TV? What would the folks at home with 'proper jobs' make of it all? Prosecuting their own legitimate concerns, on 1 November Frightened Rabbit performed the song 'The Woodpile' on Letterman's show. Rather than reflecting on what might have been a notable moment in a significant career, today Grant Hutchison regrets that it happened at all.

'Where do you turn when you [the band] are the epicentre, when you are the thing that everyone relies on for their living?' he asks. 'The pressure on you as the artist to make decisions that might benefit your own health but will not benefit someone else's wealth is a very, very hard decision to make. I wish, I *wish* I had made that decision for Scott on a few occasions. I wish that we as a band had pulled together and said, "No, this is not okay. We need to put a stop to this. If it's down to us, let's get Scott some help." And it happened a couple of times when we were on tour. If he was struggling, we would make sure he would speak to someone if it was possible. But he wasn't someone who liked to cancel shows, and [so] the only times we did that were when things were out of our control . . . But I do wish that I or someone had taken those decisions out of his hands. I wish someone had said, "Right, we're not doing this. The tour is off, or the tour is rescheduled, because we need to take a break." Because it was all on him. He didn't want to let us down or let down the fans and people who had bought tickets. You've got a tour manager there, you've got a promoter that's being commissioned, you've got an agent, a record label, and none of them are going to suggest it.'

Once again, no one took charge. Unlike Simon Neil from Biffy Clyro, who headed home before a North American tour ruined him for good, Frightened Rabbit were unable to talk themselves down from the ledge. One cut in a thousand, the business in New York might well have seemed like an issue easily overcome. After playing to three thousand people over two nights at Webster Hall in the East Village, all that was required of Frightened Rabbit was that they move themselves and their equipment fifty-two blocks north up Broadway for an appearance at the Ed Sullivan Theater that would be seen by millions of people. In an introduction aired in homes from Tacoma to Tampa, David Letterman himself would say the group's name. Conferring legitimacy, he would hold their CD up to the camera. What band wouldn't be able to do that? What band wouldn't *want* to do that? To a somewhat supportive response, Scott Hutchison had in the past spoken openly about his struggles with mental illness. By doing so, to the best of his abilities he had attempted to rubbish the notion that being in a band is a golden ticket to a privileged world. Good for him. But challenging the fundamental tenet that the show must *always* go on was a different matter. No one was ready to do that.

'I think that's the main problem,' says Grant Hutchison. 'If a band said [we want to take three months off] to a tour manager, and he relayed that to our manager, and to the label, we would then get on a call and talk about this. We'd see if there's a way we could carry on. It wouldn't be, "Okay, we hear you, we'll handle it, we'll deal with it, you just go home." They wouldn't ask, "What do you need from us? Do you need the number of people you can talk to, or the address of a rehab centre that we fund and we put money into for this eventuality?" That would be so simple . . . but there's this pressure where you feel you're letting people down. If you're not well and you've pushed yourself to your limits to carry on, you're not giving them the best version of yourself anyway. You're fed up, you're tired, you're anxious, you're not going to give the show that you could, or that they expect. And it's difficult to know who you should be able to rely on. I think giving tour managers more information – specific training, possibly, in mental health – would be a great way to go. Because the buck stops at the band, basically. There's no one saying, "Stop – this is ridiculous."

'To put it quite bluntly,' he tells me, 'people who take their lives can no longer play shows. I think [the industry] is starting to realise that looking after [vulnerable performers] also means that they're looking after themselves. I don't think it's always as selfish as that, but they *are* starting to see that they have a responsibility of care for artists. You no longer just sign a deal and then send them on their way to do whatever you tell them.'

Following the death of his brother, Grant Hutchison took to the road as the tour manager for his friends The Twilight Sad. It was an enjoyable experience, he tells me, but he missed the buzz of being one of the people the audience had paid to see. For a time he did consider a career as a 'TM', but in the end he couldn't envisage bouncing around the world as an employee of musicians who were paying him to be their mother hen. There were practical difficulties, too. To a greater extent, even, than musicians, a crew member often spends all but a few weeks of each year away from home. Equal part carny and French Foreign Legionnaire, these soldiers of the road deserve a book of their own. *Another night, I'm going mad.* Rather than spending the rest of his working life on the road, Grant Hutchison decided to make and sell cider. 'In the domestic part of my life, I've never been happier,' he says.

He's now a father. Had his wife, Jay, given birth to the couple's baby girl at a time when her husband was still a member of Frightened Rabbit, the drummer estimates that 'in the first year of [her] life I might not have been around all that much, and there's only so much control I would have had over that'. On the road in the United States supporting The National, the sight of the head-liners convening with their young families for a handful of dates here and there had prompted Hutchison to consider the 'incompatibility' of touring and family life. As well as this, he has his doubts that the relationship with Atlantic Records would have lasted longer than one more album anyway, after which the band might well have 'fizzled out'. An unintended consequence of the drastic curtailment of Frightened Rabbit's career is that the surviving members were able to attend as best they could to a life beyond music.

'If I'm being perfectly honest, I knew this is how this would end,' Grant tells me. 'I didn't know when but I was fairly certain [how]. Scott had spoken openly about his depression and his suicidal feelings, and I just knew that there was just something that made me think that this was how I would be saying goodbye to my brother. This is what he's going to do. Maybe because of that I think that the [time] we had together was actually quite long. When you look at the age he was when he died . . . knowing how many times he might have done it and turned back, probably he ended up with a lot more years in his life than he might have done. But it was definitely quite a drastic deterioration in the last few years. And his and my relationship was always very strong, but that too had started to crumble towards the end. We hadn't fallen out, or anything – well, we'd had moments over the years – but it just felt distant and just didn't feel like there was the same connection there. It definitely felt like he was checking out, I suppose.'

By comparison to the stories above, my own forlorn attempt at suicide seems barely worthy of the name. Heavily drunk in a flat that looked as if it had been in a spin dryer, I'd reached my nadir at last. All I wanted to do was sleep. Long past the point of pleasure, the only reason I was drinking – fast and hungry gulps of hard

liquor, willing myself not to vomit – was for the subsequent periods of surprisingly brief blackness. Around the bed were dozens
of empty bottles of bourbon, some of them broken. Nervous as a
kitten, each morning I'd head out to the local shop to replenish my
stock of paralysis and silence. *If I could just feel like that all the time,
I'd be sorted.* Hang. On. A. Minute. With what struck me as rational
design, beneath clearing skies at once I understood that the surest
way of securing my prize would be to kill myself. It was so obvious
that I couldn't believe that I hadn't considered it before. 'I can live
with this,' I thought. 'I can live with not living.'

Slitting my wrists with a dull knife proved unworkable. Sawing
back and forth in grim fascination, had I persisted with this method
likely I'd still be at it today. What I needed was the kind of Japanese
kitchen blades my fiancée bought me for a recent birthday. With
one of them in my hand I'd have opened myself up in a jiffy. *Crikey,
this is miles harder than it looks.* Instead, I decided to swallow all
the tablets prescribed in my name. Lithium, Phenergan, Pregabalin,
Lamotrigine, Seroquel, Zopiclone. I don't know for sure what I
was thinking, but I do know how I felt. I felt calm and accepting; relieved, even. At long last I was doing something that made
sense. Ten minutes earlier the thought of ending my own life hadn't
occurred to me. Now I was pleased of the company. So down went
the pills, and down I lay, quiet and becalmed by the surety of my
story's rightful end.

Instead, I was found in a state of near unconsciousness at the
foot of my bed. That's double handy, isn't it? For the book, I mean,
and for me. I'm willing to guess that the intervention saved my
life. A stomach pump and yet another week up at the Royal Free
probably helped, too. As if by magic, two days later I was no longer privy to the kinds of feelings that lead a person to believe that
suicide is a fitting way to leave the stage. On a noisy ward, in the
day's smallest hours, I gamely attempted sleep. *Take my hand, off*

to Never Neverland. But I couldn't sleep, so instead I had a little think. *This is getting silly now, isn't it? From here, surely there's only two ways this can go.*

After that ... after that I began to get better.

10: TUNNELS AND TREES

From the back seat of a people carrier, in 2019 Frank Turner teaches me how to use Twitter. Back in London, a girlfriend who is soon to become my fiancée has been on at me about it for ages. 'You need to be on there,' she tells me. 'It's good for your brand.' 'Excuse me?' 'Your brand.' *Okay.* I wonder if perhaps I should mention to her that in a doomed attempt to get high from spent amphetamines, as a teenager I once drank a pint of my own urine. *Will that be good for my brand? Is this the kind of thing you had in mind?* How about I write a book in which I itemise some of the very worst things that have ever happened to me? *Might that work?* Anyway, Frank and I are on our way to the Mitchell Library in Glasgow for the first night of a five-date tour promoting his book, *Try This at Home.* As the streets of one of the country's great cities roll by, with stop-the-press gravitas I announce that I'm thinking of joining Twitter.

'Give me your phone.'

'Sorry?'

'Your phone, please. Give me your phone.'

A mere decade behind schedule, that's all it takes for Frank to put me in the game. By far the most proactive person I've ever known, in the crepuscular light of early spring my expert teacher brings me up to snuff on the norms of democratic media. Tweets, retweets, trending, pile-ons, hashtags, hate storms, threads, groups, trolls. Reliably bamboozled by all instances of 'new' technology, my first instinct is to throw myself out of the moving vehicle. But by the end of the tour, I'm beginning to see the appeal. Explaining my story, onstage in Glasgow, Manchester, Chester, Yeovil and London, the singer requests that members of the audience support me in my quest to join the chorus of transnational chatter. Back in the dressing room, after each show I see that I've attracted fifty or a hundred new followers. Perfect strangers one and all, each subscriber constitutes a tiny dopamine hit of abstract validation. *Interesting*.

Driving away from the Stoller Hall in Manchester, Frank tells me that his mental health has been much improved by a recent decision not to read the comments beneath his tweets. *Oh, no, not this again.* With the noises in my own head at last abating, for the first time in an age I have reasonable cause not to worry *quite* so much about the kind of trouble I've spent years getting myself into. I'd even go so far as to say that life is suddenly looking okay. My dear friend and straight-up guardian angel Dan Silver has secured me a gig on the *Telegraph*'s Culture section. Its fine editors don't seem to mind that a lifelong opponent of the expensively educated crime syndicate that is the Conservative Party is suddenly trying his best to write up a storm on their pages. On somewhat steady feet I've even overcome my instinct for solitude by re-emerging into impolite society. *Great, what have I missed?* Well, for one thing, it seems as if I've been missing out on a social media phenomenon that can sometimes be a place of remarkable danger. Out on the road, to my rookie eyes Twitter looks like a cuddly bear. At worst, it's knockabout fun. But as many have learned, get too cute and it'll have your arm off.

In the years before the rise of social media, Frank Turner made his bones at the Nambucca pub on London's Holloway Road. A remarkable hothouse of emerging talent, other alumni include Laura Marling, Jamie T, members of The Vaccines and the folk singer Beans on Toast. Mumford & Sons were also part of the scene. After spending years paying his dues, in 2021 banjo player Winston Marshall absented himself from the internationally successful group after being lavishly criticised on Twitter for his support of the book

Unmasked: Inside Antifa's Radical Plan to Destroy Democracy by the 'discredited provocateur' (*Columbia Journalism Review*) Andy Ngo. In a statement posted on 10 March, Marshall wrote that 'over the past few days I have come to better understand the pain caused by the book I endorsed. I have offended not only a lot of people I don't know, but also those closest to me, including my bandmates and for that I am truly sorry. As a result of my actions I am taking time away from the band to examine my blindspots.

'For now,' the guitarist wrote, 'please know that I realise how my endorsements have the potential to be viewed as approvals of hateful, divisive behaviour. I apologise, as this was not at all my intention.' With that, Winston Marshall took a break from Twitter. On 25 June, he stepped away from Mumford & Sons for good.

I find it fascinating that the guitarist's self-cancellation had *nothing* to do with the means by which he earns a living. A fleeting endorsement of a book by an unethical journalist was all it took to set his world on fire. At the end of an interview with Dr Charlie Howard I ask what advice she would give a young performer about to tread onto the uncertain terrain of the music industry. 'The thing they need to have is really good boundaries around social media,' she replies. It's the first thing she says; it's out of the gate before anything else. 'They need to know how to use it without it taking over their entire personality. So they need some training on how to use social media in a way that works for them.'

The fact that I've chosen to speak to Frank Turner about social media has itself put me in a frame of mind typical of social media. Reductive and nervous, already I'm weighing up the 'optics' of one white guy asking another what it's like to be kicked about in public. For the record, along with a variety of other terrors, I *know* that sexism and bigotry are rife on Twitter. You do too. Such is the ubiquity of this stuff that even a novice like me can find it in an instant. Beautiful women and voluble people of colour seem to be particularly easy prey. In calling foul on a bargain-basement joke ('you go through men faster than Taylor Swift'), a tweet from Taylor Swift herself was met with responses such as – let's see, here's one – 'Your [sic] a joke. How embarrassing. Your [sic] like 50 years old hating on someone because you're not happy with your life . . . you wish you could get some men [sic] attention lmaooo'. Among the replies to a post in which the rapper, singer and actor Ice-T voiced his support for his 'Asian brothers and sisters' suffering violent attacks in the age of The Disease, we have: 'Mr T, thanks for trying to stir the pot with your race baiting, liberal MSM regurgitating bullshit . . .' What I cannot claim to know, however, is the extent to which Taylor Swift and Ice-T are bothered by this kind of stuff. But I *do* know how it messes with the mind of Frank Turner. What's more, I knew it many months before I started this book.

'I get meta-frustrated, if you see what I mean,' he tells me. 'I get annoyed at myself for getting annoyed. Often, anyway. Someone can send one or two abusive tweets to me – and I try not to look, but it does happen – and it's amazing how wounding that stuff can be. It's startling. It will stop me sleeping for an entire night, often. And that's just one or two instances. On the times in my life when I've become the subject of a hate storm on social media – which is many at this point in my life – I don't eat, I don't sleep. It fucks me up. My wife [Jessica] will tell you about it, it will ruin weeks of my life. Jess is training as a counselling psychologist, so she's familiar with the techniques of talking me down from this. But it is very hard to talk me down. I get *extremely* upset.'

Locked down by the state, on a Friday afternoon in the foothills of spring Frank and I spend an enjoyable hour interrupting each other via a pair of laptops. Despite a friendship that is now into its second decade, there are times when I've taken aim at the singer in print. Don't tell him this, but I've rather enjoyed doing so, too. (If there's one thing I can't stand, it's fawning client journalists.) What I find interesting is that were it not for the fact that *I* brought up these instances in his company, he and I would never have discussed them. I mention them here only to say that if you're in the market for a – checks Twitter guidebook – 'snowflake', you're at the wrong gig.

'This is important,' he tells me. 'You can't aspire to be a public figure and then complain when not everybody loves you. That's ridiculous. You have to accept that some people are going to like what you have to say, and some people aren't. So there is a level at which I'll take my [medicine]. But [on social media] there is a whole ecosystem of people who spend an enormous amount of time and effort having a go at me. They fucking hate me. *They fucking hate me.* And there's a viciousness to things that is, I think, different from what came before. In the pre-internet era, if you wanted to hound someone, at the very least you had to buy *stamps*. Do you know what I mean? Now it's just so easy.'

These days Frank Turner uses social media 'as a broadcast medium rather than a conversational tool. Rather than trying to have a conversation with hundreds of thousands of people at the same time – which isn't possible anyway – I issue statements.' The dexterity with which he does this can often be impressive. Sitting outside a pub up near Archway, towards the end of a night in the summer of 2014 the singer and I were jousting about him never having played a gig in my hometown. 'But I've played in Wakefield,' he said. 'Yes, but you've never played Barnsley.' 'We just played in Blackburn. Who does that?' 'I know, but you've never played Barnsley.' Two pints later, Frank Turner decided that in a fortnight's time he would right the wrong of never having performed a set in S70. By way of publicity, a week before the event he issued a single oblique tweet about a planned visit to an unnamed town in South Yorkshire. More clues followed. The singer's unpaid appearance at the Old No. 7 bar on Market Hill raised more than a thousand pounds for a local charity helping the children of miners attend university. On hearing the news, an audience too young to recall The Strike began chanting as one: 'If the miners are united they will never be defeated.' (Actually, the miners *were* defeated, but never mind.) Rewarding the patience of those who couldn't gain entry, the evening's final song was performed on the pavement outside.

On our short book tour in the spring of 2019, Frank plays me his new album. As the mundanity of rural England gallops by, the first thing I think, and the first thing I say, is, 'I reckon you're going to get trouble for this.' In a very modern way, like everyone else, my attention was first captured not by the music but by the *idea* behind it. In a variety of styles, and in good faith, *No Man's Land* tells the stories of twelve historical women (his mother is the thirteenth). As well as composing songs about such figures as Catherine Blake, Sister Rosetta Tharpe and Christa McAuliffe, Frank also curated a series of podcasts that provided further details about the lives of the people on the record. Released in the summer of that year, to no one's surprise the singer's eighth studio album was accused of being a rank example of 'extreme mansplaining' (*Independent*) and, according to the *NME*, a work in which its women's 'voices' 'are consistently overshadowed by Turner's [who] should've just made us a Spotify playlist'. (Not possible. Regardless of your opinion of *No Man's Land*, prior to its release only one of its subjects had ever had a song written about them.) To the bugle call of widespread if not quite universal negative publicity, the beasties of social media did their thing.

As he says, Frank had been here before. In a review of the album *Positive Songs for Positive People*, from 2015, the music critic Alexis Petridis wrote about the singer's 'pretty vociferous' online detractors dispatching '100 death threats a day' in response to 'a piece [that] appeared on the *Guardian* website collating Turner's fruitier thoughts on socialism and state funding of the arts'. This kind of tally, the author reasoned, was 'pretty impressive even by the standards of an era in which sending death threats appears to be some people's answer to pretty much everything, from the announcement of the Glastonbury bill to the romantic entanglements of Miley Cyrus'. Speaking to the writer Mark Beaumont, Turner had described the fortnight's worth of correspondence – 'death threats and hate mail' – as 'really vicious, horrible shit, all because of expressing an opinion contrary to the mainstream of thought within the entertainment or creative world. It was fucking horrible. I don't want to go through anything like that again.'

I have no doubt that the furore around *No Man's Land* was in part a continuation of the same punishment beating. I'm not sure how else one can explain the brickbats reaching their peak *before* the album was actually released. *At least give it a spin first, no? If you can't stand it, imagine how pleased you'll be that your instincts were proved to be correct.* More than half a lifetime ago, I remember being outraged at people holding life and death opinions on a book they hadn't read. Realising that I hadn't either, in what seemed (and *seems*) to me like a basic courtesy I bought and finished *The Satanic Verses*. That'd be a nicer world, wouldn't it? If we all shut up about things we hadn't seen, or read, or heard. Certainly it would have spared Frank Turner no end of grief prior to an acoustic concert at Lancaster Town Hall on 5 July 2019 (in aid of a local food bank, no less).

'There was a day when the internet kerfuffle about it was reaching its peak and I was incredibly stressed,' he tells me. 'I was sitting on tour backstage, chain-smoking cigarettes – having supposedly recently quit smoking – thinking to myself, "I'm just gonna jack this in. I can't be bothered doing this any more. Whatever my life choices have been, this is a feeling I do not wish to experience ever again." My wife Jess was so frustrated about it because she pointed out that at that night's show, which was an eighteen-hundred capacity show that had sold out, there were more people in the front row of the audience than there were people who were giving me shit on Twitter. And this was just one show on the tour. But somehow those were the people that were getting to me. What do you do about that?'

Down the high-speed cables to his new home on the Essex coast, I tell Frank Turner that it is indeed a puzzle. Perhaps it's inevitable that one will be drawn to the clamour of people who hate you, even if it comes at the expense of those who love what you do (or at least, those who have paid to see you perform). Whether or not you allow them to hold your gaze, though, is a different matter. In an antiquated instance of proto-trolling back in the nineties, a small group of readers irritated by an endless stream of self-consciously contrarian articles launched a campaign to have me sacked from my modest berth on a crappy magazine. 'Get Rid of Ian Now' – GROIN – they called it. They even printed up badges. Wearing mine with pride, I was of course delighted to be getting so much attention. Certainly I spent more time thinking about it than I did considering people who might have *liked* what I wrote. I could, of course, just as easily have been deeply upset by the group's attempt to have me removed from gainful employment. My employers might have been spooked, too. If it happened today, perhaps they would have been.

In the digital age, I was similarly thrilled that a hundred and ninety-eight *Telegraph* subscribers posted negative comments about my interview with Billy Bragg. I had no end of fun when two hundred of them flipped their wigs about a piece I'd written about punk. Just last week, a reader accused me of 'mangina writing'. What a hero. Then again, I was certainly spooked by the deep scorn of a small army of (to my mind) intransigent and spiteful Morrissey supporters angered by what I believed to be a nuanced piece about the singer's, um, iconoclastic views. But it's not really much by way of hard evidence, is it? Splashing about in the shallows like this, I haven't the faintest idea what it's like to be the target of a hate storm. So in answer to your question, Frank, I don't know *what* to do about this kind of thing. Should it ever happen to me, I'll be sure to let you know.

'Eleanor Roosevelt once said that it takes two people to be shamed, so if you refuse to participate, if you refuse to be a victim in all this [the internet trolls] tend to move on quite quickly,' Frank tells me. 'Because if the person isn't going to roll over, it's no fun. If you're not going to issue hostage-statement style apologies, then they *will* move on. Secondly, the politics of Twitter are pretty much the politics of the school cafeteria. It's about who gets to sit with the cool kids. And for me, remembering that I was never allowed to sit with the cool kids, *and never wanted to*, that's been very useful. I do not seek approval from these people, anyway; it's never been on my "to do" list to be approved by these kinds of cunts. So why am I losing sleep over the fact that they don't like me? They've never fucking liked me. They never will. It's an irrelevance. I should carry on with my life, and they should too.'

Has there ever been a more incoherent aphorism than 'sticks and stones may break my bones but words shall never hurt me'? On social media, in response to contributors who are usually guilty of nothing more than undertaking a job of work, trolls and bad faith actors seek to dominate space. Prior to joining the *Telegraph*, my Culture editor Eleanor Halls wrote what might well have been the first mainstream profile of Stormzy. (She didn't mention to me that it was the first, *I asked*. Like any number of male music writers, had it been me it'd have been the first thing out of my mouth.) Upon publication, on Twitter she attracted the attention of 'quite a well known music journalist' who accused her of 'nicking things from his article'. She had done no such thing. The man's approaches were made on her public timeline, about which she thought, 'I'm literally an intern and it says that on my Twitter, so fuck off. [But] it really threw me, actually, because we had quite a nasty spat about it.' Again, in full view of a wider public, a different male journalist broke cover to criticise the way she wrote about grime music. This is a genre that Eleanor knows well; she writes very well, too. So come on, fellas, is it not time we were honest with each other?

'[Another] thing that was quite upsetting when I was starting out was that I'd do a lot of these interviews, often with male musicians,' she tells me. 'I would do them on video and I would get absolutely misogynistic abuse for being a female [journalist] who dared to speak to a man in a professional way. If I went live on Facebook with whichever artist it was, or on YouTube, and they [the artist] would share it, a lot of their own fans just couldn't understand that a woman and a man could be having a conversation that was professional and didn't involve one of them wanting to have sex with the other, essentially. They just couldn't see me as a professional person. They either saw me as the object of their attention, or I was only interviewing [the artist] because he was the object of *my* attention. They weren't *listening* to what I was saying. And I'd spent hours preparing these questions and researching these interviews thoroughly, and then you'd read these five hundred and fifty comments at the end which are not listening to what I'm saying but are commenting on what I look like or how I'm staring at him or how he's staring at me. And you think, "Literally, *what is the point?*"'

There is, perhaps, something about the male mind that is suited to the eternally adolescent monomania of the obsessive music journalist. *Perhaps.* Even so, the dominance of the landscape by people who look like me suggests institutional stasis at best and, at worst, a mephitic boys' club in keen need of mucking out. On the *Telegraph* Culture desk Eleanor Halls noticed that she was fielding pitches from male writers unperturbed that she'd knocked them back three times two days earlier. There was, she noted, a resilience to their efforts that was less evident in female contributors. In the hope of providing support and encouragement, she began sharing stories of the times *she* had been rejected by commissioning editors. As well as launching a series of ongoing interviews and features under the banner PassTheAux, on social media Eleanor let it be known that submissions and ideas from women writers would be considered in a manner less dismissive than was evident elsewhere.

'I was inundated with tweets and emails; hundreds and hundreds and hundreds of UK female music journalists,' she tells me. 'A common thread in their emails was either, "I started off in music journalism's heyday, at the *NME*, or whatever it was, and kind of got edged out because I felt I wasn't taken seriously as a female music critic" – those ones were from women who were a little bit older – or, "I felt that I didn't have the authority or confidence to write about music." There seemed to be this confidence gap there, kind of this imposter syndrome; so much so, in fact, that they didn't have the confidence to even pitch. It was a sense of intimidation and a lack of confidence, basically, while others had just been burned by men in music journalism.

'So I was trying to put my finger on that,' she says. 'And tracing it back, I think it's tied to social kudos. When I was younger, men discovered new music; men always had control of the aux cable at parties. It was a sense of control, I think . . . I think because music when I was growing up was so dominated by men listening to indie bands and rock stars and guitar music that men felt an ownership of it. They were male musicians so they thought of it as being *their* space. Those were my anecdotal thoughts. There was a sense of ownership of the music space.'

Ownership of the music space. With a masochism that can easily pass for machismo, bands take a perverse (if often justifiable) pride in the lengths to which they will go to undertake a live campaign. In the thick of a European winter, the Bay Area punk group Rancid toured the continent in *a car* with a broken heater. Green

Day spent almost three months on the road in conditions so squalid that Billie Joe Armstrong contracted body lice. In what is surely a winning entry, the hardcore group Black Flag undertook campaigns of such penury that its members were required to eat dog food. Many of the women who endure the routine hardships of early-day touring are rewarded further with a glass ceiling. A report from 2021 co-authored by Christine Bauer, the Assistant Professor of Human-Centred Computing at Utrecht University, showed that algorithms used by streaming services prioritise male artists. In 2018 a survey by the Music Industry Research Association found that 'seventy-two per cent of female musicians report that they have been discriminated against because of their sex, and sixty-seven per cent report that they have been the victim of sexual harassment'. The same report revealed that 'sixty-three per cent of non-white artists said they faced racial discrimination'.

It might even be that bands of any kind are increasingly regarded as last year's model. In 2019 Billy Bragg told me that, 'In the twentieth century people who were marginalised had to use the platform of music, but now people have different means of getting their voices heard. Music is no longer the vanguard in that respect.' In an article in the *Guardian* about the declining number of groups in the charts, in 2021 Ben Mortimer, the co-president of Polydor Records, told the writer Dorian Lynskey that, 'If you're young and inspired to become a musician, you face a choice. If you go the band route, you need to find bandmates with a similar vision, you need expensive instruments and equipment, and you need to go out on the road to hone your craft. On the other hand, you could download Ableton [production software], shut your bedroom door and get creating straight away. Culture is shaped by technology.' I recalled these words when the Torontonian non-profit organisation Over the Bridge issued a 'Nirvana' song composed by Google's artificial intelligence programme Magenta. The vocals on the marginally convincing 'Drowned in the Sun' were sung by Eric Hogan, the frontman in the Atlanta-based tribute group Nevermind.

In 2020 I spoke with Ellie Rose Davies – otherwise known as LED – the guitarist and co-vocalist with the young alternative rock group Goat Girl, from Deptford, for an article in the *Telegraph* about the dearth of breakthrough bands from London. The co-author of one of 2021's best albums (the universally applauded *On All Fours*), she told me that, '[Our band] will always make music together and we'll keep putting it out. But in terms of it no longer being our main source of income – well, that's already the case.' I noticed that she didn't sound greatly perturbed by this. Declining the advances of a number of major record labels, Goat Girl signed a recording contract with the independent Rough Trade. Despite their album appearing in the UK top thirty, Ellie continues to work as a cook at the Grand Howl café in Hackney. Her signature dish is enchiladas. She likes working with people who aren't associated with music, she says. It's good for her state of mind to sometimes stand down from the weirdness of it all.

'It's not necessarily just that the [music business] causes all these mental health issues and then doesn't deal with them in the right way – although I do think that's true – it's also that creative people who don't necessarily fit into the cogs of our system are drawn to music, and thus to the music industry,' she tells me. 'That said, the industry *doesn't* deal with people's mental health at all well.'

One of the later interviewees for this book, in the depths of winter Ellie Rose Davies adds layers of harmony to what has by now become a universal point of view. The music business is an unusually dangerous place of work from which the members of Goat Girl have done their best to keep themselves safe. Appearing on my computer from her home near the Whitechapel Road, Ellie speaks of enduring frequent panic attacks and bouts of anxiety that would surely have been made worse by submitting to the working practices of a major label. She is, she says, in a 'fortunate position' in which 'our record company and management would never put us through any situation where we'd feel uncomfortable'. Save for 'the occasional pill at a festival once or twice a year', the guitarist abstains from drugs, alcohol and other stimulants. When a different member of Goat Girl was required to step away from the ranks for a short time to deal with *her* mental wellbeing, no one blinked.

'I think encouraging an open conversation about mental health is definitely something that has helped me,' Ellie tells me. 'It's important for people to feel that they can be straight up and honest – and having a team of people behind them who make them feel like that's okay. [But] for me there needs to be a separation between music, which is intrinsically powerful and therapeutic – not only for the musician but for the listener – and the uglier, overbearing side that controls the whole thing. There's the unequal distribution of wealth where the artist is the least well-paid person. So I wonder if the main problem is deeply rooted in capitalism and the fact that as an artist you're seen as a product. And because you're seen as a product that's sellable, you're just not going to be respected enough, I don't think. I feel like I never stop working. I find it really hard to relax because there's always something going on . . . If something is your passion as well as your job, it's difficult to know where the line is. And sometimes you don't want there to be a line, because if you had one then that would make what you do seem a bit impersonal.'

Despite innumerable protestations to the contrary, the professional musician *has* a proper job. What it isn't is *normal*. I sometimes wonder whether things could be improved by this simple change of description. If a job isn't proper, it's *improper*. Through this lens the very act of making music can appear invalid. With grateful servitude, musicians become minor partners in a business that wouldn't exist without them. The gilded stories of a vanishingly small number of groups rising to positions of genuine power are exceptional distractions. In this industry, the thumping majority of musicians are expected to tolerate things that others in the chain of command would not. They're reminded at all times that theirs is a profession of which others would dream of joining. They're expected to smile, and to suck it up. The learned behaviour of misplaced humility and masochistic endurance is doing them in.

'There needs to be someone taking responsibility,' Steph Langan of the charity Tonic Music for Mental Health tells me. 'There needs to be responsibility from different ends of the music industry. The promoters, the record labels – everyone contributing to having a structure where you can have a team of mental health professionals there to provide a good [setup] to implement policies and procedures. Now that can be very boring, but it comes down to the basic rights of the musicians. It comes down to people being treated with respect, as humans. They're not *super*-humans; they can't just go on and on and on . . . I think there needs to be a central body and a central voice [regulating this]. I don't know what that would be, exactly, but it would be someone who is responsible for making sure that these things happen.'

Based in Portsmouth, Tonic Music for Mental Health is one of a growing number of charities and organisations seeking to help musicians. Funded in part by the proceeds of concerts by The Specials (the group's singer, Terry Hall, is a patron), the organisation plans to roll out a series of 'public facing' Tonic Rider hubs at as many venues as it can afford. As well as offering their services to anyone who has bought a ticket, the team will provide a 'mental health MOT' to the bands on the bill. In work undertaken before The Disease, the charity discovered that 'nine out of ten' touring musicians maintained contact long after they'd rolled out of town. According to Steph Langan, sometimes they encountered performers 'who have broken down [because] they feel like they just can't carry on with the show. They're knackered, they're exhausted. And we can be there to talk to them in that time before the show and just chat and talk it through. Sometimes that's all people need – they just need to talk and get it out. It does give them that sense of offloading.'

Tonic Music for Mental Health's tactic of setting up shop in the venues in which bands appear is a new approach to an enduring problem. At a stroke, the troubled musician doesn't have to go anywhere to get help; rather than saying the word, *they'll* be asked if there's anything *they* need. Speaking to me from her home near the Hampshire coast, Steph Langan is right to say that sometimes people just need someone to talk to. Other times, of course, they'll need much more than this. I would be surprised if the people at work in her organisation didn't join me in worrying that the music industry's willingness to 'have a conversation' about mental health is contingent on it *not* interfering with the workings of an unjust business model. Inching towards the light, the taboos that remain are difficult to dislodge.

'Nobody says no, do they?' Steph tells me. 'I personally think that it would be a helpful model to [introduce] people who have a clinical background in mental health services. I think it would be helpful to have people who are used to working with chaotic people who are very unwell. I think there should be proper risk assessments where someone could say, "No. No. You're not going on tonight . . . Because too many people are dying. Too many people are ending their lives. Too many people are burning out and having breakdowns. At some point, something's got to change. Something's got to give. Because the industry can be incredibly toxic. Musicians are commodities. It's all about the money machine . . . and that's just not sustainable. We're all human and we all need sleep. We all need a measure of routine.'

Along with a hundred other bands, in the summer of 2017 the English sextet Creeper travelled across North America as part of the Vans Warped Tour. From coast to coast, the going was gruel-ling. Travelling vast distances in a vehicle with no suspension, to his dismay singer Will Gould found an exception to his claim that he could sleep anywhere. With a night's rest dependent on sleeping pills and alcohol, the frontman began to suffer deep anxiety. He became reluctant, even, to leave the bus. *Why wasn't he feeling happier?* 'It's really bizarre, that feeling that you should be grateful for every single thing that's happening all the time,' he tells me. 'I'm being told – it's never in so many words, but you definitely are – I'm being told a hundred per cent that you don't complain and that you should be grateful for what you've got.' Gould thought back to all the jobs he'd done while waiting his turn to earn a living from music. Making pizza boxes for three months, a placement in a call centre, selling magazines on the street, working in a factory, you name it. He recalled his years travelling to mainland Europe in a van to play hardcore punk for people in squats. 'So I thought, "Okay, well, this isn't bad,"' he says. 'I thought, "I'll just get on with this."' As best he was able, this is what he tried to do.

'On the Warped Tour I'd wake up tired and drowsy as fuck from all the sleeping tablets,' he tells me. 'Straight away I'd be drinking a pint of gin because I couldn't go onstage without drinking again. *At eleven in the morning.* Me and Ian [Miles, one of the band's two guitarists] would literally drink pints of gin. It'd look like water, but it was gin . . . I'd walk out to the show, switch it for water for the half an hour we played so it didn't look crazy, and then I'd go back to the bunk and drink until I went to sleep again. And then the next day I'd start that process all over again. And that went on for three months. Every single day.'

Discontinued in 2019, even by the standards of the music industry the Warped Tour was an uncommonly arduous campaign. In lieu of formal headliners, each day the festival's running order was drawn from a tombola; on any given morning, a group could be onstage long before lunch. Having seen the event first hand in Houston (where it was forty-two degrees), Atlanta, Pittsburgh and Salt Lake City (*twice*), on each occasion I returned to my hotel believing that I'd witnessed a working model of hell on earth. Each day scores of tour buses ferried a battalion of performers hundreds of miles so that they might play for just thirty minutes on one of numerous rickety stages erected in the parking lots of amphitheatres that all looked as if they were ordered from the same catalogue.

An ostensibly fraternal enterprise, out here bands faced constant reminders of the odds stacked against them. At the Utah State Fairpark I watched in amazement as Josh Franceschi, the singer with the English group You Me at Six, patrolled the venue asking strangers to come and watch his band's set. He had a handmade sign and everything. 'But you've headlined the Brixton Academy.' 'Yeah,' he said, 'but out here I'm nothing.' 'You're on a major label. Surely that counts for something?' 'Not to these people.' *Right. Wow.* As if reasoning with a child, Franceschi explained that without these charm offences the chances of 'YM@S' playing to literally no one were high. After two hours spent pestering strangers, at three o' clock sharp the young quintet knocked out six songs to a gathering of about thirty people. To a man, the group considered this a good result. Packing up their gear, they returned to the tour bus they were sharing with a young American band they barely knew.

Out here I'm nothing. Eight years later, on the Warped Tour in 2017, Creeper were spending too much time drinking and taking drugs. Playing in venues situated as many as thirty miles from city centres, sometimes it seemed as if there was nothing else to do. At the end of a drunken night two thirds of the way through the tour, the band were required to manhandle their now former drummer, Dan Bratton, to bed. 'He's not a very good drunk,' Ian Miles tells me. *Go to sleep, Dan, you're being annoying.* Tired of his attempts to rejoin the party, Miles threatened to shoot his bandmate with a BB gun.

Bratton's attempts to deliver a series of punches were derailed by a rugby tackle by Oliver Burdett, the group's other guitarist. 'He was just lunging towards me with his fist in the air,' Ian recalls. Incensed that he'd had a can of beer poured down his trousers, the drummer attempted to stab Burdett with a knife. 'Genuinely, I saw the rage in his eyes,' he says. Dan Bratton chased his quarry all around the venue. By now a danger to all, the group were required to lock him out of the vehicle until he'd regained control of his senses.

'Under the night-time glaze of alcohol and drugs and the atmosphere of everybody being in the same space, of everybody doing the same thing, the *normality* of it all, that wasn't out of the ordinary to us,' Ian tells me. 'That was normal behaviour. And weird shit like that was happening all over the site. It was happening with different bands, and it was happening *between* different bands. One night I set my guitar case on fire and threw it in a lake. It was people going mad, essentially. And that's just normalised. Not in public perception, just within the music industry . . . the problem is the environment. It's the environment you're in when you're in the studio, and when you're on the road, because being out of control in those situations is just so normal. I feel like I've probably had manic episodes on tour without even noticing. I would be onstage and I'd be so high, so incredibly high, that you don't even notice. I'll come offstage and I'll be buzzing. I'll be jumping around the dressing room. We'll be throwing food at each other or running around the venue.'

That was normal behaviour. In order to make their second album, *Sex, Death & the Infinite Void*, released in 2020, Creeper shuttled between their homes in Hampshire and a recording studio in Los Angeles. Each night, some of the band's members headed to Bar Sinister – 'the best club for sinful pleasure' (*LA Weekly*) – in Hollywood; come chucking out time, at 1 a.m. they'd often head to an illegal speakeasy in the city's downtown area. According to Ian, it was 'seedy and dark and exciting and fun'. Each morning, the guitarist arrived for work at WAX LTD Studios with a fresh bottle of whiskey. If the record's producer told him his playing sounded a little too tight, he'd knock back a shot to loosen things up. Listening to the record today, Will Gould says that, 'I can hear a drunk style on some of those songs. I can almost smell the whiskey through the speakers.'

Ian Miles lives with bipolar disorder. At home on the outskirts of Southampton, his wife wondered whether her husband was on the cusp of a dangerous acceleration. *Look*, she said, *you've been zooming around. You've been trying to do a million things but not finishing anything. You've been staying up really late. Honey, I think you might be in some kind of hyper-manic stage at the moment. I think we should really try and calm down and take a step back.* But with an album in the works, there was no chance of this happening. By the following month the guitarist had become 'utterly obsessed' with the idea that formal religion was conspiring with the police to raise funds with which to buy nuclear weapons that would then be handed to MI5. Armed and dangerous, it seemed obvious that these organisations planned to annihilate a world that had become too dangerous for politicians to handle. The only reason Ian was privy to this classified information was because he'd been chosen by a shadowy resistance to launch a strike at the pyramid's lower tiers.

'I walked all the way into Southampton, which is an hour and a half away on foot, and I tried to burn down some churches,' he tells me. 'I kicked a church door down. I approached the vicar and told him that I was going to do it. It was so silly. He reacted as if it happened all the time, which I'm sure it doesn't. I went in and I was screaming at him about all the falsities of religion and how he should be ashamed – blah, blah, blah – and then I ran into the main chapel area and I was screaming about how I was going to burn it down. But I'd forgotten my lighter fluid. And he just said to me,

"But the church is made of stone. You can't burn it down." And I just went, "Oh fuck!" And ran out.'

By the time he was apprehended by the police, Ian was convinced that he'd killed four Jehovah's Witnesses simply by blinking at them. Sectioned to a psychiatric care facility, he got the impression that the higher-ups at Creeper's record label regarded his misfortune as something that could be used as 'a selling point' for the upcoming marketing campaign. When it comes to the kind of stories lapped up by music journalists, they were probably right. Speaking on – what else? – Zoom from his home near the coast, on a cold spring afternoon Ian tells me that today he's able to talk about the episode only because it seems as if it happened to someone else. Speaking in near perfect sentences, he apologises for his likeably hesitant delivery. He has no need to. 'Will's much better at this kind of thing,' he says.

The next day, Will Gould bursts into my sitting room with a dozen theories about things in the music industry that are making people ill. *Poverty wages. Job insecurity. Normalised excess. Corporate theft. The relentless scrutiny of Twitter. An absence of respect for both art and artist. The travails of playing for a young audience that have never acquired the habit of paying for music.* He tells me of a tweet he read in which it was said that young listeners would be surprised to learn that all of their favourite bands are addicted to cocaine. 'I'm certainly not addicted to cocaine, but I've definitely abused substances [many] times in my life,' he says. 'And so has everyone in music that I know.' On tour since he was seventeen, the singer fell into the practice of drinking fortified wine as a means of staving off boredom and cold. Courted by a major label, in 2015 Creeper played a show upstairs at the Garage, on Highbury Corner, at which he and Ian necked two bottles of white wine apiece before going onstage. Standing in the audience, a representative from the record company asked their manager, '*What the hell was that?*' Unperturbed by the group being drunk at what was in effect a job interview, Warner Bros. signed them anyway.

'There was one night when we were on tour [supporting] All Time Low when we all dressed up as Kiss,' Ian tells me. 'We hadn't even *met* All Time Low at that point; we literally hadn't said "hi", or anything. And we put on the black and white makeup, had Kiss blaring really loud out of a boom box, and we went up to their dressing room, flung the door open and ran in singing Kiss at them and drinking beers. Now, we know about being on tour and being respectful to the bands who have taken you out. We're very good with that. What we did could have gone *really* badly [because] that behaviour is essentially unacceptable. It shows a *huge* lack of respect to the people who are taking you out on tour. Imagine if I did that working a nine-to-five job. Imagine if I just got up from my desk and had gone, "Yeah, this is a great idea" – and I'd put on makeup, got a boom box, kicked open the door to my manager's office and gone in singing at him and drinking a beer. I'd be fired instantly.'

With Ian sequestered in a psychiatric care facility, Will was required to take charge of finishing *Sex, Death & the Infinite Void*. Back in the UK, release schedules, singles, videos, tours and promotional campaigns were waiting on the album being wrapped. It all sounds very exclusive, doesn't it? It seems so very glamorous. But with the group's plans for a live campaign torn to pieces by The Disease, from his home in Manchester the singer tells me exactly how much money he made in 2020. 'And is *that all*?!' I ask. 'Yep, that is all,' he says. I made a promise that I wouldn't reveal to you the precise figure, but what I can say is that it's not enough to live on. For someone whose band scored a top-five record, the amount is shockingly low.

In some ways it strikes me as a wonder that Creeper's second album got finished at all. Describing his relationship with 'addiction and substance abuse' as 'fluctuating problems in my life', Will tells me that during its recording 'my drinking was as bad as it's ever been'. In the midst of 'a particularly dark night . . . where things really changed', he recalls vomiting in a plant pot in a hotel lobby. 'Drinking constantly every day', he was 'throwing up all the time, which is mad because I'm a singer and that's one of the worst things you can do'. One morning he rang his mother in tears. 'It was going really, *really* badly . . . I think it kind of got to the point where everyone knew that I was in trouble,' he tells me.

'And now look where we are,' he says. 'We're talking about mental health in the music industry. Even when the money was there, I imagine that back then these mental health issues were deep rooted anyway. The excess and the drinking and the drugs. But what I do think has happened is that things have been made worse by the fact that if I decided to stop now, if I decided I couldn't carry on, I run the risk of losing my entire career. *You can't stop.* You're not allowed to. Financially you can't because you have to pay your bills. But surely you should have enough money to cushion yourself. In any other industry that you worked, you'd be allowed to take a sick day; if you're really sick in an office, you're allowed to take a month off with some degree of pay. When Ian went into [a care facility], I had to carry on making that record so that he had something to come out to. I thought about breaking up the band, or putting the band on hiatus while he recovered, but his wife said to me on the phone, "If you go on hiatus, Ian's going to come out and have nothing left."'

Over the course of the first year of The Disease, I've spent more time than you might imagine thinking about Creeper. Given that I've never actually met them in person, or seen them play, it's certainly more than *I* would have imagined. Despite an unreliable eye for runners and riders, this was the group I could most easily imagine winning the race for arena-level rock popularity. Instead, they got stuck in a purgatorial holding pattern in which no one had permission to land. They've been on my mind since the start of all this. In the first week of lockdown I wrote a piece for the *Telegraph* in which I spoke to various people in the music industry about the effects of the sudden blanket ban on public gatherings. From a dozen interviews, it is the contribution of Hannah Greenwood, Creeper's keyboard player, that has stayed with me the longest. 'When [the band] aren't working, I work as a temp in an office,' she told me. 'But of course I can't do that now, either, so this has hit me from two directions. In fact, I was just enquiring about getting on Universal Credit.'

'People talk about the music industry, but is it really an industry if there's no money in it?' asks Will Gould. 'It's more like this weird hobby where people makes scraps of cash here and there. Obviously there'll be *someone* who's making money, but it'll never be us again . . . I think you could make [the industry] a safer place to be if the stakes were somehow lessened. But I don't know how you'd get to that point. The streaming thing isn't going to change. The money isn't coming back, so people have to get over that. Money is not returning to the music industry. Live music? Look at this pandemic. Look at how this has affected everyone that works in music. It's insane . . . [but] in a world where money is now sparse, in the music industry drugs and alcohol are always available. It's everywhere, all the time. You can get whatever you want. It's like having a magic ticket where you can ask for as much as you want of those things – but if you want a living wage, well, that's different. *We can't do that.* But if you want some cocaine, there's always somebody who's got some.'

Like every other musician interviewed for this book, as soon as the clouds clear, Creeper will be back on tour. In preparation, Ian Miles has asked the mental health services about the possibility of being prescribed impulse-calming beta-blockers. *Nothing doing,* he was told, *with your addictive personality you'll be hooked on them in no time.* Instead, he practises mindfulness and Cognitive Behavioural Therapy. 'The point,' he says, 'is that what I'm feeling now is so insignificant. It's valid, but in the grand scheme of things, in time [I'll see that] I shouldn't get so caught up in it.' Convening a meeting at his home, the guitarist asked for the help of his bandmates in limiting him to two drinks prior to a show. After the gig, well, we'll see. (Seeing how on past campaigns Ian was slugging a bottle of gin a day, the matter surely needs addressing.) As well as this, Creeper intend to requisition one of their two backstage rooms as a quiet space to which people can retreat from the turbulence of what is an otherwise extreme environment.

'To have that, almost like a spa, will be a healthy thing,' the guitarist tells me. 'Because when you're in a tight-knit group of people there's politics between everybody. Two people in the band will fall out with the other four and so they'll be talking about them, and so on. And all of that manifests itself in wanting to drink, to not talk about that too much.'

Ian has no idea to what degree these safeguards might work. Listening to him speak, I'm somehow reminded of news footage of people fortifying their homes with sandbags. They can't say if their efforts will protect them from the coming flood, but to do nothing is unacceptable. Dropping in on tours, I've noticed that experienced campaigners find ways of managing the pressure. On days off in Europe Chris Wolstenholme from Muse travels home to the suburbs of London to be with his wife and their six children. Green Day have separate dressing rooms and individual tour buses. Frank Turner finds a quiet place in which to read a book for an hour. Warming to the theme, Ian recalls the time Creeper supported Blink 182. Contrary to the American group's enduring frat boy image, singer Mark Hoppus drank only a single shot of whiskey before heading to the stage. 'Maybe it's not so hard to do that, to take control of it,' Ian says. I tell him that it's not my business to dispense advice, but that if I were him I would hold tight to this memory.

'I would say that the creative mind is a vulnerable mind,' says Dr Charlie Howard. 'So people who are coming into the industry already have a vulnerability, and that vulnerability is magnified by the pressure put on them from the industry, from the culture around them with drink and drugs, from all sorts of things. They find themselves on tour for extended periods, and they're lonely being away from their families, and so the thing that started as a vulnerability has more and more petrol thrown on it. So eventually things just become too much. And I think that you'd have to be pretty extraordinary for these sorts of things not to affect you. It seems to me that they're extraordinary pressures that are placed on artists.'

I honestly didn't think it would end this way. Before I'd written the first word of this book, in general terms I thought I knew the trajectory of its story. I was certain that its two themes would follow a similar path. The music business and I had been unwell; as I got better, it did too. Turns out I was wrong. A hundred thousand words later, it seems as if only one of us has emerged fully into the light. In saying this, I don't mean to undervalue the good work of people trying hard to prevent musicians from falling ill, or helping them should they do so. On the contrary, the things they've told me have been my muse. I couldn't have asked for better company.

I had no idea I would feel so protective of the artists. Certainly, I never have before. Seeking to speak to younger people – admittedly, a fast-growing constituency – I picked Goat Girl and Creeper at random. A liking for their music was pretty much the measure of it. I had no idea that the first group had decided to keep the music business at arm's length. I didn't know that the second had placed themselves at such terrible risk. Not for a second do I seek to conflate the experiences of nine English musicians with those of every young person who steps out onto a stage. But what I do know is that the hopes of every emerging artist have been savagely diminished by an infrastructure that is rigged to the point of scandal.

In a review of Sir Bob Geldof's autobiography *Is That It?*, in 1986 Clive James wrote that 'when a pop act becomes successful there are only two kinds of money it can earn – not as much as you might think and more than you could believe'. Thirty-five years later, no one I know expects the latter. The chances were always slim, anyway, but in my youth a band could at least dream of being lavishly remunerated doing something they love. Today I'd say that any musician who earns a living from his or her art can justifiably call themselves a rock star.

On the hunt for sensitive information, I asked Frank Turner how long he could survive were he reliant only on the streaming revenues of the *No Man's Land* LP? I also requested a ballpark estimate of the proportion of income derived from streams and record sales compared to that pulled in from live campaigns. An established artist, each of Frank's last four albums has debuted in the British top three; as well as this, his records have appeared on the charts in Australia, Austria, Belgium, Canada, Germany, the Netherlands, the Republic of Ireland, Switzerland and the United States. The response is printed with his permission.

Income from record sales and mechanical royalties combined doesn't factor highly in my income. It's more about [merchandise], publishing and live [work]. This is a situation I've grown accustomed to/accepted over time, but I think the pandemic has certainly shown up some of the glaring flaws in the existing setup – labels making more money while artists go broke. Clearly, something's amiss. But to return to your initial question: not long. Maybe that's because I've grown accustomed to some creature comforts in my life; it's also because [No Man's Land] was not my most successful record by any stretch. But even the question 'Could you survive on streaming royalties alone from your entire catalogue?' gets a cautious 'not really' in reply.

Seeing as I started with them, let's have Metallica play us out. After all, they *did* see this coming before anyone else. When an unapproved version of the song 'I Disappear' was played on US radio in 1999 the group's lawyers dispatched cease and desist notices to station managers up and across the country. In searching for the source of a leak that had somehow bypassed Elektra Records' formal channels of distribution, the musicians and their label discovered to their horror that the track was available for free on the brand new online music-sharing platform Napster. As fast as that, the future was here. Within nine months of the programme's launch five million people had downloaded its software; a transnational treasure trove, anyone plugged into its global network was afforded free unlimited access to the online music libraries of every other user. With unlimited hubris, the company's chief executive officer, Eileen Richardson, described the platform as 'the MTV of the internet'. There was one crucial difference: Music Television paid royalties.

Metallica went to war. On 13 April 2000 the group filed a suit against the company and three universities whose computer networks permitted the use of its software. Drummer Lars Ulrich issued his own statement. 'From a business standpoint,' he concluded, 'this is about piracy – aka taking something that doesn't belong to you; and that is morally and legally wrong. The trading of such information – whether it's music, videos, photos, or whatever – is, in effect, trafficking in stolen goods.' The resulting furore was as startling as it was predictable. By the time *Kerrang!* flew a journalist to Los Angeles for an audience with Ulrich at the Sunset Marquis, the matter, at least for the group's record company, had become a question of damage limitation. In an interview with my friend Paul Brannigan, Ulrich said, 'On a deeper level this issue says a lot about where our society is at right now. People have this relationship with the internet and think that if something is on it they have a right to it. That's wrong – it's a privilege to have that access ... Should all music not be free, then? Can we just throw open the doors at Tower Records and do away with the cash registers? There's some imbalances here that just make no sense.'

As Lars Ulrich pointed to the future, the world stared at his finger. The problem for Metallica is that it was just so easy to caricature them as rapacious rock stars. 'There's a lot more issues at stake here [than personal wealth],' the drummer protested. 'If people grab songs from the internet and then don't buy that record, it's going to be really hard for new artists to break through ...' For once, Ulrich was only half right. The breakthroughs still happen, they just do so without breakthrough money. So fragile is this new financial order that in 2020 bands were blown to pieces by a year away from the road. Declining to name names, Will Gould says that people in groups far more popular than Creeper have told him that insolvency is drawing near. 'I hate to be pessimistic about it,' he says, 'but I think we're in a new world where these things are in place now. Consumers themselves don't want to change that because they've grown up with things as they now are.'

In their own sweet time, Metallica went mad the old fashioned way. Arrested development, sex and drugs, alcohol and egomania, that kind of thing. Following James Hetfield's discharge from rehab, in the summer of 2003 I interviewed the group in Dallas on their first tour for three years. Six months before the world was allowed to see them at their lowest ebb, in the film *Metallica: Some Kind of Monster*, the quartet were already figuring out ways to marry the requirements of their frontman's fragile state of recovery with the day-to-day realities of a rolling rock band. At the Texas Stadium Hetfield told me that he 'could easily fall back [into the habit of] hanging out with the boys in the strip club [but] you know, I spent far too long believing I was God. And, really, I didn't do a particularly good job, did I?' Each week on the road in North America, Metallica played three consecutive stadium concerts before flying home for four days' rest. Minutes before taking to the stage, I was gifted the chance to watch them start their engines playing 'Battery' in a locker room belonging to the Dallas Cowboys. Come the end of the night, Hetfield was back once again in the suburbs of San Francisco.

They're still taking care. Stirred by the animal magnetism of a middle-aged man dressed in a Metallica t-shirt, on a summer's afternoon in 2019 my fiancée expressed surprise at the length of the group's most recent European campaign. 'Look again,' I said. 'You see? The tour lasted three months, but they flew home three times for breaks of at least two weeks.' As it turned out, for once the group's noble and dogged attempt to strike a healthy balance between personal and public life did them no good. In a statement issued in the autumn of 2019, Metallica announced, 'As most of you probably know, our brother James has been struggling with addiction on and off for many years. He has now, unfortunately, had to re-enter a treatment program to work on his recovery again.' (The full details of the episode are really quite unpredictable. I wish I could share them with you.) The reader's response to this information is the difference between viewing a glass as being half full or half empty. To my eye, the overall achievement of Hetfield's sixteen-year streak of abstinence is only slightly diminished by a (to date) lone relapse. The real headline is that, aside from this, Metallica have found ways to protect themselves from the music industry's wild environment. That it may never be entirely safe, for them or for anyone, is the result of deficiencies elsewhere. If nothing else, at least they're being paid properly for their troubles.

I wish I could say for sure exactly how *I* became well. I wish I could tell you of a sunlit epiphany so powerful that it righted the course of my listing life. My father's grave would be a good spot for this kind of thing, I imagine. That'd be suitably journalistic. I can picture myself looking down at the dates on his grey marble headstone and thinking, 'Remember how strongly you felt that sixty-one was no age at which to die? Way you're going, you'll be lucky to make it to fifty.' But visiting Eric isn't like that. Heading down to Ardsley Cemetery to 'pay my respects' involves clearing the leaves and cigarette butts from around his little plot and standing nervously over him for as long as seems fitting. *Five minutes? Ten? What's the form here?* In a way it's like looking into the future. In the end we're all just dust and bones.

In search of an explanation as to how things got straightened out, I'm reminded of a phrase beloved of the American punk scene. 'Don't be a dick,' they say. Don't do it. It could just be, then, that I gave that a go. I will admit that by the time I came to this decision I didn't have many chips left to play with. In the Last Chance Saloon, my line of credit was not at all good. The thing about trashing the scenery with the kind of ruthlessness I brought so easily to bear is that people stop trusting you. Every conversation is imbued with subterranean meaning. 'How are you doing?' translates as, 'Are you about to go crazy again and fuck everything up?' Let me tell you, going mad is maddening. *I'm not a fucking wild animal, you know?* Oh, really – *really?* – is that so? Well, then why am I acting like one?

It wasn't a particularly smooth landing. As things began to bottom out, a mutual friend contacted Nico, my last and most reliable drug seller, and pleaded with him to strike me off his rounds. *He's going to kill himself,* was the gist of it, *this needs to stop.* We had a rum old game going on, too, Nico and I. Whenever he pulled up on my street, I'd attempt to account for my four- or five- or six-gram purchase by telling him I was heading out to a happening. It must have looked like I went to more parties than Gore Vidal. Sometimes I'd say that I had friends coming round after the pubs shut. *Fellas with appetites, you know?* I told these lies because I didn't want my delivery driver to think ill of me. I didn't want him to know that I'd developed a death wish.

Anyway, this sudden sanction put quite the wrinkle in our operation.

'Sorry, mate, shop's closed,' he told me on the trumpet.

Profound silence. Stopped clocks. *'What?'*

'Can't come down no more, Ian, not after what [name redacted] told me the other night.'

'How about—'

'You rein it in a bit?'

'Exactly!'

'Yeah. He said you'd say that. I don't think that's gonna work though, is it? At least not for now.'

Part of me was relieved. In a doomed attempt to help myself, I'd already deleted Nico's number from my phone at least a dozen times. I'd scrubbed evidence of text messages, too, for all the good it did me. But try as I might, I just couldn't cut the cord. With yet another ravenous midnight surging towards me, I'd text our mutual friend and ask for our seller's details just one more time. Time after time, just one more time. Honestly, could I have made it any more obvious that things were getting out of hand? Suitably spooked, one night my friend came calling in the tiny hours of a hot weekend. Hearing the trill of my phone through the letterbox, after ten minutes' knocking and hollering he told me that he was off to find a copper. *Oh please. There's no way he's going to do that.* Fifteen minutes later, the two uniformed officers who were threatening to break down the door proved harder to ignore. *What to do?* The flat looked like King Kong had swung through it. Certainly I was going to have my hands full accounting for the pyramid of cocaine on a plate in the kitchen. Fighting back panic, I opened the door to the width of my head. Hanging onto the frame, I tried to explain that I was having a rough night, and that I was sorry for having caused such a fuss. Doubtless pleased at being spared the hassle of dealing with an overdose, or a dead body, the two PCs left my friend alone to try to sort things out.

'The fuck is wrong with you?' he wanted to know. All things considered, it seemed a reasonable question.

'I don't know. I really don't.'

'Ian, let me in.'

'I can't do that, pal. I just can't. I need you to leave me be.'

Whether by accident or design, what I was doing was painting myself into a corner. I *wanted* to run out of road. On six or seven occasions I scoured the streets of Camden Town looking for furtive young men selling overpriced packets of powder. Guided into alleyways late at night, I knew I was placing myself in perilous situations. On each occasion I declined the phone numbers proffered for future use. 'Don't need 'em,' I thought, 'because this is the last time I'll be doing this.'

Within a month it was.

It took me about a year to train myself to resist the liquid temptations of the late-night shop just yards from my front door. In the end, I treated it like a game. Sitting on the settee at midnight watching the baseball, or the ice hockey, from North America, I'd think, 'I just need to get to one o' clock when the Green Door Food Bazaar closes for business.' It really was as simple as that. At first, failure ran up quite the score against success. Defences breached, I'd hammer away at a brand new bottle of Jack Daniel's until every drop was gone. But as the weeks crawled past I learned to savour the quiet but pronounced feeling of accomplishment at being able to forego the merchandise lurking (literally) round the corner. In a small but far from discountable way, this became a high.

Slowly re-emerging into music business society, to my surprise I discovered that I didn't at all mind being the only person in a bar not taking a drink. I found that I rather enjoyed having my choices reduced to Diet Coke or fruit juice. I learned to take pleasure in being capable of reading a book on the tube ride home. To my delight, but not surprise, without exception my efforts to sort myself out received the unconditional support of every one of my friends and acquaintances. As we have seen, alcohol and excess is prevalent in the music industry. But so too is kindness and empathy.

With a greater degree of quietude than you might think, I am of course glad to be rid of it all. It's good to no longer feel quite so ashamed. Tired and sick of my carrying on, I sometimes wonder if a part of my mind staged a backbench revolt against a deranged executive branch pulling madly at the levers of power. It might even be that I just got bored of myself. There are times, certainly, when I don't feel very different from the person who ran wild for all that time. After almost three years of mental and physical sobriety, I can still feel a restless presence brooding within me. There is still a part of me that seeks only to *destroy*. There it goes now, look, darting through the shadows, banging on the walls, trying its best to get something going. Fucking little hoodlum.

But it ain't coming in. Not today, anyway.

I consider myself lucky that I was able to reverse most of the physical damage I brought to bear on myself. I have a lesion in my mouth where I fell over in a state of near unconsciousness and almost bit right through my tongue. My doctor told me that she'd never seen an injury like that before; she even had to phone a specialist at UCHL for advice on the best course of treatment. My left arm bears a pair of train track scars running north to south. The bone remains pinned together up by the shoulder. My left nostril feels as if it's been put to sleep by Novocain. But that's about it. Incredibly, even my liver somehow battled its way back to full match fitness.

There was just the one thing I felt sure I could never piece back together. In one of my late-period hurrahs, on the evening before

I was due to speak with a young English band for the cover of *Kerrang!* I polished off yet another bottle of Tennessee whiskey. The following morning I estimated I had just enough time to top myself up with another. 'It'll be fine,' I thought. My interview wasn't until mid-afternoon, anyway. If I got the booze down fast enough I'd have enough time for a few hours' sleep before I headed out to my job of work. By then I'd be right as rain.

Only it didn't work out like that. In the fading light of an autumn evening, I came to fully clothed on the settee with an avalanche of missed calls and texts by my side. It's difficult to describe the cocktail of panic and despair that flooded through my system as I tried to make sense of the day's damage. By standing up a band and inconveniencing their record company, I'd made *Kerrang!* appear shoddy and unprofessional. This was a big deal. Stranded on the equator between rock and a hard place, (then) acting editor Sam Coare's fury at my actions was mitigated only slightly by a concern for my personal wellbeing. All I could do was surrender to shame. I was so ashamed, in fact, that I didn't bother asking for another chance. After embarrassing myself, I saw no profit in embarrassing him.

When Sam's editorship was made official, I sent a text telling him he deserved the gig. As the successor to James McMahon, I knew he had his hands full improving both the magazine and the morale of its browbeaten staff. I also felt – correctly, as it goes – that he had the chops to handle this task. By way of reply, he suggested that perhaps the two of us might go out for lunch. I believed he knew what I'd been up to since the last time he shouted at me. Rather than drugging and drinking myself to death, I'd occupied my time writing a book. (*Smash! Green Day, The Offspring, Bad Religion, NOFX and the '90s Punk Explosion* was published by Da Capo Press in the penultimate week of 2018.) Twelve hours a day, six days a week, the incremental construction of its 291 pages had given me a longer lasting and much more complicated high than anything available on the street. The sustained concentration required to prevent its narrative from crashing into the rocks had helped keep me straight in what might have otherwise been a fragile state of nascent recovery. In the book's latter stages it dawned on me that the story I had opted to tell was ultimately a happy one. From a cast of misfits and addicts, the groups I'd written about had each found their own way of surviving the music industry without going mad.

By way of apology, the following month I stood Sam a cheeseburger at the Gourmet Burger Kitchen at the Angel Centre in Islington. Once more in the company of the man in charge, for the first time I considered the sheer scale of my investment in what might be about to happen next. For almost two decades *Kerrang!* had allowed me to travel the world in search of stories that I wrote as I saw fit. I had accomplished this work as well as I knew how. Inspired by a remarkable degree of creative freedom, my sense of pride at being a member of the team had only blossomed with age. It had been *such* a laugh. At once, the possibility that I no longer had a place there felt like a loss that couldn't easily be faced. By the time the lunch plates had been cleared the editor had reached the relevant item of business.

'You know you'll always be welcome at *Kerrang!*, right?'

'Actually, Sam, if I'm being honest with you, I didn't know that. I thought . . . you know . . .'

'Don't be a cunt.'

Relief.

'I can come back, then?'

'Yeah, why not? We'll have to start you off slow, though. You'll need to earn back some trust.'

'Obviously.'

'I'll tell the section editors we're bringing you home.'

The day was a Friday. With a brand new issue in its bed, an invitation was extended for me to join the editor and the rest of the staff in a nearby pub on Chapel Market. This was how Sam's new regime marked the end of every working week. This was how it rolled. Colleagues as friends in a happy place of business, *Kerrang!* restored once more to its natural state.

At the bar I was asked if I fancied a drink. *Did I?* Tell you what, I didn't half put a dent in that cranberry juice and soda.

BONUS TRACK: ANOTHER STATE OF MIND

My fiancée, who works in publishing, reckons I should go out on a song. 'It's probably not a good idea for you to leave your readers feeling depressed,' is what I think she said. I'd go and check, but on this grey morning she's gone back to bed. Last night she invited some friends over for a gathering in the back garden. Hammering away at the keyboard like Schroeder from *Peanuts*, I could hear them from the desk in the bedroom. *Are they listening to S Club 7?* (Beware any music journalist who can't get past a pop group's naff packaging, by the way. In the seventies and early eighties, even ABBA received a rotten press.) Hearing my approach, they instructed the smart speaker to play Sleater-Kinney.

'I've finished the final chapter.'

'Well done! Is it happy?'

'I think so. I pulled it out of the nosedive right at the death there.'

A moment's quiet as the group estimated the impact of my presence on their happy night.

'Honey, are you drunk?'

'Actually,' she said, 'I'm *half* drunk. If you want to know the truth, I wish I was more drunk than I actually am.'

'You should go and work in the music industry. Those folks know how to get the job done.'

The reason my fiancée floats unnamed through the body of this book is because she didn't much fancy having her private business hung out for all to see. That said, I have been given clearance to tell you that at the start of our second date she received a briefing about some of the things that have ailed me. Instead of running for the hills, she decided to stick around. *Honey, I'm tougher than the rest.* In the summer of 2019 she accepted my down-on-one-knee proposal of marriage at Embankment station – the meeting point for our glorious first date – with a few tears but little hesitation. I got yanked to my feet for causing a scene. I produced two tickets to see Kiss. *Ta da!* Tell me I don't know how to treat a lady.

Last week we went to a Camden Council office on Southampton Row to register our wedding. Squinting at my passport, the man behind the desk told me that he used to be in a band about whom I once wrote a positive review. He asked me what I'm up to these days, to which I replied that I was half a week away from finishing a book about how the music industry ruins lives. He nodded his head; it had given him a breakdown. That said, as people so often do, he harbours hopes of getting back in the game. While at work in a different office, he recalled watching a parade of young fans queuing to see Creeper at Koko. 'I looked at them all and thought, "Oh, God, what have I done with my life?"' he said.

If he's reading this, I wish him well. I hope he finds what he's looking for.

I reckon marriage might just work for me. In the teeth of three lockdowns, certainly, my fiancée and I have managed to maintain our groove. Winter walks to nowhere, takeout food on a Friday night, cleaning the flat on a Sunday morning. What's not to love? In the absence of live music, late at night the two of us munched our way through some of the wonders of modern television. Bathed in the vivid glow of tubal light, sometimes I played the 'I've been there' game. Let me tell you, she can't get enough of that.

'That's Detroit that is. I've been there. It was like being a character in *Grand Theft Auto*.'

'Good for you.'

'Moscow, look. I've been there. Our translator was worried about kidnappers.'

'I know. You've told me, like, five times.'

'Melbourne. I've been there. I wanted to go and see Ramsay Street but it was raining.'

'How about we play the quiet game instead?'

'Oh, I'm useless at that.'

In a book already overburdened with tragedy, I hesitate to tell you that music journalists no longer get to travel the world free of charge. That's not the only thing that's changed, either. I could be wrong, but I doubt that a nineteen-year-old from a redbrick background could today come to London and strike up a paying career writing about people in bands. The opportunities are fewer; the accents have changed. *I have an artist's hands, though I'm a working man. But my craft has been forgotten by the age.* I'm pleased that readers no longer need me to tell them what it is I think they should listen to. I'm even more pleased that I can still earn a living writing as well as I'm able about the people who *make* the music.

I always knew that the writing itself was my favourite part of the job. As I waited for this book to come back to me from its copy-editor, the *Telegraph* allowed me to compose a piece about how, as a child, the Motörhead live album *No Sleep 'Til Hammersmith* changed my life. Talk about a treat. I doubt he'd approve, but these days I'm most likely to hear Lemmy's voice from my earphones while out running. Every evening I cover many miles: up the hill to Hampstead and down to Golders Green, or over Tower Bridge and along the South Bank to the Palace of Westminster. This too is an addiction, of course, a perennial pursuit from which I take a grim and silent pleasure. Determined to protect me from myself, without my consent my iPhone has taken to turning down the volume in my cans. But we're not having it, Lemmy and I, so up we go, back to full crank. *Everything louder than everything else.* Just last night, amid the gloom of a reluctant summer,

I listened in as he told me to 'be a man, fix the glitch'. To be honest with you, I think I'd let things get a bit beyond a glitch. But I did my best, Lemmy, and I fixed it.

A man I don't like once gave me some good advice. 'Don't spend too long trying to connect what happened with your dad with what's going on in your head,' he said. 'The healthcare professionals will do that for you.' The only exception to this otherwise universal truth was a psychiatrist over in Swiss Cottage who tended to me as my illness was losing, but not relinquishing, its grip. With an air of agreeable impatience he wanted to know why I was taking so damn long to cross the finish line. *Ian, really, what's the problem here?* Imagine my relief when at last I was able to tell him that there had been no episodes of even minor concern since the last time I had seen him.

'Really? Nothing?'

'Not a thing.'

'Remind me, how long has that been now?'

A smile. 'I suspect you know how long it's been. It's been just shy of nine months.'

'That's very good, isn't it?'

'Yeah. It's not bad.'

Come the end of my visit, I was no longer in the care of the mental health services.

That night I took my fiancée to see Elvis Costello & the Imposters at the Hammersmith Apollo. 'Music critics like Elvis Costello because music critics look like Elvis Costello,' David Lee Roth once said. He might even have had a point. Kitted out in my Lock & Co. trilby and prescription Wayfarers, outside the venue I posed for a picture beneath a marquee bearing the headliner's name. Watching the show from the tenth row, my plus one told me that Costello was different from how she'd imagined he would be. 'I thought he'd be more, I don't know, *hostile*,' she said. 'But he actually seems quite nice.' Maybe. But just listen to the tension in the music. Check out the agro in those songs.

Even when it's as good as this, music cannot absolve the failures of the industry that promotes it. Its bottomless wonder doesn't make it all worthwhile. But it does stand apart from it all. It remains unsullied. When I'm listening to it, I can sometimes convince myself that each iteration is the very pinnacle of creative achievement. Iconic Swedish pop music, or strident rap from Long Island; punk rock sung by a college lecturer at Cornell University, or full-tilt metal from Huntington Park; a post-rock masterpiece by a band from London, or a thing of deconstructive wonder from a trio up in Ayrshire. *Oh, I just don't know where to begin.* At any given moment, you'd be amazed at the number of artists who have a momentary shot at being the very best thing in the world.

That night at the Hammersmith Apollo the crown belonged to Elvis Costello. Waiting for the crowd to disperse, at the end of the night I took a moment to watch the road crew break down the equipment on the stage. Under the glare of the house lights, even the grandest productions are merely industry and hardware there to be spirited away. Floating through the air, the moments you remember for the rest of your life cannot be captured. They can't even be touched. They're there, and then they're gone. No matter how hard I try, I lack the vocabulary to explain what happens in a truly great show. Even the people making the music don't know what it is. Probably it's the closest thing to magic you will ever see.

As if proving their existence, out on the road bands leave messages on dressing-room walls. With Sharpies and stickers, they make themselves known. Thousands of miles from home, I've seen their faces brighten at the sight of a dated inscription from a familiar name. *Look who was here just last month.* Just weeks before The Disease became the biggest story in the world, I saw the words 'Sweet Children' written up in the rafters of the iconic independent music venue 924 Gilman Street, in Berkeley. In 1989 the group became Green Day. The only venue in the area that allowed young teenagers through its doors, for the young Billie Joe Armstrong the experience of appearing on its stage was about something other than music. 'It was about a community and a movement,' he once told me. 'Gilman was the first time that I learned anything in my life. Before Gilman, everything I'd learned up until that point was bullshit.'

With remarkable tenacity, for coming up to forty years Gilman Street has disobeyed the music industry's traditional rules of engagement. Within its walls, the ties that bind performers and audiences to a bedlamite culture have always been resisted. There's even a sign at the door that says so. In large stencilled letters it reads, 'No alcohol, no drugs, no violence, no fucked-up behaviour.'

My own visit felt like a pilgrimage. On a mild Sunday night in the thick of winter, I watched a young man sing songs about his disappointing life. Standing just feet from the stage, even at the time I realised there was every chance that I would never hear from him again. But as he locked into his groove, for more than a moment he too became the greatest thing in the world.

CREDITS

Thank you for reading my book. I hope you liked it. It's funny, but at the outset it used to take me about ten minutes to explain what it was I thought I was writing about. Inching forward, I managed to tighten it up a bit. 'It's about how the music industry makes people ill,' I'd say. 'Will you speak to me, please?' Those who did are the ones I wanted. There was no make-do-and-mend. The candour with which people availed themselves gave me sustenance through many a frigid night. Everyone told me something I didn't know. It is an honour to be trusted with their voices.

I think of them as part of the band. Seeing as we're now at the end of the show, I'd like you please to give a big hand to Dunstan Bruce, Ellie Rose Davies, Eleanor Goodman, Will Gould, Tom Gray, Eleanor Halls, Charlie Howard, Grant Hutchison, Steph Langan, Chris McCormack, Ian Miles, Simon Neil, Stuart Richardson, Frank Turner, Jennyfer Walker and Ginger Wildheart. As well as answering my questions, Jeordie Shenton was patient enough to guide me through a jungle of academic research. From psychologist to singer, each person played their instrument without dropping a note. I'm now going to leave this analogy alone.

As an A-level student, I used to buy novels simply because they were published by Faber & Faber. My God, I must have been insufferable. The very epitome of metropolitan sophistication – *Theft*, *Moon Palace*, *Life is Elsewhere* – not for a second did I imagine they employed Thin Lizzy-loving Derby County fans. Angus Cargill, my editor, is exactly that. Armed only with a pencil, many are the times he's protected me from the worst of my excesses. Stylistic excesses, thank God. A patient and astute guiding hand, he's also my friend.

I am indebted to Ian Preece for his insightful and judicious copy-editing. I trust that my occasionally distant relationship with the rules of grammar hasn't caused him undue offence. I also owe him an apology for redrafting entire chunks of this book – by which I mean all of it – at the point at which he believed he'd finished his work. I hope one day he will come to appreciate that it was his tasteful interventions that inspired me to do so.

Thanks also go to Libby Marshall, from Faber & Faber, who was kind enough to read this manuscript at a somewhat formative stage. Her input and observations helped me see the text in a sharper light. At a later stage, the help and input of Anne Owen, Dan Papps and Paul Baillie-Lane brought the book into the hands of the reader. I'm also incredibly grateful to Pete Adlington and Jack Smyth for the brilliant cover. And to Hannah Marshall for marketing.

To my delight, my agent, Cathryn Summerhayes, understood this project at the point at which it was nothing more than a Word document written at the back of a plane on a flight to New York. *The Bookseller* tells me she's one of the hundred most powerful people in publishing. With an air of post-watershed informality – would we say Tourette syndrome? – I'm proud to be one of her authors.

With crashing predictability, writing this book took *much* longer than I thought it would. Without the support of a team of patient and talented editors at the *Telegraph* and *Kerrang!* I doubt I would have finished it at all. And when I say finished, what I mean is started. Either way, I'm grateful to Sam Coare, Eleanor Halls, Luke Morton, Ross Jones, Cal Revely-Calder and Nick Ruskell for sparing me the kind of anxieties that have been known to haunt the freelance mind.

Paul Harries has been my friend and colleague for more than two decades now. In the lobby of an expensive hotel in

Philadelphia, in the holiday season of 2002, he said, 'Imagine if we got a bill for all these trips we've been on. All the flights, the meals, the drinks, the cabs, the lodgings, the whole bit.' Tell you the truth, part of me thinks this might yet happen. But if we do end up in debtors' jail, I can at least count on the company of a loyal and talented comrade.

In the month before The Disease, Dan Silver and I went to see the American ska-punk band The Interrupters at the Forum in Kentish Town. At the end of their set, using *Kerrang!*'s rating system, he turned to me and said, 'That was a four-K show.' Despite not having worked at the magazine for almost twenty years, he's still a lifer. It gets into your blood that way. In attempting to define our relationship, not for the first time I'm reminded of us playing ice hockey video games. We never played against each other, we were on the *same* team. United and strong, I will never have a truer friend.

I'm grateful to my comrade and fellow Faber & Faber author Paul Brannigan for his unsolicited but emphatic encouragement at a crucial stage of this book's gestation. His deep generosity of spirit kept me warm on my long trudge towards the finish.

The young musician referred to at the very end of the story is Kevin Nichols. I'm sure he wouldn't mind if you gave him a listen.

In the telling of this story I've spared my mother the role she played in helping me stay alive. Save for this brief expression of gratitude, I see no need to drag her through things for a second time. By her side, always, was my stepfather. After years of worry, I suppose we can say that at least we got somewhere in the end. I don't know if it's much, but I do hope that it's something. I'm sorry I was oblivious for so very long.

I'd also like to place on record my gratitude to Wendy Ainslie, Paul Brannigan, George Garner, Alistair Lawrence and Jennyfer Walker for their help in keeping me alive.

Pathogens permitting, by the time you read this the woman I refer to as my fiancée will be my wife. As if striking up a relationship with a man on the exit ramp of mental illness wasn't enough, in the thick of three lockdowns she's had to put up with me writing a book about it all. Kept apart from family and friends, I can only marvel at her capacity for living with someone who clambers into bed at four in morning having spent half the night moving sentences around. For me it's been like playing Tetris; for her, solitaire. Given the extent of the palaver, my admiration for her patience and understanding is by now boundless. So too is my love.

With light in our eyes, I hope she'll meet me by the bandstand for the first, and last, dance.

Ian Winwood, Camden Town

SOURCES

CHAPTER 1

12 *I haven't been really good at long-term goals*: James Hetfield, Metallica, *Quebec Magnetic* DVD, Blackened Recordings, 2012

12 *Don't tread on me*: 'Don't Tread On Me', Metallica, written by James Hetfield and Lars Ulrich, 1991, Elektra

18 *They're dirty, noisy, obnoxious, ugly, and I hate them*: Metallica tour programme, 1986

23 *Can't get enough*: 'Motorhead', Motörhead, written by Ian Fraser Kilmister,

24 *I was so wasted*: 'Wasted', Black Flag, written by Greg Ginn and Keith Morris, 1979 SST

CHAPTER 2

32 *I know I'm dying*: Layne Staley and Adriana Rubio, *Layne Staley, Angry Chair: A Look Inside the Heart & Soul of an Incredible Musician*, Xanadu Enterprises, 2003

32 *Heroin was Staley's demon and his muse*: Jason Cohen, 'The Man Boxed In: Layne Staley, 1967–2002, *Spin*, July 2002

35 *I'm just looking for another good time:* 'Kickstart My Heart', written by Mötley Crüe, Nikki Sixx, 1989, Elektra

36 *This is how low it gets*: Nikki Sixx and Ian Gittins, *The Heroin Diaries: A Year in the Life of a Shattered Rockstar*, Simon & Schuster, 2007

37 *The place was crawling with vermin*: Mötley Crue with Neil Strauss, *The Dirt: Confessions of the World's Most Notorious Rock Band*, HarperEntertainment, 2001

38 *It wasn't as if I said*: Steve Lamacq, 'The Last Time I Saw Richey', *Guardian*, 29 September 2000

42 *Around to see a man and a woman*: Allan Jones, *Can't Stand Up For Falling Down*, Bloomsbury, 2017

45 *Four-day, five-day marathon*: 'Motorhead', Motörhead, written by Ian Fraser Kilmister, 1977, Chiswick

CHAPTER 3

59 *We're shooting through the ceiling*: 'Cheyenne Sunrise', The Hold Steady, written by Craig Finn and Tad Kubler, 2008, Vagrant

67 *The truth of the matter is that most bands*: *The Clash: Westway to the World*, 3DD Entertainment, 2000

68 *Heroin fucking ruined [Richards] for years*: Paul Brannigan, *Thinking Out Loud: The Wit and Wisdom of Lemmy*, Aurum Press, 2009

67 *What a waste*: 'What A Waste', Ian Dury & The Blockheads, written by Ian Dury and Rod Melvin, 1978, Stiff Records

68 *Is it worth it?*: 'Shipbuilding', Elvis Costello & The Attractions, written by Elvis Costello and Clive Langer, 1983, F-Beat

68 *All good clean fun*: 'Motorhead', Motörhead, Ian Fraser Kilmister, 1977, Chiswick

68 *Lou Reed should burn in fucking hell*: ibid.

69 *I believe that if you can do without them*: ibid.

74 *Nobody gives a damn when you're down on your luck*: 'Hollywood (Down On Your Luck)', written by Phil Lynott and Scott Gorham, 1981, Vertigo

CHAPTER 4

77 *How does it feel, young Steven:* David Mitchell, Utopia Avenue, Sceptre, 2020

77 *In terms of hard cash, it means a lot:* ITN News, 16 January 1986

78 *Record contracts are just like:* Daniel Kreps, 'Prince Warns Young Artists: Record Contracts are 'Slavery'', *Rolling Stone*, 9 August 2015

CHAPTER 5

108 *In the city there's a thousand faces:* 'In The City', The Jam, written by Paul Weller, 1977, Polydor

110 *A decorated splatter brightens the room:* 'Seasons In The Abyss', Slayer, written by Tom Araya and Jeff Hanneman, 1990, Def American

120 *Hello darkness, my old friend:* 'The Sound Of Silence', written by Simon & Garfunkel, Paul Simon, 1965, Columbia

CHAPTER 6

138 *That ain't working, that's the way you do it:* 'Money For Nothing', written by Dire Straits, Mark Knopfler and Sting, 1985, Vertigo

CHAPTER 7

158 *Running wild in the streets:* 'Wild In The Streets', Circle Jerks, written by Garland Jeffreys, 1982, Frontier

158 *It hits you, like a hammer:* 'Thunder & Lightning', Thin Lizzy, written by Brian Downey and Phil Lynott, 1983, Vertigo

166 *[Corgan] is a media slut:* Everett True, 'Live review of Smashing Pumpkins at the Metro in Chicago', *Melody Maker*, 4 September 1992

171 *Was always looking for the next big thing*: Quote supplied privately by author and journalist Mark Blake

176 *In at the deep end, hang on tight*: 'Let's Get Rocked', Def Leppard, written by Joe Elliot, Rick Savage, Phil Collen, Robert John "Mutt" Lange, 1992, Mercury

178 *The aspiration starts now*: Martin Amis, *Inside Story*, Jonathan Cape, 2020

180 *Man, It's So Loud In Here*: 'Man, It's So Loud In Here', They Might Be Giants, written by John Flansburgh and John Linnell, 2001, Restless

CHAPTER 8

191 *That's some catch, that Catch-22*: Joseph Heller, *Catch 22*, Simon & Schuster, 1961

208 *He's the most tip top – Top Cat!*: 'Top Cat', Hoyt Curtin, 1962, Colpix Records

208 *Move over for a damage case*: 'Damage Case', Motörhead, written by Ian Fraser Kilmister, Eddie Clarke, Phil Taylor, 1979, Bronze

214 *I feel the apocalypse is within my sight*: 'The Jackson Whites', written by The Wildhearts, Ginger Wildheart, 2009, Backstage Alliance

CHAPTER 9

219 *I get knocked down, but I get up again*: 'Tubthumping', written by Chumbawamba, Chumbawamba, 1997, EMI

219 *[Chumbawamba are] a collection of*: Well Done, Now Sod Off, 2000

221 *I tell you it was all a frame*: 'E.M.I', Sex Pistols, written by Johnny Rotten, Steve Jones, Glen Matlock, Paul Cook, 1977, Virgin

223 *Not very good pop stars*: ibid.

227 *[Since] necrophagy in rock is a tradition*: Greil Marcus, *In the Fascist Bathroom: Writings on Punk 1977–1992*, Penguin, 1992

229 *The risk of death for musicians in their twenties*: Wolkewitz, M., Allignol, A., Graves, N. and Barnett, A. G., 'Is 27 really a dangerous age for famous musicians? Retrospective cohort study', *BMJ*, 2011, No. 343

229 *Musicians [of all ages]*: Bellis, M. A., Hughes, K., Sharples, O., Hennell, T. and Hardcastle, K. A., 'Dying to be famous: Retrospective cohort study of rock and pop star mortality and its association with adverse childhood experiences', *BMJ Open*, 2012, No. 2(6)

229 *Musicians had a mortality rate*: Kenny, D. T. and Asher, A., 'Life expectancy and cause of death in popular musicians: Is the popular musician lifestyle the road to ruin?', *Medical Problems of Performing Artists*, 2016, 31(1), pp. 37–44

229 *Musicians' expected involvement*: Shenton, J., 'Musicians' cognitive appraisals of risky, impulsive and self-destructive behaviours', BSc dissertation, University of Suffolk, 2017

234 *When the lights go down . . . all you hold dear remains*: 'Feel', written by Duff McKagan, Duff McKagan, 2019, Universal Music Enterprises

234 *No one sings like you anymore*: 'Black Hole Sun', Soundgarden, written by Chris Cornell, 1994, A&M

246 *Take my hand, off to Never Neverland*: 'Enter Sandman', Metallica, written by James Hetfield, Lars Ulrich & Kirk Hammett, 1991, Elektra

CHAPTER 10

252 *Extreme mansplaining*: Roisin O' Connor, 'Frank Turner Review, No Man's Land: More a Case of Extreme Mansplaining', *Independent*, 16 August 2019

252 *Are constantly overshadowed by Turner's*: Will Richards, 'No Man's Land review', *NME*, 14 August 2019

258 *Seventy-two per cent of female musicians*: Music Industry Research Association, 'Inaugural Music Industry Research Association (MIRA) Survey of Musicians', Princeton: MIRA, 2018

258 *If you're young and inspired*: Dorian Lynskey, 'Why are Bands Disappearing: "Young People Aren't Excited by Them"', *Guardian*, 18 March 2021

273 *When a pop act becomes successful*: Clive James, *Snake Charmers in Texas*, Jonathan Cape, 1988

275 *From a business standpoint*: Paul Brannigan and Ian Winwood, *Into The Black: The Inside Story of Metallica*, Faber & Faber, 2015

275 *There's a lot more issues at stake here*: ibid.

BONUS TRACK

286 *Honey, I'm tougher than the rest*: 'Tougher Than The Rest', Bruce Springsteen, written by Bruce Springsteen, 1988, Columbia

288 *Oh, I just don't know where to begin*: 'Accidents Will Happen', Elvis Costello & The At-tractions, written by Elvis Costello, 1979, Radar

288 *Be a man, fix the glitch*: 'Life's A Bitch', Motörhead, written by Ian Fraser Kilmister, Phil Campbell, Mikkey Dee, 2004, SPV/ Steamhammer Sanctuary

288 *Music critics like Elvis Costello*: 'The 50 Greatest Rock Star Insults by Telegraph reporters', *Telegraph*, 21 December 2017